The Invisible Handcuffs
of Capitalism

THE INVISIBLE HANDCUFFS
OF CAPITALISM

How Market Tyranny Stifles the Economy
by Stunting Workers

by Michael Perelman

MONTHLY REVIEW PRESS
New York

Library of Congress Cataloging-in-Publication Data

Perelman, Michael.

The invisible handcuffs : how market tyranny stifles the economy by stunting workers / by Michael Perelman.

    p. cm.

Includes bibliographical references and index.

ISBN 978-1-58367-229-7 (pbk. : alk. paper) – ISBN 978-1-58367-230-3 (cloth : alk. paper) 1. Labor. 2. Work. 3. Capitalism. I. Title.

HD4904.P386 2010

331.13–dc22

                            2010050845

Monthly Review Press

146 West 29th Street, Suite 6W

New York, New York 10001

www.monthlyreview.org

www.MRzine.org

5 4 3 2 1

Contents

Acknowledgments

All books are collective, but I am fortunate in working with a wonderful collective, beginning with Blanche Perelman, whose tolerance and support has let me obsess about the causes and consequences of economics' neglect of work, workers, and working conditions. Next comes Michael Yates, who was far more than an editor, relentlessly prodding me to think harder and more clearly. He deserves a fair share of any credit due to this book. Edward Roualdes gave up a vacation in Hawaii to work with me on the manuscript, catching me when I was insufficiently clear. David Ward also gave detailed editorial suggestions, as did my colleagues Richard Ponarul and Samir Nissan offered valuable suggestions. My first editor, Margo Crouppen, helped me during the early stages.

Setting the Stage

The Invisible Handcuffs tells a unique story about the damage that capitalism inflicts on society. Many authors have addressed the cultural, social, ecological, or ethical shortcomings of markets, such as the unequal distribution of income. Others have stressed the inherent instability of capitalism, which leads to recurrent economic crises.

This book does something different. It takes aim at capitalism in terms of its own basic rationale—the creation of an efficient method of organizing production. In particular, *The Invisible Handcuffs* concentrates on a largely ignored dimension of market inefficiency: how the failure by economists and employers alike to adequately take work, workers, and working conditions into account has led to actions that have stifled the economy.

The inattention of mainstream economists to work, workers, and working conditions has not been accidental. It has been a key part of a centuries-long effort, beginning at least as far back as Adam Smith, to construct an ideology that would shield markets from criticism.

Some mainstream economists have dared to look in this direction, but they have been treated harshly. So most economists have practiced self-censorship and shied away from examining work, workers, and working conditions. There have been sharp disagreements about minor points, but these have only helped to obscure the virtual unanimity about larger issues.

There have been times, especially during economic crises, when the usually closed ranks of economists have opened a bit. During the recent "Great Recession" for example, many people saw or at least suspected that the fanciful economic theories had helped to bring about the economic crisis. However, we shall see how similar "awakenings" have accompanied past crises, but once these passed, the old ideology, again masquerading as science and as always buttressed by imposing mathematical models, reasserted itself. Ironically, this return to orthodoxy made the economy even more vulnerable to crisis.

The approach of this book is historical, because this is especially useful in understanding the continuing hold of mainstream economic theory. As William Faulkner wrote in *Requiem for a Nun*, "The past is never dead. It's not even past."

An Ideological Fairy Tale

Almost 250 years ago, Adam Smith, often described as the father of modern economics, introduced the idea of the invisible hand, which has since become a popular metaphor for expressing unbounded faith in capitalism. He proposed that the market coordinated people's activities in such a beneficent way that one might well imagine that an invisible hand was at work creating an economy that was both fair and efficient.

Smith maintained that within the rules of the market, people were free to do as they pleased. He recognized that the market did impose discipline, but he insisted that it did so fairly, in the sense that the market did not favor any persons or groups.

Smith's argument has a certain power and persuasiveness, and, because he was skilled in rhetoric, a subject he taught at his university, he was able to convincingly present the economy as a voluntary system, carefully excluding dramatic economic changes that were already under way, literally in his own neighborhood. But as we will see, Smith's idea of an invisible hand guiding the economy toward a desirable social outcome took hold because it fit the needs of those powerful persons who owned the land, raw materials, and capital upon which everyone else depends.

Building upon Smith, later economists created a more sophisticated theory, while still maintaining the basic ingredients of Smithian economics, especially his emphasis on individual commercial transactions (buying and selling) as the central feature of capitalist economies. Production itself, which is always a social and not an individual process, was excluded.

The dogmatic insistence on framing the economy this way obscures any consideration of fundamental questions about work, workers, and working conditions. For example, economists may look at workers in terms of the level of wages or the extent of unemployment (the absence of a buyer-seller transaction in the job market), but the actual content of people's existence as workers on the job passes unnoticed. Even where economists take note of workers' skills, they reduce it to the level of a commodity—identifying skill as "human capital, "to be sold to a willing buyer.

Within this narrow market perspective, social relations become invisible. Workers are not just creatures that inhabit the workplace. They live within families, a class, and a society. If these relationships are ignored, the potential for substantial progress in grasping the economy is virtually nil.

An Ideology Comes Unglued

Although the ideological victory of mainstream economics has been effective in staving off critiques, it has been a mixed blessing for employers and their allies in government. While economics has helped shield them from criticism as well, it also has mesmerized them into believing things that are not true. They, too, have neglected work, workers, and working conditions, and this has made for bad management and bad policy. People in power became lulled into ignoring the importance of the productive activities that form the foundation of a strong economy.

The subject of conflicts between ideological and productive needs runs through this book. The ideology of economics intersected with the personal needs of the people who run the economy. These "captains of industry" enjoyed believing that their authority was the result of their own talents and hard work. Measures that could make workers more productive might threaten to undermine either the rationale for or the authority of the capitalists. So when they had to choose between justifying their position and improving workers' productive potential, they opted for the former.

Instead of Adam Smith's imagined harmonious economy, the real world is one in which the interests of employers and workers are sharply at odds. Ideology may be able to partially cover up the nature of this conflict, but ideology cannot eradicate it. Instead, hidden from view, the conflict festers, poisoning all aspects of society. This corrosive aspect of capitalist social relations compels business and public agencies to take strong measures to impose their will on recalcitrant workers; however, the effort to control labor increases hostility within the workplace. At the same time, such measures create an atmosphere that destroys respect, as well as the free flow of information, both of which are essential in an efficient modern economy. They also force the system's apologists to construct still more elaborate rationalizations for its goodness.

In contrast, a rational economy would offer workers a helping hand, not just in terms of providing a higher standard of living, but even more important, making sure that workers have every opportunity to develop their potential.

This neglect of workers' potential, both at the workplace and in society at large, represents an enormous loss—both social and economic. One problem in moving forward is the opposite of Adam Smith's invisible hand. What we might call "invisible handcuffs" blind workers from realizing how capitalism both constrains their potential and degrades their quality of life.

The more technologically advanced an economy becomes, the more destructive the invisible handcuffs become. Both the economy and society suffer because of the tragic neglect of work, workers, and working conditions. Modest political reforms and a more humanistic scheme of management might seem to be able to remedy this problem, but such efforts will, at best, make modest improvements. These invisible handcuffs will continue to undermine society by stunting workers and thereby stifling the economy. Nonetheless, these handcuffs are an integral part of a market economy.

For the most part, this book concentrates on the United States, where the market economy has perhaps evolved the furthest. Certainly, the current U.S. economy falls short on an infuriating array of counts. Here is the most powerful economy in the world, yet it seems powerless to meet the most pressing needs of its people. The list of pervasive problems includes obscene poverty, inadequate health care, climate change, and environmental damage.

Policymakers do not pay sufficient attention to such problems. When they do address them, they end up going to great lengths to nurture the market rather than people; yet to their surprise, the relative economic strength of the U.S. economy still seems to be eroding. In this context, the importance of looking at the economy from the perspective of workers should be undeniable. Today, when the world faces such difficult threats, society cannot afford to waste a resource as valuable as human potential. This book is intended to highlight the urgent need to cast off the handcuffs in order to benefit from previously unutilized human potential.

The Bearded Slave

Mainstream economics represents a barrier to meeting the urgent challenges that we face. Breaking through the solid front of the discipline is a difficult but urgent task.

Economists have been trained to resist such efforts. Their education promotes a maddening uniformity. Heated debates do occur, but almost always within a narrow framework. A few marginalized schools of economics exist at the fringes of academia, but they exert little influence on the discipline as a whole. For example, for decades no Ivy League economics department has hired anybody who deviates significantly, much less radically, from mainstream thought.

Some individual economists dissent from market fundamentalism on specific issues, such as global warming. Others even accept a role for government spending, especially in the midst of a crisis, to increase the quantity of commercial transactions in order to generate more employment. But for the most part, even when the economy is in obvious disarray, the economics profession presents a solid phalanx, insisting on the primacy of market transactions at the expense of the process of production. As a result, matters of work, workers, and working conditions fall from view.

One purpose of emphasizing commercial transactions is to ensure that the "handcuffs" remain invisible, but this choice has unintended consequences. By excluding the study of work, workers, and working conditions, economists lose sight of the productive system on which the economy depends. This not only leaves them unable to recognize destructive economic tendencies, but it also encourages business and political leaders to take measures that undermine the economy by limiting people's potential.

Although the dogmatism of economics seems as hard as a rock, the situation is not hopeless. Jacob Riis, a posthumously celebrated social reformer, recalled his therapy to avoid discouragement:

> I would go out and look at a stone-mason hammering away at his rock perhaps a hundred times without as much as a crack showing in it. Yet at the hundred-and-first blow, it will split in two, and I know it was not that blow that did it, but all that had gone before.[1]

This book is intended as one among many blows that will ultimately crack the prevailing dogma that prevents the development of an economy that can nurture and tap in to people's potential. It does not describe how this kind of economy will work. Developing the details of the future organization is far more challenging than helping to make way for the transition; however, awareness of the current wasted potential must precede the transformation of the present system of social relations.

Michelangelo's wonderfully evocative, half-finished sculptures, known as *The Slaves*, made a deep impression on me when I saw them in Florence forty years ago. These works do not display the uniform delicacy and detail of his *David* or the frescoes of the Sistine Chapel, but the very incompleteness of these four massive statues, intended for the tomb of Pope Julius, is a major source of strength. The *Awakening Slave* depicts a powerful body, seemingly waking, while still encased in stone. The effect of the *Bearded Slave*, struggling to free himself from his marble boulder, which had once completely engulfed him, is even more dramatic.

Everybody irritated by a boss's foolish command or a corporation's ridiculous bureaucratic demands has taken a first step toward an awakening. These annoyances are symptomatic of a much larger problem associated with an outdated system of command and control at the workplace. Once that realization kicks in, you can sense your inner *Bearded Slave*. I like to think that many economists are also like the *Bearded Slave*, deep down struggling to emerge from the self-censorship that engulfs the discipline.

Capitalist society also has something in common with the *Bearded Slave*, except that what covers its inner potential is man-made. It is capitalist control that encrusts society with unsightly layers of waste and inefficiency. This book includes many such examples. Hammering away at this crud might make the system more productive, but more often than not the waste and inefficiency serve a purpose—to maintain the existing system of control.

With enough blows, the irrationality of this system will be exposed. An irresistible vision of a humane system with rich social relations—something more beautiful than Michelangelo's statues—will first come into view and then replace capitalism.

A Brief Note on
the Characterization of Economics

This book describes economists as if they were an entirely homogeneous group, which is not entirely accurate. A tiny minority of marginalized economists remain critical of the capitalist system. A larger number of more conventional economists, some of whom have won Nobel Prizes, have been able to recognize particular shortcomings, though without understanding the systemic nature of the invisible handcuffs.

For example, the work of behavioral economists and neuroeconomists is generating interest for the development of a more realistic analysis of how people actually make decisions. This research shows why the fundamental assumptions of human behavior that economists use are thoroughly unrealistic. Although one of these scholars, the psychologist Daniel Kahneman, won the Nobel Prize in economics, the critical insights of these groups have been no more able to budge the mass of the economics profession than the generations of institutionalist economists (the progeny of Thorstein Veblen) who preceded them.

The stubborn resistance of economics to adapt to scientific evidence reflects a long-standing solidarity on the part of the discipline. Even in macroeconomics, which generates contentious economic debates, Paul Krugman's textbook acknowledges, "the clean little secret of modern macroeconomics is how much consensus economists have reached over the past 70 years."[2]

For this reason, this book will treat economics and economists as if they were homogeneous, despite the existence of a small number who do not completely fit the stereotype.

Overview

The first chapter, "The Anti-Worker Theology of Markets," begins with a discussion of the theological defense of markets by sources as far apart in time and in stature as Edmund Burke and George W. Bush. According to such people, market relations ensure not only efficiency but also higher qualities, such as freedom and justice. For the true believers, questioning markets is akin to blasphemy. However, a more appropriate theology of markets might come from Greek mythology, from the legend of the sadistic Procrustes, whose story is introduced in this chapter.

The second chapter, "Disciplining Workers in the Procrustean Bed," begins to moves away from theology toward reality, by examining a less attractive aspect of the market (and one that the ideologues refuse to attribute to the market): disciplining workers. The chapter describes both direct discipline in the workplace and obvious forms of control, such as the Federal Reserve's intentional creation of unemployment to make labor fearful of being fired—what Alan Greenspan, then chairman of the Federal Reserve Board, referred to as the traumatization of labor. Such policies are ironic, considering that policymakers pretend that all social objectives—whether higher wages, better working conditions, environmental protections, or even the quality of life—must give way to the promise of job creation. The two concluding sections of the chapter offer quantitative estimates of some of the human and economic costs of labor discipline.

The third chapter, "How Economics Marginalized Workers," analyzes the development of economic theory's justification of its inattention to work, workers, and working conditions. It explains why economics chooses to treat work as nothing more than the absence of leisure and how economic theory reduces workers to an abstract input—labor—comparable to coal or steel. This perspective is especially destructive because the abstractions of economics block its practitioners and those whose vision is shaped by economists from recognizing the potential of real people.

Chapter 4, "Everyday Life in a Procrustean World," discusses the impact of the narrow market perspective on everyday life. It examines the enormous amount of time that jobs consume, as well as the extension of controls on people's behavior outside the workplace. These controls are also counterproductive, because they interfere with people's opportunity to improve their own abilities and capacities. This chapter shows how mainstream economics has tried to convince working people themselves to adopt the same perspective as economists, instructing them to identify themselves as individual consumers while seeing their own work as nothing more than a loss of leisure. In effect, workers are supposed to ignore work and their relationships with other workers.

The fifth chapter, "International Procrusteanism," briefly extends the analysis to the international economy, showing how much of the rest of the world must comply with the demands of the United States for market-friendly policies.

Chapters 6 and 7 put the subject in historical perspective by looking back at the economic vision bequeathed by Adam Smith. "Adam Smith's Historical Vision" looks at Smith's analysis based on how he thought that societies evolved until they reached the ultimate form of market organization. In this intensely ideological work, Smith cast markets in a highly favorable light. Markets are harmonious, fair, efficient, and give everybody an opportunity to succeed. In this way, Smith provided the ideological foundation for the defense of markets.

Chapter 7, "The Dark Side of Adam Smith," shows how Smith realized that his vision of a harmonious society depended upon the prior existence of a successful coercion of labor to accept the discipline of the workplace. In his time, violent measures were often required to leave people with no other option than to accept the new conditions of wage labor. Even after people became corralled into wage labor, Smith realized that controls had to reach deeper into people's lives, even including state regulation of religion. In short, for all his positive rhetoric about freedom, Smith's ultimate concern was to control people in order to make them obedient workers. This reading of Smith lends further support to chapter 2's emphasis on the role of discipline.

This chapter also explains why Smith had to distort his work by excluding any discussion of modern industry. He did this in order to allow him to offer his vision of marketplace freedom and liberty, and, later, accounts for how economists simplified Smith's writings. They removed its uncomfortable ideological implications, leaving an effective, but unrealistic, propagandistic shell.

Chapter 8, "Keeping Score," looks at the concept of the Gross Domestic Product, a seemingly straightforward measure of the progress of an economy. We review the evolution of this concept, showing how, just as with Adam Smith's theory, the Gross Domestic Product focused on convenient matters that put the market in the best possible light. Just as is the case in economic theory, Gross Domestic Product accounting sweeps work, workers, and working conditions under the rug, along with any notion of the importance of social relationships. By using such a measure to gauge economic success, the concept of Gross Domestic Product served to strengthen the case for destructive, market-friendly policies.

The chapter ends by contrasting the Gross Domestic Product with the results of a recent field of "happiness studies," in which social scientists, including some economists, recognize the disconnect between the GDP and a satisfying quality of life.

Chapter 9, "The Destructive Nature of Procrusteanism," is the capstone of the book, surveying some of the innumerable ways in which capitalist discipline proves to be counterproductive, even in terms of its narrowly conceived objective of increasing the quantity of commercial transactions included in the Gross Domestic Product. For example, unwieldy bureaucracies driven by purely financial motives are incapable of efficiently organizing, let alone inspiring, people. These bureaucracies are not merely a managerial mistake but, as will be shown, a natural outgrowth of an advanced market economy.

These shortcomings of the great corporations that dominate the modern market economy fall into two classes. The first class consists of the destructive effects of efforts to control labor, natural to the present capitalist system. The more interesting, second set of defects represents the ways in which the present organization of production does not just waste labor but also stunts workers' potential.

The final chapter, "Where Do We Go from Here?" offers some hints about the future possibilities of people working together to create a better life. These propositions fly in the face of prevailing opinion. However, if we continue with the obsessive efforts to control labor, we will harm the interests of society as well as the interests of those who seem to be benefiting from current practices.

CHAPTER ONE

The Anti-Worker Theology of Markets

The Theological Defense of Markets

Academic economists present a great mystery. How can they muster so much brilliance and intelligence to deny any suggestion of market imperfections? These dogmatic defenders of markets warn that any measures to address economic deficiencies—other than the knee-jerk remedy of expanding market powers even further—are certain to disrupt economic efficiency. Others may acknowledge market problems, but they insist that the root cause must be people's personal shortcomings. The proper response is to demand more from the people, not the system.

This blind devotion to the market is a kind of religion. Like the adherents of many other religions, economists can be intolerant of those who do not accept their worldview. As Margaret Thatcher, the ultra-conservative British prime minister, popularly known as the "Iron Lady," once explained, "Economics are the method. The object is to change the soul."[1] This call for spiritual uplift inspired neoliberalism, an extremist mindset in which public policy must give way to the interests of the market.

However, when markets implode, and eventually they always do, many fundamentalists temporarily throw aside their faith in markets. They call on the government for support—never for selfish reasons, of course, but only to return the market to health once more. Once the crisis has passed, their absolute faith in the market is restored. As Charles Darwin once observed, "ignorance more frequently begets confidence than does knowledge."[2] The stubbornness of market fundamentalism reflects a theological view that markets are an end in themselves rather than merely a means to an end. Even the mildest challenge to the market reeks of heresy. Edmund Burke, perhaps the most famous British statesman of the eighteenth century, set the tone for this theological defense of markets, confidently declaring, "The laws of commerce . . . are the laws of nature, and consequently the laws of God."[3] The *Journal of Markets and Morality* continues to promote this theological tradition.

From a less elevated perspective, business and political leaders commonly join the familiar litany of praise for the market, bandying about lofty terms: freedom, democracy, and justice, not to mention efficiency and prosperity. When first running for president in 1999, George W. Bush offered a simpler formulation, simply declaring that "trade and markets are freedom."[4]

Surely, nobody could object to allowing people to enjoy freedom, democracy, or any other positive quality attributed to the market. Fundamentalists ask why anyone would be foolish enough to challenge the existing economic system, one that presumably represents the pinnacle of social organization—or at least it would, if ill-considered taxes and regulations did not interfere with what President Ronald Reagan called "the magic of the marketplace?"

But adults should not believe in magic. Despite Reagan's fanciful rhetoric, the market is a harsh taskmaster. Frederick Winslow Taylor, the father of scientific management, famous for devoting his life to using a stopwatch to cut split seconds from workers' tasks, gave a more realistic verdict of the modern situation, observing, "In the past the man has been first; in the future the system must be first."[5] Does this system really serve people's essential needs? I do not think that it does. Let us begin to see why.

A Different Theology

Consider a different theology—an ancient Greek legend. A bandit named Damastes terrorized people near Eleusis in Attica. People called him Procrustes, or "The Stretcher," because he compelled unwary travelers who fell into his hands to spend the night on an iron bed. He sadistically murdered his guests by stretching short men to fit the dimensions of the bed, or, if they were tall, cutting off as much of their limbs as necessary to fit them into the bed. His sadism supposedly turned the surrounding countryside into a desert. Procrustes' reign of terror was eventually cut short when Theseus, a heroic figure who became king of Athens, subjected Procrustes to his own bed treatment.

Mythological references might seem out of place in a book on the economy, but economic language has become so perverted that reframing it in an unfamiliar context seems appropriate. After all, Taylor's expression—"the system must be first"—suggested that the modern economy requires that people conform to its dictates. In effect, his stopwatch tightened the screws on the Procrustean bed.

German sociologist Max Weber, hardly a radical, vividly captured this harsh spirit of the Procrustean world, observing, "The market is the most impersonal relationship of practical life into which humans can enter. . . . Such absolute depersonalization is contrary to all the elementary forms of human relationship."[6] One of Weber's most famous expressions is his metaphor of the iron cage (actually a mistranslation of a less poetic "shell as hard as steel"):

> Today's capitalist economic order is a monstrous cosmos, into which the individual is born and which in practice is for him, at least as an individual, simply a given, an immutable shell, in which he is obliged to live. It forces on the individual, to the extent that he is caught up in the relationships of the "market," the norms of its economic activity.[7]

Contemporary rhetoric offers an excellent example of this market imperative. The word *reform* has become synonymous with the elimination of protections against unfavorable market outcomes. In effect, people must learn to adjust to the market rather than make any attempt to have the market adjust to people's needs. Procrusteanism is the set of practices intended to force people to accept market discipline.

The Procrustean Heritage of Economics

Associating Procrusteanism with the market might seem jarring to many readers, but it has actually been part of a subtext of economics for centuries. Many early economists believed that because people are driven by potentially dangerous passions, the market offered a socially beneficial outlet for their urges.[8] For example, Adam Smith, whose first book was about psychology, introduced his famous description of the invisible hand thusly: "It is not from the benevolence of the butcher, the brewer, or the baker that we expect our dinner, but from their regard to their own interest."[9] In the same vein, John Maynard Keynes wrote, "It is better that a man should tyrannise over his bank balance than over his fellow-citizens; and whilst the former is sometimes denounced as being but a means to the latter, sometimes at least it is an alternative."[10]

Francis Ysidro Edgeworth, an influential Oxford economist, expanded upon the association between the passions and the market. Although he was less clear than Smith or Keynes about the market as an alternative to antisocial behavior, his basic message was unmistakable:

> The first principle of economics is that every agent is actuated only by self-interest. The workings of this principle may be viewed under two aspects, according as the agent acts without or with the consent of others affected by his actions. In wide senses, the first species of action may be called war; the second, contract.[11]

Economists in the eighteenth and early nineteenth centuries clearly understood that people would naturally resist employment as wage laborers if they could maintain themselves outside of the market. They proposed strong measures to deny people alternative means of support, including the confiscation of the land upon which people had traditionally provided for their own needs.[12] The intention was to make people so destitute they would be desperate to work for wages. Then, once wage labor became sufficiently common, people would begin to think of it as normal and take it for granted.

Once workers became habituated to wage labor, economists could ignore the coercive side of the market and treat it as a purely voluntary system. In the process, they banished any suggestion of either coercion or irrational behavior, except on the part of those who might be foolish enough to resist total engagement with the market. Here is how the Reverend Thomas Robert Malthus described the egalitarian relationship between workers and their employers:

> The man who does a day's work for me, confers full as great an obligation upon me, as I do upon him. I possess what he wants; he possesses what I want. We make an amicable exchange. The poor man walks erect in conscious independence; and the mind of his employer is not vitiated by a sense of power. [13]

Nonetheless, Malthus was not above recommending harsh measures to ensure that workers would be so destitute that they would have no choice but to accept the amicable bargains that would await them.

The brutal measures that were required to transform society to the point that people took wage labor for granted did obvious damage. However, once people accept market life as the norm, the Procrustean bed begins to fall from view. The ongoing negative consequences of markets became less noticeable. Even the people the system harms most directly come to accept it as natural, almost as if they were voluntarily donning a pair of invisible handcuffs.

These handcuffs, and their unintentional consequences, remain invisible, but that does not mean their damage is insignificant. As we shall see, so long as the causes of the alienation, insecurity, and powerlessness that go along with capitalism remain invisible, free-floating anger becomes common. Procrusteans have mastered the art of diverting this anger into a powerful reinforcement of the system.

There is another kind of damage. The Procrustean project of squeezing more profits out of people ultimately turns out to be self-defeating, so much so that it threatens the health and vitality of society, along with the very economy it is intended to promote.

Beyond the Procrustean Economy

In the spirit of Weber—at least the mistranslated Weber—the market functions as a Procrustean bed. Why would anybody willingly lie down in such a bed? Those who accommodate themselves to the system often suffer a cruel fate, as the discussion of workplace deaths and diseases in chapter 3 will demonstrate. However, the system punishes those who refuse to adjust themselves voluntarily to it. This helps people to come to see this world as natural and allows overt Procrustean control to be largely replaced by the invisible handcuffs.

At times, however, when Procrusteans overplay their hands or the system malfunctions, the handcuffs become visible once again. As was true before capitalism was firmly established, some elements of society stand up against the demands of the market and others may appear ready to do so. In response, the Procrusteans stand ready to impose their will, unleashing violent repression when necessary. For example, in Uruguay, when such repression was in full force, the journalist Eduardo Galeano observed, "People were in prison so that prices could be free."[14]

Unlike the irrational sadist Procrustes—a parasite that destroyed its victim with no apparent purpose—those who control the capitalist economy are rational, singlemindedly devoted to the making of money. Toward this end, the Procrusteans routinely call upon the state to use its monopoly of force to keep everybody in line, while loudly proclaiming that the modern economy is the height of freedom as well as rationality. After all, people can freely choose to work where they want and buy what they want—and nobody commands anybody (except on the job).

Business leaders, politicians, and economists are quick to explain that the logic of the system is immutable. They come down hard on anyone who dares to question Procrustean rationality, even though they themselves are generally immune from the harsh demands of Procrusteanism. This posture helps to make the boundary between the realm of Procrustes and the invisible handcuffs even fuzzier. How can anyone rationalize why hours of work have not radically decreased despite the proliferation of modern, labor-saving technology? How can anyone reconcile increasing job insecurity and stagnating wages with market efficiency? Are these conditions the natural functioning of the labor market or the intentional manipulation of Procrusteans?

We will make the case that ultimately the market is Procrustean and, like Procrustes, destroys its surroundings. Viable alternatives do exist. They might seem impossibly utopian, but only because the gate-keepers of the Procrustean economy stubbornly refuse to accept any dialogue or even the possibility of a dialogue. As Margaret Thatcher adamantly proclaimed, "There is no alternative." The iron bed must remain in place. Everyone must learn to accept the dictates of the Procrustean economy—to voluntarily don the invisible handcuffs. There is no choice in the matter. To defy the logic of the market would be suicidal—at least in an economic sense.

As we shall see, the truth is otherwise. The Procrustean ideology is as absurd as it is inhuman. Let us begin now to see how. First, let us critically evaluate the market. Then let us point ourselves in a more positive direction. Only after people get beyond the idea that the system must be first can society tap into people's potential and create a more fulfilling way of life. With sufficient intelligence, courage, and imagination, we can get the kind of economy we deserve—an anti-Procrustean one in which the productive system will finally adjust to meet society's most pressing needs.

CHAPTER TWO

Disciplining Workers in the Procrustean Bed

Jobs! Jobs! Jobs!

The most compelling defense of the inverted priorities of Procrusteanism concerns jobs: any policy that dares to give people's pressing needs priority over the rigid imperative of the market will surely result in a loss of jobs. In fact, the promise of job creation drives the rhetoric of almost all economic policies. Business demands tax breaks, relief from environmental protection, and a host of other special treatments, while the rich demand tax cuts for themselves, all in the name of creating jobs, even when the evidence for the job creation is weak or nonexistent.[1]

For all their talk about job creation, the largest corporations—the businesses that win a disproportionate share of the benefits from playing the job card—actually create few jobs. According to a report published in 2000, toward the end of a period of unusually vigorous job growth, the top 200 corporations worldwide employed a mere 0.78 percent of the world's workforce, even though their sales accounted for 27.5 percent of world economic activity.[2] That business is not particularly good at creating jobs—especially good jobs—should come as no surprise. Wall Street rewards corporations for eliminating jobs, not creating them. Profits rather than jobs are the highest priority for business leaders. However, big business is exceptionally skillful in collecting subsidies based on the false hope of job creation—often in amounts in excess of $100,000 per job, even when the jobs are short-lived or nonexistent.[3] For example, when Northwest Airlines threatened to move from Minnesota, the state granted the company $828 million for a repair facility with 1,500 jobs. Once the agreement was in place, the company accepted an immediate loan of $270 million as part of the deal. Not long after, it announced that the facility and the jobs were on hold.[4] After the company went bankrupt in 2005, it showed its compassionate side. Management supplied its laid-off workers with a handbook for surviving during hard times, offering valuable tips, such as not being "shy about pulling something you like out of the trash."[5]

Even when jobs are created, the quality of the jobs is poor, something ignored by policymakers. Many of the jobs in the giant corporations do not provide health care or a living wage. The CEO of Wal-Mart, the world's largest private employer, confessed that a full-time worker might not be able to support a family on a Wal-Mart paycheck.[6] As a result, millions of its employees must rely on government assistance. In July 2003, California assemblywoman Sandy Lieber released copies of employee handouts from Wal-Mart explaining how to use an employment verification service when applying for Medicaid, food stamps, and other public services. According to the Democratic Staff of the Committee on Education and the Workforce, one 200-person Wal-Mart store may result in a cost to federal taxpayers of $420,750 per year—about $2,103 per employee over and above the costs imposed on state and local governments.[7]

Despite the poor record of large corporations in providing good jobs, business attacks any legislation intended to raise wages or improve working conditions as a "job killer." The use of such clever terms effectively cuts off any discussion with those who might be foolish enough to advocate such policies. In light of the absence of effective regulations to prevent workplace fatalities, more attention should be given to killer jobs rather than job killers. Such alternative phrasing cannot gain traction in the present political climate, because those who dare to question the wisdom of the Procrustean economy seldom manage to get a public hearing.

Although employment in the United States has increased during the last three decades, hourly wages corrected for inflation peaked in 1972 at $8.99, measured in 1982 dollars. By 2007, hourly wages had fallen to $8.32. Well-paying blue-collar jobs had been disappearing for years.[8] Then, decent white-collar employment suffered the same fate. Both trends helped to give us an unprecedented stretch of thirty-five years without an increase in real wages.

In addition, jobs have become more insecure. A few decades ago, many people had long-lasting careers. They could feel reasonably certain that as long as they performed their job well, they could continue with the same employer and probably also advance to better positions.

Today, businesses now openly regard workers as disposable commodities. Downsizing, outsourcing, and plant closings have become routine events. The *Wall Street Journal* casually noted that "many management theorists" maintain that "the whole concept of a job—steady work at steady pay from the same employer—must be discarded."[9] Just after AT&T announced the layoff of 40,000 workers, James Meadows, vice president for human resources and responsible for administering the job cuts, explained corporate thinking about job mobility:

> In AT&T, we have to promote the whole concept of the workforce being contingent, though most of our contingent workers are inside our walls. "Jobs" are being replaced by "projects" and "fields of work" are giving rise to a society that is increasingly "jobless but not workless." . . . People need to look at themselves as self-employed, as vendors who come to this company to sell their skills.[10]

Meadows's honesty points to the shallowness of business's professed interest in job creation. For people like him, business supplies plenty of opportunities. If people cannot take advantage of these, something is wrong with them. If not enough opportunities are available, some interference is upsetting the smooth functioning of the market. Masters of Procrusteanism never apologize for the way the system treats ordinary people.

Work! Work! Work!

Although jobs are at the forefront of economic policy dialogues, the nature of the work itself gets little consideration. After all, work raises troubling questions. With all of the advances in technology, why do people still have to work so hard? Although the physical demands of most modern labor are light compared to those who worked in William Blake's "dark Satanic mills, "work in pre-capitalist societies had certain advantages over labor today. Before markets became dominant, people worked relatively few yearly hours. During harvest times, work was long and hard, but during much of the year, free time was abundant. Joan Thirsk estimated that in sixteenth- and early seventeenth-century England, about one-third of the working days, including Sundays, were spent in leisure. [11] Innumerable religious holidays punctuated the tempo of work throughout Europe. Karl Kautsky estimated that there were 204 annual holidays in medieval Lower Bavaria.[12] In short, modern technology has not so much been used to relieve people of the burdens of work as to extract more work from people.

Modern technology has eliminated many awful jobs. Relatively few people in the United States work in dangerous, subterranean coal mines. Yet many modern jobs put workers at risk for more subtle but equally lethal conditions. In so-called "clean rooms" for semiconductor production, workers lack adequate protection from the toxic chemicals that surround them, while they wear "bunny suits" to protect the silicon from the workers' bodily impurities.

The contrast between jobs and work is striking. Many people work long hours in poor conditions, while millions of people are left looking for jobs. Shouldn't a successful economy emphasize the development of technology that makes work easier, rather than creating technology intended to make a smaller number of people work more intensively? Why wouldn't a successful economy apply modern technology to make work less stressful? Such questions are rarely raised in polite society.

As I will explain later, modern economics frames the world in a way that precludes questions about the nature of work by adding its own Procrustean twist. Economics devalues work by reducing people to one-dimensional consumers who maximize their "utility"—economists' strange term for enjoyment—by using their budgets (however limited) to select bundles of goods suitable to their personal tastes. Within this framework, work represents nothing more than the loss of utility that people experience because they choose to sacrifice leisure to get utility from consumption. In effect, the clock becomes the sole indicator of working conditions.

When Workplace Procrusteanism Subsides

Ironically, despite the constant drumbeat of business advocates calling for tax cuts and subsidies to aid corporations in their holy quest to create jobs, employers actually need a large pool of unemployed workers. When unemployment is low and the fear of getting fired subsides, workers' bargaining power increases. Employers recognize pools of unemployed workers as a valuable tool for increasing their bargaining power.

Because most people do not enjoy taking orders and have a natural tendency to assert some independence, workers can become rebellious when workplace authorities do not treat them with respect, especially when they feel confident that comparable jobs are readily available.

In the late 1960s, when unemployment was unusually low, Procrustean authority was far less effective. For example, in 1968, Bill Watson, a sociologist, spent a year working in a Detroit automobile factory, where he witnessed several dramatic examples of the lengths to which workers went to challenge management. In one case, workers revolted against the production of a poorly designed six-cylinder model car. After management rejected employee suggestions for improvements in the production and design, the workers initiated a "counterplan," beginning with acts of deliberately misassembling or omitting parts. Workers in the inspection section made alliances with workers in several assembly areas to ensure a high rate of defective motors.

In the process, workers and foremen argued over particular motors. Tension escalated. Workers went ahead and installed defective motors in cars, thereby forcing management to remove them later. The conflict ended only when a layoff allowed management to move the entire six-cylinder assembly and inspection operation to another end of the plant.[13]

In a second instance, the company attempted to save money by building engines with parts that had already been rejected during the year. Workers in the motor-test area lodged a protest, but management hounded inspectors to accept the defective motors. After the motor-test men communicated their grievances to other workers, they began to collaborate in intentional sabotage. Inspectors agreed to reject three of every four motors. Stacks of motors piled up at an accelerating pace until the entire plant shut down, costing the company more than ten hours of production time to deal with the problem. When management summoned inspectors to the head supervisor's office, the inspectors slyly protested that they were only acting in the interest of management.

Watson's third example is the most telling of all. During a model changeover period, management scheduled a six-week inventory buildup, keeping only fifty people on the job. These workers would have earned 90 percent of their pay if they had been laid off. Workers reacted to the opportunity and attempted to finish the inventory buildup in three or four days instead of six weeks. They trained each other in particular skills, circumventing the established ranking and job classification system to slice through the required time.

Management responded harshly, forcing workers to halt, claiming that they had violated the legitimate channels of authority, training, and communication. If workers had been given the opportunity to organize their own work, Watson claims that they could have completed the task in one-tenth the scheduled time. Management, however, was determined to stop workers from organizing their own work, even when it would have been finished more quickly and management would have saved money because of the speed-up.[14] So much for the idea that market forces lead to efficient choices!

Watson also described how workers engaged in hose fights at the workplace and organized contests to explode rods from engines. These incidents illustrate the enormous costs associated with a conflictive system of labor relations. One might argue that the particular managers that Watson described were unusually shortsighted, but something else was at stake. To admit that workers have something to contribute beyond blindly carrying out the demands of management undermines the ultimate rationale for management's domination. As a result, managers often instinctively resist all encroachments on their authority, no matter how much this authority impedes productivity.

Watson's story communicates a sense of the intense joy and exhilaration that workers felt from having the opportunity to organize their own activity. He applauded the industrial sabotage as "the forcing of more free time into existence." He explained:

> The seizing of quantities of time for getting together with friends and the amusement of activities ranging from card games to reading or walking around the plant to see what other areas are doing is an important achievement for the laborers. Not only does it demonstrate the feeling that much of the time should be organized by the workers themselves, but it also demonstrates an existing animosity. . . .

While this organization is a reaction to the need for common action in getting the work done, relationships like these also function to carry out sabotage, to make collections, or even to organize games and contests which serve to turn the working day into an enjoyable event.[15]

Watson's experience may not have been particularly unique. In the 1980s, the United States automobile industry had to dedicate an estimated 20 percent of its plant area and 25 percent of its workers' hours to fixing mistakes.[16] The industry had two options available. It could intensify its supervision over workers or it could actively engage its employees by giving them more control over their jobs. The first option is not only expensive, it further alienates the workers, perhaps encouraging other forms of sabotage. The choice made, that of more intensive supervision, suggests that the automobile industry seems to have adopted the attitude Watson experienced.

One could argue that the behavior Watson described was evidence of the need for a firm hand to control rebellious workers. That rebellion, however, may have been less a product of outrageous and unacceptable behavior by these workers than a natural response to the Procrustean response to the conflict inherent in the relationship between labor and capital.

Imagine how much the company lost just because management stubbornly refused to take advantage of the workers' on-the-spot knowledge of the business. But to do so would have weakened the dysfunctional Procrustean hierarchy that allows managers the privilege of seeing themselves as superior to their underlings.

In fact, management's perception is less relevant than that of the workers. Once you get beyond the theology of capitalism, the ultimate justification for this mode of production is that the efficiency of markets can offer the best possible life for people. Part of the illusion of efficiency is that capitalism is a meritocracy—that the best people rise to positions of authority. Consequently, maintaining the legitimacy of authority is crucial for capitalism.

The proper maintenance of authority is an old question. Machiavelli's *The Prince* may be the classic text on the subject. His chapter 17 asks whether it be better to be loved than feared. He concluded "it is safer to be feared than loved."[17] Machiavelli's conclusion is just as applicable for capitalist management as for a medieval prince. In this sense, a certain amount of Procrusteanism is a necessary requirement for the capitalist workplace.

The key insight from Watson's experience is the degree to which the workers were able to organize themselves in spite of management.

Had their objective been to earn profits, their efforts would have qualified as entrepreneurial—and far more so than is usually expected from workers who lacked the formal qualifications usually associated with leadership.

The Federal Reserve to the Rescue

Business leaders understood why workers, such as Watson and his colleagues, openly challenged management. They had little fear of getting fired because unemployment rates were very low. Although they would never admit to such crass motives, business leaders know that maintaining a substantial level of unemployment gives them a strategic advantage. Losing a job posed few risks for Watson's colleagues since many equally attractive jobs were available at the time. Where jobs are harder to find, workers are less likely to behave in ways that displease management, including demanding higher wages.

Since the end of the Second World War, the responsibility for creating the "appropriate" level of unemployment has fallen to the Federal Reserve. Officially, the Federal Reserve has a dual mandate to prevent inflation and to maintain full employment. In reality, the Fed concentrates on fighting inflation by vigorously preventing full employment.

A board of seven governors, appointed by the president and approved by the Senate, theoretically runs the system, but the Fed is actually quite Byzantine. "Constitutionally, the Federal Reserve is a pretty queer duck" was the verdict of the populist Texas congressman Wright Patman. Martin Mayer, author of *The Bankers* and other excellent books on finance, went further, observing that "the Federal Reserve would be a queer duck even without any Constitution, for a more awkward and complicated mixture of private and public, executive and legislative, national and regional could not possibly be imagined."[18]

In addition to the Federal Reserve Board, each of the twelve regional banks has a president, selected by bankers. These regional presidents, directly representing the interests of the banking sector, wield enormous power.

The chief policymaking arm of the Federal Reserve, known as the Federal Open Market Committee, consists of a rotating pool of seven of the governors and four of the regional bank presidents plus the president of the New York Federal Reserve Bank. This committee makes the key decision regarding monetary policy—whether to make credit scarce or abundant.

The decisions of the Open Market Committee have a powerful effect on the economy. When the committee makes credit tight by restricting the supply of money, interest rates increase, which then discourages businesses from borrowing to finance spending on building, plants, equipment, and the like. In addition, higher interest rates depress consumers' purchases of cars or houses on credit, because their monthly payments depend on the rate of interest.

Shrinking consumer purchases, together with the higher cost of borrowing, further discourages business from investing. As a result, the economy slows down, replenishing the pool of unemployed workers.

In effect, then, the Fed represents a collaboration between the bankers and government, free to make policy without congressional oversight. The only requirement placed on the Federal Reserve is that the chairman has to appear twice a year before the House and Senate. Just imagine the uproar if anyone suggested that labor unions have the power to determine the course of the economy with virtually no oversight.

In addition, all other things equal, high interest rates tend to redistribute wealth from the poor to the rich, because the rich as a whole are net lenders, while the poor are net borrowers. Even during the 1990s, a time when interest rates were low, over one-seventh of wage earners' salaries went to pay interest on their loans.[19]

Business does not want the economy to slow down too much, since economic growth is ultimately necessary for a sustained expansion of profits. Therefore, when the Open Market Committee deems it appropriate, it once again expands the money supply in an attempt to increase the pace of economic growth, at least until the economy begins to run short of unemployment.

Ideally, the Federal Reserve would like to maintain a Goldilocks economy, in which economic growth is just right—strong enough to increase profits, but slow enough to keep workers in check. When business is pleased with economic performance, the press portrays the chairman of the Federal Reserve Board as a hero. For example, the journalist Bob Woodward titled his book on Alan Greenspan, *Maestro*, as if the economy were his symphony orchestra.[20] After the economy fell apart on his watch, Greenspan's reputation withered.

The Hidden Procrusteanism of the Fed

One thing is fairly certain: when business fears that the economy is beginning to grow fast enough that workers might feel confident in demanding better wages or working conditions, the Federal Reserve is sure to step in and tighten the money supply.

Restrictive monetary policy does not operate in the open. One of the beauties of the monetary weapon is that few people make the connection between what the Open Market Committee decides and their own situation. Nobody seems to be responsible for the resulting hard economic times. How could the economy seem Procrustean when Procrustes is nowhere to be found? When the economy slows down, the boss can tell the workers, "Sorry, guys, but there's nothing I can do. I would love to be able to comply with your demands, but business is not good."

Workers are likely to resent people who directly discipline them, such as a supervisor or even the boss of the whole operation. Few workers, however, will ever think to vent their anger at the faceless president of a branch of the Federal Reserve Bank or one of the equally unknown members of the Board of Governors. No wonder that conservatives often regard the Federal Reserve's fight against inflation as one of the nation's highest economic priorities.

Insofar as discipline is concerned, the system works like a charm—at least for business interests. This game becomes even more effective because the Federal Reserve projects an image of standing above the political fray. The Fed speaks in terms of its mandated responsibility to maintain long-run growth, minimize inflation, and promote price stability—all of which sounds reasonable—while ignoring that part of its mandate to create full employment.

The Federal Reserve uses price stability as a code word for holding wages in check. Paul Volcker, former chairman of the Federal Reserve Board, was clear about this relationship: "In an economy like ours, with wages and salaries accounting for two-thirds of all costs, sustaining progress [in reducing inflation] will need to be reflected in the moderation of growth of nominal wages."[21]

The targets of restrictive monetary policy do not include rising prices for assets, such as houses or stocks. Instead, rising asset prices are interpreted as signs of economic health, even though these prices may be the result of speculative excesses that will ultimately destabilize the economy. Nor are the multimillion-dollar salaries of executives a concern.

When Richard Nixon was running for president in 1968, he insisted that inflation was the country's number one problem. After his election, he enlisted his Council of Economic Advisors to identify those adversely impacted by inflation. According to the council's chairman, Herbert Stein, "If anyone was being severely hurt, the available statistics were too crude to reveal it." [22]

Of course, Dr. Stein understood as well as anybody what David Ricardo, the most important economist of the early nineteenth century, wrote about the harm of inflation:

> The depreciation of the circulating medium (meaning inflation) has been more injurious to monied men . . . It may be laid down as a principle of universal application, that every man injured or benefited by the variation of the value of the circulating medium in proportion as his property consists of money.[23]

As later research has shown, a modest level of inflation is beneficial for the economy because it allows business more flexibility in dealing with workers. Employees are resentful when business demands wage cuts. Inflation allows business a back door for reducing wages—at least what wages can buy. In this way, management can alter the wage structure, rewarding some workers, with higher wages while letting the real wages of less-favored workers erode.[24] In addition, a number of studies indicate that inflation does no damage to the middle or lower classes as a whole. Although inflation does harm those on fixed incomes, inflation (within limits) is associated with higher economic growth, bringing more prosperity, especially to unskilled workers. Inflation, however, does have a detrimental effect on the rich, because it erodes the value of their financial assets.[25]

Creating Unemployment

Economist Edwin Dickens has written a series of significant articles analyzing the minutes of the meetings of the Open Market Committee of the Federal Reserve Board, dating back to the 1950s. Dickens's research shows convincingly that the Federal Reserve's partisan behavior is designed to tilt the economy in the direction of the wealthy by making workers more compliant. Dickens reported numerous occasions when participants voted to tighten the money supply just before major union contracts were about to expire. The minutes indicate that the specific intent was to force employers to be less generous with their wage offers during contract negotiations. [26]

A recent study formalized Dickens's work by attempting to distinguish whether the policy actions of the Federal Reserve were a response to inflation or to low unemployment. The study concluded that "a baseless fear of full employment" rather than the prevention of inflation was the guiding principle of the Federal Reserve.[27] The conclusion of this study should come as little surprise to people familiar with the Federal Reserve's obsession with the danger of high wages.

Defenders of such policies justify the temporary restriction of job creation, contending that the Federal Reserve is merely trying to curb excessive growth. According to this school of thought, the Federal Reserve is simply preventing the kind of excesses that lead to severe recessions or depressions. Slowing down growth today may be necessary to provide for a higher, sustainable growth rate in the future. Most economists argue that the cumulative effect of even a fairly small increase in growth rate can be substantial, more than enough to compensate for a temporary slowdown.

The periodic slowdowns that the Federal Reserve engineered to undermine wage growth are unlikely to stimulate economic growth. According to a study by the Bank for International Settlements, slowdowns actually seem to diminish rather than promote long-term growth.[28] Over and above the dramatic effects of intentionally engineered slowdowns, the more steady effort to keep wages in check also probably reduces the rate of growth. As economists continually warn, the cumulative effect of a reduced rate of economic growth can be substantial. This loss must count as another cost of Procrusteanism.

In the 1920s, John Maynard Keynes described the effect of this sort of monetary policy on workers:

> The object of credit restriction . . . is to withdraw from employers the financial means to employ labour at the existing level of wages and prices. The policy can only attain its end by intensifying unemployment without limit, until the workers are ready to accept the necessary reduction of money wages under the pressure of hard facts.[29]

Keynes's description of this policy seemed to frame it as a form of Procrustean class warfare:

> Those who are attacked first are faced with a depression of their standard of life, because the cost of living will not fall until all the others have been successfully attacked too; and, therefore, they are justified in defending themselves. . . . They are bound to resist so long as they can; and it must be war, until those who are economically weakest are beaten to the ground.[30]

Keynes concluded: "It is a policy, nevertheless, from which any humane or judicious person must shrink."[31]

Sado-Monetarism

The Federal Reserve's fight against wages can be intense. In 1979, shortly after taking the reins at the Federal Reserve, Paul Volcker announced new operating procedures and a determination to hold inflation in check.

At first, many powerful people doubted whether Volcker would be willing to follow through with his plans, which were sure to create enormous casualties. A front-page story in the *Wall Street Journal*, "Monetary Medicine: Fed's 'Cure' Is Likely to Hurt in Short Run by Depressing Economy, Analysts Say," expressed this sentiment. The paper noted:

> Among those who are skeptical that the Fed will really stick to an aggregate target is Alan Greenspan . . . who questions whether, if unemployment begins to climb significantly, monetary authorities will have the fortitude to "stick to the new policy."[32]

Around this time, possibly in response to the article, Volcker invited the editor of the paper's editorial page, his deputy, and the features editor to a lunch at the New York branch bank of the Federal Reserve. Volcker asked his guests, "When there's blood all over the floor, will you guys still support me?" The deputy editor responded affirmatively, later proudly recollecting, "There was blood indeed, as overextended Latin borrowers and American farmers were caught out by a return to a sound dollar. But we held fast."[33]

Volcker's militaristic analogy (expressed privately to the staff of the *Wall Street Journal*) let the cat out of the bag. The effort to tame inflation was, in reality, mostly a class war, what might be called "sado-monetarism." Indeed, Volcker himself had intended to spill blood. Volcker expressed his intentions in another way:

> [Volcker] carried in his pocket a little card on which he kept track of the latest wage settlements by major labor unions. From time to time, he called various people around the country and took soundings on the sta-

tus of current contract negotiations. What is the UAW asking for? What does organized labor think? Volcker wanted wages to fall, the faster the better. In crude terms, the Fed was determined to break labor. [34]

Volcker tightened the money supply so extremely that the United States experienced what was then the worst economic downturn since the Great Depression. Volcker only let up when the collateral damage became too great. Mexico, which owed a great deal of money to U.S. banks, seemed to be on the brink of bankruptcy, threatening the U.S. banking system. Citibank was effectively bankrupt.

Later, Michael Mussa, director of the Department of Research at the International Monetary Fund, looked back fondly at Volcker's accomplishment. Mussa continued the military analogy, praising Volcker's victory in vanquishing "the demon of inflation":

> The Federal Reserve had to show that when faced with the painful choice between maintaining a tight monetary policy to fight inflation and easing monetary policy to combat recession, it would choose to fight inflation. In other words, to establish its credibility the Federal Reserve had to demonstrate its willingness to spill blood, lots of blood, other people's blood.[35]

Interestingly, the intended enemy of this war—the workers—went unmentioned in this recollection, as did the collateral damage to farmers and the Latin Americans. But what had workers done to make the state treat them as enemies? Were these people culpable of some evil act for wanting more than a pittance?

The Federal Reserve serves the needs of the powerful. Its role is to protect capital against the interests of labor. In order to maintain labor discipline, the Federal Reserve Board is entrusted with the task of maintaining a level of unemployment high enough to keep workers fearful of losing their jobs.

The Treatment of a Different Kind of Worker

Just compare the bloodlust of those leading the attack on labor with the lax disciplinary mechanisms for the corporate elite. Based on an extensive survey of major corporations, Michael Jensen, professor emeritus at Harvard's Graduate School of Business, found 94 percent of all contracts for chief executives prevent them from being fired for unsatisfactory work without a big severance package. Remarkably, in 44 percent of the contracts, this protection included those convicted of fraud or embezzlement.[36] This should be a national scandal. As Warren Buffett told his shareholders:

> Getting fired can produce a particularly bountiful payday for a CEO. Indeed, he can "earn" more in that single day, while cleaning out his desk, than an American worker earns in a lifetime of cleaning toilets. Forget the old maxim about nothing succeeding like success: Today, in the executive suite, the all-too-prevalent rule is that nothing succeeds like failure.[37]

Soon afterward, Stanley O'Neal proved Buffett to be correct. In 2007, after announcing an initial estimate that his firm had lost almost $8 billion that quarter, Merrill Lynch let him go with $161.5 million in stock, options, and other retirement benefits. One compensation expert said, "I wish my performance was so bad that I could get $160 million to leave."[38] As the economic crisis unfolded, O'Neal's successor and a host of other failed executives collected comparable rewards.

Sado-monetarism is not so much a matter of monetary discipline, as most economists would have it, but of class discipline. Earlier, in the 1960s, Harry Johnson, a conservative professor from the University of Chicago, writing in a journal dominated by the conservative perspective of his school, offered a shockingly honest evaluation of the class bias of monetary policy:

> From one important point of view, indeed, the avoidance of inflation and the maintenance of full employment can be most usefully regarded

as conflicting class interests of the bourgeoisie and the proletariat, respectively, the conflict being resolvable only by the test of relative political power in the society and its resolution involving no reference to an overriding concept of the social welfare.[39]

The Dread of Unemployment

The level of unemployment provides a rough indication of the difficulty of getting a new job. But what about the probability of getting an equally desirable job? Recent economic changes have made such prospects increasingly unfavorable. In today's job market, losing a well-paying job generally means downward mobility—having to settle for less desirable employment in the future.

Not surprisingly, unemployment takes a heavy toll on people's psyches. Unemployment and the threat of future downward mobility mean humiliation not only for the worker but also for the entire family. Losing access to what one considers a normal level of consumption can be a wrenching family experience. Children and spouses suffer embarrassment when they are unable to afford the kind of consumption to which they had become accustomed.

Being unemployed is more stressful than divorce or marital separation.[40] People can get over the pain of divorce or separation, but the psychological toll of unemployment lingers. Psychologists have found that people who have lost a limb are naturally unhappy about their condition, but, after a while, they return to their previous level of happiness. But the unemployed do not. Richard Layard, a respected British economist who recently turned to the subject of happiness, observed:

> So unemployment is a very special problem. Moreover, it hurts as much after one or two years of unemployment as it does at the beginning. In that sense you do not habituate to it (though it hurts less if other people are out of work too). And even when you are back at work, you still feel its effects as a psychological scar.[41]

Psychologists also know that dread—anticipatory fear of a likely experience—can be even worse than the event itself. So long as workers feel a strong dread of unemployment, a lower threshold of unemployment will be sufficient to make workers compliant.

This psychological knowledge played an important role in setting economic policy during the late 1990s. At the time, the economy was growing. Low-interest rates first fueled the dot-com bubble, and then, after its collapse, led to the housing bubble. Unemployment was creeping downward. Wages were increasing, but only modestly. Even so, business feared that unemployment was headed to dangerously low levels, yet Alan Greenspan, chairman of the Federal Reserve Board, refused to increase interest rates, knowing that despite lower unemployment, the dread of unemployment by itself was sufficient to keep wages in check.

One major factor in the intensification of dread was the effect of globalization. Greenspan understood he did not have to use the powers of the Federal Reserve to create unemployment. The pool of unemployment had expanded to include hundreds of millions of workers outside the United States. Workers who make strong demands are likely to be met by an employer threat to move production offshore. In this environment, the danger of higher wages and a decline in labor discipline were insignificant. This realization gave Greenspan confidence to keep interest rates low. The high stock market and housing prices were not a matter of concern for him.

Traumatized Labor

Greenspan's confidence was a reflection of what George Orwell called "the haunting terror of unemployment." In Orwell's words, "the working man demands . . . the indispensable minimum without which human life cannot be lived at all. Enough to eat, freedom from the haunting terror of unemployment, the knowledge that your children will get a fair chance."[42] Greenspan explained his monetary strategy in similar, but less eloquent terms, bluntly noting the state of what he called the "traumatized worker." He was not referring to the traumatization of the unemployed workers, but rather that of the employed workers who dreaded the possibility of unemployment.

Traumatization refers to a condition that causes people to suffer serious disorders—the kind with potentially grave consequences. The association of post-traumatic stress disorder and the threat of unemployment might seem far-fetched, if the source were someone less eminent than Alan Greenspan.

As Bob Woodward reported, Greenspan saw the traumatized worker as "someone who felt job insecurity in the changing economy and so was resigned to accepting smaller wage increases. He had talked with business leaders who said their workers were not agitating and were fearful that their skills might not be marketable if they were forced to change jobs."[43]

With wages held in check while the economy boomed, inequality soared during the late 1990s. In 1997, responding to a question from Representative Patrick Kennedy, Greenspan, who made a science of public evasiveness, blamed the resulting growth in inequality on technology and education, excusing his own contribution:

> It is a development which I feel uncomfortable with. There is nothing
> monetary policy can do to address that, and it is outside the scope, so far
> as I am concerned, of the issues with which we deal.[44]

I do not believe that Greenspan ever used the expression "traumatized worker" in his public pronouncements. He always chose his words carefully, and he perfected a language that was legendary for its obscurity. Still, his less inflammatory words still conveyed the same message. For example, he testified before Congress: "The rate of pay increase still was markedly less than historical relationships with labor market conditions would have predicted. Atypical restraint on compensation increases has been evident for a few years now and appears to be mainly the consequence of greater worker insecurity."[45]

Greenspan was correct in his assessment of the situation facing workers. He had numbers to back him up, reporting:

As recently as 1981, in the depths of a recession, International Survey Research found twelve percent of workers fearful of losing their jobs. In today's tightest labor market in two generations, the same organization has recently found thirty-seven percent concerned about job loss.[46]

Greenspan was not the only official at the Federal Reserve who appreciated the benefit of low unemployment without wage increases. One of the governors of the Federal Reserve, Edward W. Kelley Jr., spoke at a meeting of the Open Market Committee about "the good results that we are getting now." He went on to say:

I don't know how much has to do with the so-called traumatized worker. How long is the American workforce going to remain quiescent without the compensation increases that it thinks it should get? When employment is as strong as it is right now, I don't think we can depend on having permanently favorable results in that area. This has been a rather big key to the present happy macro situation where we have a high capacity utilization rate and a relatively low inflation rate. We all feel rather good about that.[47]

Economists also realized what was happening to labor. Not long after Greenspan's comments about identifying speculative bubbles, Nobel Laureate Paul Samuelson told a conference sponsored by the Federal Reserve Bank of Boston that "America's labor force surprised us with a new flexibility and a new tolerance for accepting mediocre jobs."[48]

Work stoppages offer a quantitative measure that suggests how effectively labor was tamed. Between 1966 and 1974, the number of work stoppages involving a thousand workers or more never fell below 250. The average was 352, with a peak of 424 in 1974. Work stoppages then began to fall off rapidly, reaching a low point of fourteen in 2003, and rising slightly to twenty-one in 2007.[49] Then as the economic crisis took hold, many workers had to accept serious declines in wages and benefits.

One might expect that lower wages would cut into consumer demand, but, according to a study in the *Journal of Consumer*

Research, "people use consumer purchases to compensate for psychological states of insecurity."[50] Many families had to take on considerable debt to maintain their standard of living, and this debt reinforced the dangers of unemployment.

Worker acceptance of mediocre jobs at modest wages paid handsome dividends for business, creating more demand (through debt) while making workers even more fearful of losing their jobs. In addition, workers' insecurity also meant that they were less likely to quit in search of better employment, allowing employers to avoid the costs of recruiting and retraining replacement workers. Perhaps best of all, employers could enjoy this bounty without having to call upon the Federal Reserve to slow down the economy.

William McChesney Martin, chairman of the Federal Reserve between 1951 and 1970, used to say that the job of the Fed was to take away the punch bowl when the party gets going. With labor traumatized, the Federal Reserve no longer had to maintain a watchful eye over the economy. Instead, the Fed carelessly spiked the punch bowl with low interest rates and limited oversight of the financial system, fueling a series of bubbles during the Greenspan years. If economists paid a small fraction of the attention they paid to the purchase price of labor to labor's contribution to the process of production, perhaps policymakers would pay more attention to the system of production and be less likely to allow such bubbles to get so far out of hand.

The bursting of those bubbles ultimately traumatized much of the world. Although Greenspan was confident that labor was in no position to challenge capital, many of the rest of the economic pundits were still obsessed with keeping labor tamed, so much so that they were unable to pay attention to the impending disaster.

In stark contrast to the sadistic attitude toward labor, when speculative excesses or some other miscalculation create adverse economic conditions that threaten to harm powerful business interests, especially in finance, the Fed is almost certain to rush in to the rescue, throwing money at business interests while letting labor hang out to dry.

More Discipline

Public policy has further traumatized workers. Since the 1970s, the U.S. government has shredded the social safety net. Access to supports such as welfare and public housing is fast becoming a thing of the past. To make matters worse, governments are making laws to make life difficult for those without employment. For example, some cities have criminalized feeding groups of poor people unless those organizing the food distribution have a permit, but then city officials refuse to issue the necessary permits when requested.

Workers are aware of these negative signals regarding the harsh consequences of unemployment. To capture the reality of this disciplinary environment, Jared Bernstein, today chief economic advisor to Vice President Biden, coined the expression YOYO economy—meaning that workers are told "you're on your own."[51]

Prisons also serve to reinforce the discipline of the workplace. The United States presently incarcerates more than two million people. Some prisoners represent a serious threat to society, but most do not. Given the popular association of marijuana with a lackadaisical work ethic, the harsh penalties connected with this substance may be relevant to efforts to maintain discipline.

Whether by design or not, the fate of prisoners and the homeless stands as a stark warning, not just for those who might find themselves without employment, but for those people who might otherwise dare to resist the Procrustean way of life. Be thankful for your employment or you might have to share the fate of those unfortunate people.

The Lethal Costs of Discipline

Although traumatization may be useful in disciplining the working classes, the heightened levels of stress takes a toll on workers' health. Unemployment increases workers' level of mortality.[52] A study of younger workers who were part of a mass layoff confirmed the lethal effect of job loss. These workers had persistently 15 to 20 percent higher mortality rates than others in their cohorts.[53]

The dread of unemployment creates stresses that affect others besides the workers themselves. Family members and others are drawn into the depression, anger, and even diseases that traumatization inflicts on workers. The recent expression "going postal" suggests how the traumatization of the unemployed can harm people outside the family.

Sado-monetarism threatens health in other ways. Because the purpose of this branch of Procrusteanism is intended to aid the rich at the expense of the poor, nobody should be surprised that it is associated with increases in both poverty and inequality. Richard Wilkinson is at the center of a rich literature that identifies the negative health effects of inequality.[54] Here again, the causal link is stress, which inequality spreads throughout society. This stress harms the rich as well as the poor, suggesting further evidence of the dysfunctionality of capitalism, even by the standards of its intended beneficiaries.

Even though traumatization may harm the rich as well as the poor, the initial impact of a sado-monetarist tightening of the economy strikes the jobs of low-wage workers, pushing people who were just getting by into destitution. Over and above stress-related maladies, the poor often live crowded together in unhealthy conditions without nearby sources of good food. Lack of access to quality medical care compounds the health threats of poverty.

The effect on children is most tragic. Recent neurological research has shown that poverty affects the prefrontal cortex of children's brains.[55] This part of the brain is critical for problem solving and creativity. The lead author reported that the damage to this part of the brain was comparable to what might occur from a stroke.

Sadly, the enormous losses caused by the harsh efforts to discipline workers in a capitalist society go unnoticed. As the economy continued to sink in the late 2000s, the number of foreclosures and the increase in unemployment were of the same order of magnitude, but public attention was not equally proportioned.

The press has devoted far more attention to the losses that people have suffered because of the crash of the real estate market and the subsequent destruction of their pension funds. For example, a website featured in the *Wall Street Journal*, Greenspan's Body Count, tallies deaths linked to the real estate bust, but not to the health effects of traumatization.[56] Foreclosures are a tragedy, but so are job losses and the perpetual fear of unemployment.

Earlier forms of organization also had inhuman consequences and defects. One need only think about the widespread use of slavery. Even before slavery took hold in the colonies, the authorities in England applied harsh punishment to their own countrymen who lacked proof of employment. According to a statute of 1572, beggars over the age of fourteen were to be severely flogged and branded with a red-hot iron on the left ear unless someone was willing to take them into service for two years. Repeat offenders over eighteen were to be executed unless someone would take them into service. Third offenses automatically resulted in execution.[57] Although some people had qualms about such brutal methods of organizing labor, for the most part such practices seemed both normal and profitable. Only gradually did people recognize that such crude measures represented a barrier to economic development. Similarly, people were slow to realize that the problem with slavery was not that a few slave owners were cruel and sadistic, but rather that the system as a whole was flawed.

The coercive systems of the past ended not because of humanitarian scruples, but because of their inherent inefficiency. For example, Adam Smith partially rested his case for a market society on the grounds of the counterproductive nature of overt coercion, such as with slavery.

Smith was correct that more subtle market coercion is more effective than crude Procrustean measures. However, he failed to develop his insight more deeply, to realize that harsh measures, whether or not they involve physical brutality, are ultimately self-defeating. The same fate awaits marketplace Procrusteanism.

In the future, people may well look back to the present time, wondering why people were so slow to realize the inherent irrationality of the current system of organizing labor. The responsibility for this wakeup call should lie, in part, with economists, who, as the next chapter discusses, have gone out of their way to obliterate considerations of work, workers, and working conditions.

CHAPTER THREE

How Economics Marginalized Workers

The Condition of Workers

Economists defined their discipline as a science of choice, built upon an elaborate—albeit unrealistic— theory about how consumers determine what commodities to purchase. Factors such as the influence of other people or advertising are usually excluded from the economists' theoretical analysis.

Economists extended their science of choice to the workplace, where they grounded their theory on the assumption that the relationship between employer and employee was a voluntary arrangement. Each worker is assumed to decide whether the consumption that an hour of work makes possible is worth more than the sacrifice of an hour of leisure.

Within this theory, what happens in the workplace is a matter of indifference to both workers and economists. The same lack of interest applies to workers' aspirations or any other aspects of their lives. Even worse, the theory treats each worker and each employer as an individual, excluding any class-based forces. Instead, individual workers simply choose between using their time for leisure and accepting a wage with which they can purchase commodities.

Economists never conspired to exclude work and working conditions from their theory. They were open in their hostility toward anything concerned with production and the workers who made that production possible—for example, Lionel Robbins, who published the most influential book written on the proper way to do economics, or in his words, "to delimit the subject-matter of Economics." He expressed contempt for those who veered off the path of transaction-based economics in the direction of work, workers, and working conditions: "We have all felt, with Professor Schumpeter, a sense of almost shame at the incredible banalities of much of the so-called theory of production—the tedious discussions of various forms of peasant proprietorship, factory, organization, industrial psychology, technical education."[1] No mainstream economist has ever directly challenged Robbins's position.

Instead, they had powerful motives that led them in the same direction. First, they were trying to win professional prestige. Toward this end, economists could represent their simplified choice mathematically, making their theory appear to be scientific. Second, they were also intent on constructing a theory that would respond to (or still better, evade) critics who regarded capitalism as unjust, especially with respect to its treatment of workers. Within this theory, economists were able to put aside any criticisms about unfairness or exploitation.

Thoughtful economists expressed reservations about the realism of this treatment of the workplace. For example, Frank Knight, an influential figure in shaping the conservative Chicago school of economics, warned:

> Time does not in any sense measure the alternative or sacrifice, and . . . its employment in any use is a sacrifice in the first place only because there are other uses for it, which are the real sacrifice; but it is measurable, and our intelligence, forced to have something quantitative to feed upon, like the proverbial drowning man catches at any straw.[2]

Knight's readers might be expected to feel more sympathy for the potentially drowning economists than for the workers, whose conditions economists were attempting to obscure.

Economists are not totally unmindful of workers. They agree that workers might be well advised to get more education in order to increase the value of their time. Here, too, the emphasis is on individual responsibility. Alan Greenspan suggested that deficiencies in education were the root cause of inequality. Note that education does not enter into economists' theory of the relationship between labor and capital. Instead, workers are treated as if they were capitalists, accumulating what economists call "human capital."

The absence of work, workers, and working conditions leaves a gaping hole in economic theory. Perhaps the most striking reason for including working conditions in any analysis of the economy comes from shocking statistics on industrial accidents. Consider the 1969 testimony of Secretary of Labor George Schultz, a University of Chicago labor economist and dean, who later became Secretary of the Treasury and Secretary of State and then head of Bechtel, the world's largest construction firm. Schultz was testifying about the extent of industrial accidents during the Nixon administration. He informed Congress that 14,000 workers died annually from industrial accidents. Putting this figure into context, he remarked, "During the last four years more Americans have been killed where they work than in Vietnam."[3] Schultz's comparison gives new meaning to the concept of class warfare.

Congress enacted the Occupational Safety and Health Act in 1970, the year after Schultz's testimony. Even so, by 2006, almost 350,000 more workers had died on the job. Despite the decline of employment in dangerous occupations and the rising share of service work, occupational deaths continue at an unconscionably high rate. In its annual Workers' Memorial Day statement, the Centers for Disease Control reported:

Daily, an estimated 11,200 private-sector workers have a nonfatal work-related injury or illness, and as a result, more than half require a

job transfer, work restrictions, or time away from their jobs. An estimated 9,000 workers are treated in emergency departments each day
because of occupational injuries, and approximately 200 of these workers are hospitalized.[4]

While less dramatic than deaths from injuries, occupational diseases cause almost ten times as many deaths as industrial accidents—
about 60,000 per year in 1992.[5] For example, over the last decade
about 400 coal miners perished on the job. Over the same period,
more than 10,000 miners succumbed to job-related diseases, especially black lung disease.[6]

Although the government does not tabulate such data, the
American Public Health Association estimated in 1990 that 350,000
new cases of occupational diseases developed from toxic exposures
each year.[7] A more recent study estimated that in 2004, an estimated
200,000 people in California alone were diagnosed with a preventable
chronic disease attributable to chemical exposures in the workplace;
another 4,400 died prematurely as a result. These diseases produced
an estimated $1.4 billion in direct and indirect costs. Direct medical
costs of chemical and pollution-related diseases among children and
workers totaled over $1 billion.[8]

Economists' success in reframing the nature of the labor market to
exclude matters of work, workers, and working conditions is matched
by the media and the law. The media rarely notice deaths in the workplace or the prevalence of poor working conditions. The legal penalties for occupational deaths are remarkably small. The maximum punishment for causing a worker's death by *willfully* violating safety laws
is a six-month sentence, half the maximum for harassing a wild burro
on federal lands.[9]

In this environment, employers find it profitable to cut back on
maintenance expenditures. leaving workers vulnerable. A former
Justice Department prosecutor lamented that since 1970 "only 68
criminal cases have been prosecuted, or less than two per year, with
defendants serving a total of just 42 months in jail."[10] This laxity is
even more shocking in light of companies that have been involved in

multiple incidents.[11] What is more, the official data probably understate the actual toll that industry takes on workers. One recent study, based on the experience of the state of Michigan, estimated that available government data fails to capture between 60 and 70 percent of occupational injuries and diseases.[12]

In a Procrustean economy, a unique pathology exists for both work and unemployment. Even though unemployment has deleterious health consequences for individual workers, recessions can actually decrease mortality.[13] Being employed might be more stressful than being unemployed!

Yet economists pay virtually no attention to the afflictions of labor, especially when compared with their hysterical warnings about the dangers that moderate inflation might pose for bondholders.

The Public as Collateral Damage

Just as the stress from working conditions can affect the population at large, so too can the toxic exposures that workers face. The hazardous materials that businesses disperse in the workplace add to the toxic soup of potentially lethal pollutants that assault the general population.

The Bhopal tragedy, in which a Union Carbide subsidiary's pesticide plant released forty tons of methyl isocyanate gas, killing between 2,500 and 5,000 people, was the most dramatic example. The vast majority of the lives taken in this disaster were of people who did not work in the factory. The United States has never experienced anything on this scale, although a similar plant explosion, at the Bayer CropScience Institute plant in West Virginia's Kanawha Valley, came perilously close to surpassing Bhopal. The plant, which made the same chemicals as the Bhopal plant and was once owned by the same company, had a long history of safety citations. According to a congressional report, an explosion that killed two workers "turned a 2 1/2-ton chemical vessel into a 'dangerous projectile' that could have destroyed a nearby tank of deadly methyl isocyanate."[14]

When such disasters occur, workers suddenly come to the fore-front—not so much as victims, but rather as the culprits who are sup-posed to bear the ultimate responsibility for the damage. Unmentioned is that the nearly forty-year effort by employers to dis-empower unions left workers and regulators with less opportunity to effectively push for improvements in workplace safety.

The treatment of airline pilot Chesley B. Sullenberger III is an exceptional case because he got public praise for his efforts. With his plane disabled by a collision with a flock of birds, he steered the craft away from populated areas and miraculously managed to land the plane on the Hudson River without a single fatality. Suddenly, his image was everywhere in the media.

When he appeared before Congress on February 24, 2009, Sullenberger testified about a different kind of challenge. After giving his condolences to those affected by the tragic crash of Continental Connection flight 3407 in Buffalo twelve days before, the captain com-plained:

> Revolving door management teams . . . have used airline employees as an ATM [leaving] the people who work for airlines in the United States with extreme economic difficulties. It is an incredible testament to the collec-tive character, professionalism and dedication of my colleagues in the industry that they are still able to function at such a high level. It is my personal experience that my decision to remain in the profession I love has come at a great financial cost to me and my family. My pay has been cut 40%, my pension, like most airline pensions, has been terminated and replaced by a PBGC guarantee worth only pennies on the dollar. . . . I am worried that the airline piloting profession will not be able to continue to attract the best and the brightest.[15]

The experience of the crew of the Continental Connection flight 3407 confirmed Sullenberger's warnings. The co-pilot of the crew commuted to her base in Newark, New Jersey, from Seattle. Her salary was less than $17,000 a year. For a while, she held down a second job in a coffee shop while working as a pilot.[16]

The pilot was also a commuter. He slept in the Newark Airport crew lounge to save money. Although he had the previous day off, he "was coming off weeks of late-evening and early-morning flying schedules, often sandwiched around only a few hours of rest."[17] According to the National Transportation Safety Board, the company that operated the flight employed 137 Newark-based pilots: ninety-three of them identified themselves as commuters, including forty-nine who commuted greater than 400 miles and twenty-nine who lived more than 1,000 miles away.[18]

After the accident, which took the lives of the pilots and all of their passengers, much of the blame landed on the pilot. Because the company that employed him had been so lax, it endured a short period of bad press. Unfortunately, Captain Sullenberger's words soon will be forgotten, along with the loss of the commuter flight, and companies will continue to claw some extra profits by squeezing workers. People might realize that this arrangement puts others at risk, but memories are short.

The Early Primacy of Labor

Before modern technology was important in production, considerations of labor were of great importance to economic thinking. The early political economists (as economists of the time were known) advocated policies to increase the amount of work, which, in turn, would make the nation more prosperous. Either directly or indirectly, they supported policies to drive people from their traditional occupations in the countryside. Such measures would prevent people from producing goods for their own needs, forcing them to work for wages. These economists were also unanimous in their support for extending the workday as long as was humanly possible.

This perspective led many early economists to measure economic success in terms of hours of labor. Even as economics became more sophisticated, much of this labor perspective persisted, reaching a high point with David Ricardo's 1817 *Principles of Political Economy*.

These economists also followed the commonsense idea that labor would be the natural choice as a standard of value. The money price of a product can fluctuate substantially over time, and the value of money itself changes with inflation or deflation. Consequently, William Petty, the most creative seventeenth-century economist, and even Adam Smith argued (although not consistently in Smith's case) that an hour of labor was an hour of labor, regardless of economic conditions. Thus labor offered a more accurate measurement of a commodity than any alternative.

In addition, economists needed a simple way to take account of the broad array of factors that make up an economy. Labor inputs, both direct and indirect, are one thing that all products bought and sold in a market economy have in common. For this reason, early economics used labor as a measure of value.

Although this crude labor standard of value recognized the importance of work, economics still ignored working conditions and promoted measures that were inconsistent with workers' well-being. This cavalier attitude should not be surprising. Not only were economists unfamiliar with workers' day-to-day experience, they made no effort to learn about such matters. Workers were commonly seen as little better than beasts of burden. At one point, Adam Smith lumped workers together with working cattle.[19]

Petty's work illustrates how economists used this labor measure. In his primitive efforts to calculate the total production of a country (the Gross Domestic Product, as we would call this measure today), Petty in 1692 traced all production to a combination of land and labor: "All things ought to be valued by two natural Denominations, which is Land and Labour." Then Petty suggested measuring the value of land by the number of years of work required to purchase it: "Having found the Rent or value of the *usus fructus* per annum [a right to use the property of a third party for a year according to Roman law], the question is, how many years purchase (as we usually say) is the Fee simple naturally worth."[20] In his youth, Petty went much further in exploring the nature of work. He was one of the founders of the world's leading scientific body, the British Royal Society, as well as the major organizer of the society's program to produce an encyclopedic history of the trades. The idea was to precisely document the work of various trades in order to improve efficiency and learn about the scientific principles that workers used. After a promising start, the project was abandoned and remains unfinished after more than three centuries.

The History of the Trades Project could have had a valuable influence on economics. Unlike Petty, however, other early economists overlooked the underlying complications in their labor-based theory. For them, labor was simply labor. Differences of skill or the intensity of work did not often enter into their analysis. Petty, too, later fell into this perspective.

Interest in work was about to fall from view altogether because political economists were becoming more sensitive about the need to explain away the increasingly sharp divide between employers and their workers. A few decades before Ricardo, Smith had already laid the groundwork for a method of economics that saw the world in terms of the circulation of commodities rather than production. Smith's influence was a decided step backwards. As Smith's efforts took hold, the Ricardian approach of rooting economics in labor first ebbed and then disappeared altogether.

Even Smith was not consistent in this respect in avoiding considerations of work, workers, and working conditions beyond his passing approval of a labor standard of value. For example, he gave a nod in the direction of working conditions when he observed, "The real price of every thing, what every thing really costs to the man who wants to acquire it, is the toil and trouble of acquiring it."[21] He took note of the toll that work took on workers, observing that carpenters in London could only work at full capacity for about seven years.[22] Such observations made him seem like less of an ideologue than he really was.

The Brewing Conflict between Labor and Capital

Much of modern economic theory developed during the contentious times of the late nineteenth century when both modern technology and labor's increasingly militant organization was creating a strategic need for a new kind of economic theory. The early perspective of measuring production as the sum of hours worked seemed quaint once industry successfully began to harness the potential of fossil fuels. The spread of railroads across the landscape in the second half of the nineteenth century was emblematic of the emerging technology. Railroads both made possible and demanded radical changes in technology throughout much of the economy.

Railroads integrated the United States into a unified economy. One prominent historian described the country before the spread of railroads as "a society of island communities."[23] Railroads allowed agriculture to spread across the West. Arthur Twining Hadley, a noted economist who was also president of Yale University, estimated that before the railroad, shipping wheat more than two hundred miles was uneconomical.[24]

Agricultural expansion, in turn, provided a growing market for industry. In 1830, one year's wear-and-tear for horseshoes and other farm implements required 100,000 tons of pig iron, while total U.S. consumption of pig iron was only 200,000 tons.[25]

Suddenly, railroad construction demanded a massive supply of materials, setting in motion the formation of the modern steel industry. By the 1860s, railroads consumed half the iron rolled in the United States. By 1880, the production of rails would consume three-quarters of the nation's steel.[26] As Henry Adams wrote in the early twentieth century:

> From the moment that railways were introduced, life took on extravagance . . . for it required all the new machinery to be created—capital, banks, mines, furnaces, shops, power-houses, technical knowledge, and mechanical population, together with a steady remodeling of social and political habits, ideas, and institutions to fit the new scale and suit the new conditions. The generation between 1865 and 1895 was already mortgaged to the railways, and no one knew it better than the generation itself.[27]

Just as was the case in agriculture, transportation costs previously prohibited most factories from selling very far beyond their local markets. With the construction of a national railroad network, massive factories could now sell their wares in far-off places. In addition, railroads provided industry with broader access to crucial inputs such as coal.

Railroads opened up new ways of making money. Railroad securities dominated the New York Stock Exchange. Despite massive public subsidies that allowed unscrupulous operators to get rich at the public trough, the cost of financing long-haul railroads still exceeded what a handful of partners could muster. The people who organized these huge investments had to turn to the stock exchange to tap in to a larger community of investors, who had no contact with the industry's day-to-day operations.

Other industries soon tapped the stock market to finance their growing scale of operations. Because of expanding markets and greater access to credit, the average factory in the United States doubled in size, measured by wage earners per establishment, between 1869 and 1889.[28] In this new environment, industry began to assemble large masses of workers in gargantuan workplaces. In these new factories, modern machinery, not labor, seemed to be the motor force that drove the production process. Although workers were producing outputs that would have been unimaginable in Smith's day, their wages were far from commensurate with their increased productivity.

In the shadow of this new form of industry, class lines were hardening. Traditionally, workers had a chance to prosper by beginning as independent artisans and eventually becoming small employers in their own right. In modern industry, traversing the path from the shop floor to the main office was unlikely, even with the utmost perseverance.

For those endowed with sufficient money, finance offered a more direct road to success than did industry. Investors and unscrupulous promoters grew fabulously wealthy, although they had no direct connection with the labor process.

Workers in the United States were increasingly incensed by the gross disparities in the world around them. They were expected to labor long and hard for little pay. At the same time, the rapidly growing fruits of modern productivity flowed almost exclusively to factory owners and speculators, who flaunted their fortunes in ostentatious displays of wealth that seemed to mock the poverty of the workers who made their wealth possible.

Workers began identifying themselves as an oppressed majority. They courageously expressed their dissatisfaction, even though the state would regularly call on the National Guard and the police to violently repress their protests.

The elites faced other signs of unrest. Poor farmers, protesting against business excesses, proved that they could organize, shocking the nation when their populist movement won a successful wave of congressional and gubernatorial elections in the South and Midwest in the late nineteenth century.

The Challenge to Economics

Economists also faced a serious theoretical challenge. In 1867, Karl Marx published a powerful case for workers' rights, *Capital*. Marx followed traditional economics in using an analysis of value based on labor, but he argued that economists failed to see the logical consequences of their own theory. Workers are supposed to enjoy the fruits of their labor, but according to the rules of the market (and given that workers must work for the capitalists because the latter own the means of production necessary for life), the working class must work many more hours beyond the time required to produce its own consumption goods. This extra labor time, which produces profits, interest, and rent, represents exploitation.

Political events made the challenge that Marx posed more pressing. A dramatic uprising culminated in the Paris Commune in 1871, only four years after his book appeared. The Commune's takeover of Paris shocked much of the world by demonstrating workers' revolutionary potential. The British bourgeoisie credited Marx, a heretofore unknown German refugee residing in London, with an exaggerated influence on the uprising.[29] Just a few months after the formation of the commune, the British journalist John Rae, best known for his 1895 *Life of Adam Smith*, warned the public:

> It is a curious and not unmeaning circumstance that the country where Karl Marx is least known, is that in which he has for the last thirty years lived and worked. His word has gone into all the earth and evoked in some quarters echoes which governments will neither let live nor let die; but here, where it was pronounced, its sound has scarcely been heard.[30]

Rae later included this essay in a book, *Contemporary Socialism*, which made enough of an impression on the influential Cambridge economist Alfred Marshall that he included it in a relatively short list of books recommended for students in his newly reformed program in political economy.[31]

Rae was partially mistaken in his assessment of Marx's reputation among economists. For example, in 1879, the Radical Republican Senator George from Massachusetts credited a meeting of the International Working Man's Association led by Karl Marx with keeping England from joining the Confederate cause during the Civil War, thereby significantly contributing to the preservation of the Union:

> The International Association of European and American Workingmen has this title to respect among others, that it has established among the nations of the world a relation, that it has recognized a kindred between man and man, growing out of the common bond of labor, greater, more powerful, more binding than any mere national attachment, or than any tie which connects the subject to the sovereign. America is the last nation that ought to be ungrateful for that sublime accomplishment.[32]

In addition, the bright young U.S. economists who formed the American Economics Association all studied in Germany. They were not only familiar with Marx but also quite respectful of him. For example, the twenty-three-year-old Arthur Hadley, who was about to launch an illustrious career, wrote:

I have lately been much interested in Karl Marx, though I am very far from agreeing with him. His book seems to me to have a higher scientific aim than almost any work on political economy in the last half century. Like Ricardo, he seeks natural laws, not artificial maxims. Much of what he advances is I think a legitimate development of Ricardo's position. Holding some of the worst errors of the socialists, he is singularly free from others.[33]

Hadley was not unique in this respect. These economists could not help but be influenced by the repeated bankruptcies of the railroads, and they advocated measures to control the competitive forces that led to these. Marx's economics was more relevant to this phenomenon than mainstream economics. Without acknowledging Marx, these economists advocated the creation of trusts, cartels, and monopolies, as well as government regulation to protect the railroads from the ravages of competition.

Ironically, these same economists were simultaneously defending and refining mainstream economics rather than the railroads. They published articles and textbooks to "prove" that an unimpeded market economy is both just and efficient. In effect, they produced one kind of economics for political and business leaders and other economists and another for workers, telling them why they should accept the market.

Thus, after many decades in public obscurity, considerable attention turned to attacking the theories of Karl Marx. The major economists of the day turned their back on the grievances of workers and set out to answer workers' protests by "proving" that even if the system was not equitable, at least it was just.[34]

Consumers in Command

In the 1870s, three leading economists—William Stanley Jevons in Britain, Leon Walras in Switzerland, and Carl Menger in Austria—independently concocted a new kind of economics. In their theory, "the new starting point became, not the socioeconomic relations between men as producers, but the psychological relation between men and finished goods."[35] In Jevons's words, "The theory presumes to investigate the condition of a mind."[36] The economy is viewed as a collection of individual firms and consumers, each of which has an initial endowment of capital or wealth, which they use to make voluntary exchanges. Transactions occur only when both seller and buyer think they will be better off by completing the exchange. Jevons explained how this new theory reinforced the exclusion of work, workers, and working conditions: "Value always depends upon degree of utility and labour has no connection with the matter, except through utility."[37] As we shall see, even appending the slight concession to the role of labor earned Jevons strong rebukes.

Accordingly, business, subject to the harsh discipline of the market, has no choice but to submit to the dictates of the all-powerful consumers. Jevons explained this reasoning:

> The capitalist, like the merchant, is but an intermediary, who gets goods ready for the consumer, and presents him in the price a complete bill of costs. . . . The supposed conflict of labour with capital is a delusion. The real conflict is between producers and consumers. The capitalist employer is a part of the producing system, and his conflict is naturally with the consumer who buys from him. But his function of acting as discounter of the labourer's share gives rise to a further conflict with the labouring class. Thus it comes to pass that the capitalist is buffeted about and bears the whole brunt of the economic battle, while the consumer always smarts in the end.[38]

Within this theory, introspection—in this case, the consumer's subjective evaluations of consumer goods—drives the economy rather than the actual process of production. Production continues, as it must in any economy, but within this framework it does so in the background. Given the technology of the firms and the preferences of the consumers, economists take for granted that the firms somehow combine their labor, capital, and raw materials (their factors of production) to produce a mix of commodities that suits the tastes of their customers.

Contemporary economists have gone further, treating the imbalance between workers and employers in the workplace as a voluntary arrangement rather than an exercise of power. Two respected economists—one of whom was the instructor in my freshman class in economics—compared the relation between employer and employee to that between shopper and grocer:

> The firm has . . . no power of fiat, no authority, no disciplinary action any different in the slightest degree from ordinary market contracting between any two people. . . . He [an employer] can fire or sue, just as I can fire my grocer by stopping purchases from him or sue him for delivering faulty products. . . . To speak of managing, directing, or assigning workers to various tasks is a deceptive way of noting that the employer continually is involved in renegotiation of contracts on terms that must be acceptable to both parties. Telling an employee to type this letter rather than to file that document is like my telling a grocer to sell me this brand of tuna rather than that brand of bread.[39]

It did not occur to these economists that individual retail customers are unlikely to traumatize grocers merely by threatening to "fire" them.

Other economists take this sort of thinking to a still more absurd level by claiming that workers preferred what were obviously coercive measures. One proposed that "factory discipline [was] successful because it coerced more effort from workers than they would freely give. . . . The empirical evidence shows that discipline succeeded mainly by increasing work effort. Workers effectively hired capitalists to make them work harder."[40]

Another economist, Clark Nardinelli, declared that children in the factories would voluntarily choose to have their employers beat them. In Nardinelli's words: "Now if a firm in a competitive industry employed corporal punishment the supply price of child labor to that firm would increase. The child would receive compensations for the disamenity of being beaten."[41] Similarly, Steven Cheung maintains that riverboat pullers who towed wooden boats along the shoreline in China before the revolution of 1949 agreed to hire monitors to whip them to restrict shirking.[42]

Using such far-fetched analyses, economists can present capitalism as a harmonious system devoid of conflict, since exchanges are actions in which both parties presumably improve their situation and can walk away if they do not. As economist Abba Lerner, observed, "An economic transaction is a solved political problem."[43] Exchanges are actions in which both parties presumably improve their situation, since each has the alternative to walk away.

Exploitation is nowhere to be found in this narrative, nor is labor. Potential workers may only be seen bargaining for a wage before work commences and collecting a wage after work has ceased, when they are ready to begin exercising their role as consumers. What happens in the workplace falls outside the boundaries of economics.

Unfortunately, economists still had a problem. They could not measure tastes or the pleasures of consumption. For this reason, economists fell back on that flat-sounding, unmeasurable term, utility. Economists conceive of utility as a quantitative measure by which consumers can compare the degree of satisfaction of eating an apple with the pleasure of hearing a symphony.

Economists do not consider their inability to measure utility to be a problem. Instead, they assume that consumers are rational beings, aware of the relative utilities of the many choices they face. Given the assumptions of the model, if producers do not offer consumers what they want at a price they can afford, their potential customers will purchase different goods that provide higher utility per dollar. In light of their need to sell their products, producers have no choice but to make every effort to supply what consumers want: good-quality merchandise at an affordable price. Any producer that violates this market imperative will be driven from the market.

In the imaginary world of economic theory, utility comes only by way of purchasing commodities on the market. In effect, work, workers, and working conditions have no place in this theory, with one exception. The theory does allow that workers sacrifice leisure by being on the job. The lost utility of leisure—the disutility of work—is independent of the actual experience on the job, even though work may involve being maimed or killed.

Economists seldom realize that, like work, leisure can be productive and that fulfilling work might actually create more utility than leisure. None of this matters within the theory because economists simply assume that work is nothing more than the loss of leisure.

Economists' Theoretical Barricades

At the time this new—neoclassical—theory was emerging, economics was not held in high regard. In 1870, Jevons opened the meeting of Section F (Economic Science and Statistics) of the British Association for the Advancement of Science with his somber presidential address, complaining:

> There is no one who occupies a less enviable position than the Political Economist. Cultivating the frontier regions between certain knowledge and conjecture, his efforts and advice are scorned and rejected on all hands. If he arrives at a sure law of human nature, and points out the evils which arise from its neglect, he is fallen upon by the large classes of people who think their own common-sense sufficient; he is charged with being too abstract in his speculations; with overlooking the windings of the human heart; with undervaluing the affections. However humane his motives, he is lucky if he escape being set down on all sides as a heartless misanthrope.[44]

A worldwide economic crisis began in 1873, three years after Jevons's talk, sinking the reputation of economics still deeper. Walter Bagehot, longtime editor of London's *The Economist*, wrote:

> Political Economy is not altogether satisfactory. It lies rather dead in the public mind. Not only does it not excite the same interest as formerly, but there is not exactly the same confidence in it. Younger men either do not

study it, or do not feel that it comes home to them, and that it matches with their most living ideas. New sciences have come up in the last few years with new modes of investigation, and they want to know what is the relation of economic science, as their fathers held it, to these new thoughts and these new instruments. They ask, often hardly knowing it, will this 'science' as it claims to be, harmonise with what we now know to be sciences, or bear to be tried as we now try.[45]

Consider the verdict of Henry Varnum Poor, financier and cofounder of the rating agency Standard & Poor's, one of the ratings agencies at the heart of the current crisis. Originally, Poor's company informed investors about the conditions of the railroads, then the dominant U.S. industry. Poor described the standing of economics in the popular mind at the time:

I am aware that Political Economists have always been regarded as cold-blooded beings, devoid of the ordinary feelings of humanity,—little better, in fact, than vivisectionists. I believe that the general public would be happier in their minds for a little time, if Political Economy could be shown up as imposture, like the greater part of what is called "Spiritualism."[46]

Francis Amasa Walker offered a similarly negative evaluation of the state of economics. Walker was the best-known U.S. economist of the last decade of the nineteenth century, whose resumé included positions as a general during the Civil War, head of the census in 1870 and 1880, president of MIT, and the president of the American Economic Association during its first seven years. Walker published a popular article in 1879, exploring, in the words of Robert Solow, a Nobel Laureate in Economics, "why economists seemed to be in bad odor among real people."[47]

Walker lamented that Anglo-Saxon economics had turned its back on the continental tradition. He charged that economics had become so abstract that it had nothing to offer. Business people knew that this so-called science could not assist them in learning how to become wealthy. Moreover, a dogmatic insistence on laissez-faire in labor markets caused economics "to forfeit all popular respect and sympathy for the science itself, especially on the part of the working classes." Walker concluded that "a certain school of economists are undergoing a very serious crisis. . . . The interests of humanity are in no danger; the friends of the happiness of human beings have no reason to feel special anxiety or distress on that account."[48]

Walker's complaint illustrates how economists were challenged from all sides. Their critics accused them of being too abstract and remote from the concerns of the real world. Business people rebuked them for not offering practical advice, while workers understood that economists were siding with business in its struggle with labor.

Perhaps the cruelest blow came in 1877, when Sir Francis Galton proposed expelling political economy from the same British Association for the Advancement of Science that Jevons addressed a few years before. Into this hostile environment stepped Alfred Marshall, a central figure in formalizing modern economics in a way that excludes work, workers, and working conditions.

Economists' Scientific Pretensions

At Cambridge University, where Marshall taught, "professors' lectures were considered to be mainly ornamental."[49] When Marshall began teaching there, students of political economy took their examinations in either moral philosophy or history. Economics proper made up a relatively small fraction of the examinations. To add insult to injury, economics examinations lacked the prestige and prizes granted to the examinations in mathematics and the classics.[50]

To make matters worse, political economy was a broad field without defined disciplinary boundaries. Sir John Robert Seeley, the prime minister's appointment to the Regius Professorship in Modern History, exemplified this problem when he used his Inaugural Lecture to emphasize the policy role of his chair, convinced that political economy fell within the scope of his discipline of history.[51] At first,

Marshall embraced Seeley's vision, immersing himself in historical research; however, by 1885, when Marshall gave his own Inaugural Lecture at Cambridge, he had undergone a conversion. Marshall became obsessed with winning prestige for the study of political economy. Key to this endeavor was to win university approval for the creation of a separate examination for students of the subject. By 1887, an English economist explained to American readers:

> Professor Marshall's personal and indirect influence has been even more wide-spread than his book. Half the economic chairs in the United Kingdom are occupied by his pupils, and the share taken by them in general economic instruction in England is even larger than this.[52]

Marshall launched a crusade to formalize the teaching of his subject. Toward this end, he tried to give political economy a scientific gloss by using a new term, economics, in the title of his 1879 *The Economics of Industry*, written jointly with his wife. In this work, they partially explained their motive: "Political interests generally mean the interest of some part or parts of the nation" rather than the nation as a whole.[53] The more scientific-sounding expression, "economics," was also expected to convey an affinity with the science that economists had long sought to emulate—physics.

Marshall was not the first economist to use "economics" in a book title. Two long-forgotten authors of lesser known works had preceded him in this respect. The first of these writers, Julian M. Sturtevant (1877), president of Illinois College, seems to have written nothing else about economics and left no mark on the discipline.

The second was Henry Dunning Macleod (1887). None of the leading economists had much respect for Macleod's work, the style of which was at once inconsistent, idiosyncratic, and bombastic.[54] Although Macleod did some interesting work regarding credit and economic development, one somewhat sympathetic writer observed that Macleod "remained so completely outside of the pale of recognized economics."[55] Nonetheless, Macleod left an indelible mark on economics by giving the subject its name.

Marshall, however, seems to have taken the term economics from an earlier article by Macleod rather than from his book. The attraction of this article was that it set out to ground a science of economics in exchange rather than production, while, at the same time, linking the subject to physics. As Macleod explained in his book, "economics is a science which treats of the laws which govern relations of exchangeable quantities."[56] Macleod also stressed economists' affinity with physics.

Macleod wrote to the eminent physicist James Clerk Maxwell, about the commonality of physics and economics. Maxwell caustically replied, sarcasm dripping from his pen, "We are in the same boat. . . . Instead of reducing economics to physics, I endeavour to impress upon beginners in physics the principles of book keeping."[57] Macleod was not alone in reaching out to physicists. Already by the 1860s, the new physics of energy was becoming "the primary metaphor for the discussion of the physical world."[58] Economists quickly (mis)appropriated the mathematics of physics to economics. In the words of one critic of this effort, "To put it bluntly, the progenitors of neoclassicism copied down the physical equations and just changed the names attached to the variables."[59] Physicists found the economists' work sadly lacking, partly because the economists' model allowed for unlimited growth, while the physical system that they were emulating was restricted by such constraints as the conservation of matter and energy.[60]

Despite its lack of regard for Macleod as an economist, the discipline followed Marshall in accepting Macleod's lead in recasting political economy as economics—the science of exchange. In the process, the subject matter gradually narrowed down to a study of how the amalgam of individual behaviors in the marketplace affected what we call the economy.

Rebranding Economics

Marshall's success in rebranding political economy as economics was not immediate. In the final edition of his *Principles of Economics*, he still used the phrase "political economy":

> Political Economy or Economics is a study of mankind in the ordinary
> business of life; it examines that part of individual and social action
> which is most closely connected with the attainment and with the use of
> the material requisites of well-being.[61]

Eventually, however, Marshall succeeded in transforming the
teaching of economics.[62] A book on Marshall's influence in this regard
concluded:

> Marshall's outstanding achievement was . . . his success—gained by tac-
> tical skill, eloquence and tenacity—in keeping his colleagues' eyes on the
> goal of an economics whose range, precision and predictive reliability
> would compare with that of the natural sciences.[63]

This goal has obviously thus far eluded economists.

Marshall was ideally suited to revolutionize economics because
he appeared so unrevolutionary. A later Cambridge economist
observed, "Marshall certainly was a great moralizer but somehow
the moral always came out that whatever is, is very nearly best."[64]
Another commentator noted that Marshall rendered the new economics "safe and soothing,"[65] especially because he attempted to
demonstrate a continuity between the old and the new economics,
as suggested by his reference to "Political Economy or Economics."
At the same time, Marshall's presentation seemed to be able to
make the subject more scientific, while answering both criticisms of
the subject—that it was too abstract and too remote from people's
real concerns.

Marshall's fuzziness served him well. His *Principles of Economics*
contained no mathematical equations, yet still appeared "rigorous," a
word typically interpreted by economists as a synonym for a mathematical treatment. Even so, Marshall peppered his writings with contradictory remarks, expressing the importance of breaking out of the
narrow perspective of economics.

Finally, Marshall stressed the need to keep people's actual lives in
mind, especially in the sense of a Victorian appeal for self-improve-

ment of the masses. For example, in a fragment published shortly after his death, Marshall observed:

> Wealth exists only for the benefit of mankind. It cannot be measured adequately in yards, nor even as equivalent to so many ounces of gold; its true measure lies only in the contribution it makes to human well-being.[66]

Marshall's legacy is rife with ironies. Shortly before his death, after dinner on Christmas Day 1923, Marshall said to his wife, "If I had to live my life over again, I should have devoted it to Psychology. Economics has too little to do with ideals."[67]

Although Marshall may have been acutely aware of the importance of understanding economics in a broader social context, within a short time the mainstream of the discipline let that part of Marshall's vision fall from view. Marshall's own expressions of humanism shielded the Procrustean core of economics from closer inspection—in effect, making the handcuffs seem like a handshake. In this way, Marshall's work was crucial for making economics into the arid, impersonal subject that it has become.

As a result, economists today no longer feel a need to consider abstractions such as human well-being or other ideals. Occasional lip service to humanitarian sentiments does nothing to undermine the position of Procrustean economics as the sole arbiter of human welfare. Instead, such words serve to reassure readers that accepting conventional economic analysis is almost a philanthropic duty.

In a final irony, during the 1960s and 1970s, Cambridge, the school where Marshall's efforts were felt most strongly, became a vigorous center of some of the most influential challenges to the arid economics of the twentieth century.

Self-Congratulation of Economic Theorists

Economists are proud of the theoretical advance of their subject. They congratulate themselves that their discipline is more like a true science than the other social sciences. In the process, they have managed to exorcize the ghost of Karl Marx. They also celebrate their success in proving the just nature of the economy—that we all get exactly what we deserve. They claim to have "proved" that the economy will work efficiently because business will offer products that satisfy the individual preferences of consumers.

The exclusion of labor was central to making the case that the system was just. Wages were treated as part of a voluntary transaction, just like any other. The disutility of the leisure that workers sacrificed to go to work must be lower than the utility of the money they earned. Otherwise, workers would not have been willing to accept the bargain that employers offered.

On closer inspection, most of economists' claims of success do not hold up so well. Even accepting their unrealistic assumptions, economists still cannot prove that the market system is efficient in the way that most people understand efficiency. Instead, economists define an efficient economy to be one in which nobody can be made better off *without harming anybody else*. This restrictive definition rules out any consideration of redistribution. To take a dollar from the richest person in the world, who would hardly notice the loss, and give it to a starving person would not constitute an improvement by this standard. In contrast, a policy that would make this same rich person better off by $1 billion would represent an increase in efficiency, even if nobody else got anything. Because nobody else was made worse off, what could be the problem?

Lest you think that my example is fanciful, consider the verdict of Harvard economics professor Martin Feldstein, who was Ronald Reagan's chief economic advisor and for decades controlled the National Bureau of Economic Research, an important economics organization that dates back to the early twentieth century. In an article titled "Reducing Poverty Not Inequality" Feldstein described the proper response to an imagined increase in inequality occurring because a small number of affluent people received $1,000 each at no cost to the rest of society.

For Feldstein, only a "spiteful egalitarian" would not welcome such an improvement in society.[68] The windfall for the rich person would still count as an improvement in efficiency, even if it would harm the (non-market) quality of life for many others. An example would be if the wealthy could use their funds to bid up rents that could drive many people out of their neighborhoods. In effect, then, this new kind of economics became a science of justifying inaction in the face of popular demands for a more equitable society.

Most economists are dismissive of any theory not built on what they consider solid micro-foundations—economists' jargon for the patently unrealistic model I described. Mainstream economists seem to feel especially threatened by the suggestion that work, workers, or working conditions could be a legitimate subject of economic inquiry. As a result, any serious challenges to their theoretical position face a hostile response.

In one famous case, in 1944 Richard Lester published an article questioning whether labor markets operated in the manner that mainstream economics suggested. Lester had extensive experience in industry, having just served as chair of the Southern Textile Commission of the National War Labor Board. Using government data and surveys of industry leaders, Lester found evidence at odds with the assumptions of mainstream economic theory.[69] His results suggested that an increase in the minimum wage would be unlikely to increase unemployment, a conclusion that infuriated major defenders of the faith.

George Stigler, a leader of the Chicago school of economics and a Nobel Laureate, led the attack. Thomas Sowell, an admiring student of Stigler's and an important figure in the conservative movement, once likened Stigler's style of debate to a "Demolition Derby."[70] This debate provided confirmation of that characterization. Stigler "made unequivocal claims that lacked any strong empirical evidence, as if such statements were so intuitively obvious as to brook no argument."[71]

Symbolic of his combative nature, Stigler captioned a picture of John Stuart Mill, describing him as "perhaps the fairest economist who ever lived: He treated other people's theories at least as respectfully as his own, a mistake no other economist has repeated."[72]

Stigler and his allies used enough invective to satisfy their colleagues that Lester must be wrong because his data was inconsistent with their theory.

Lester's challenge to orthodoxy was silenced, so much so that, looking back at his performance almost three decades later, Stigler could write with evident pride, "The idea that minimum wage laws were the expression . . . of the well-informed desires of particular regions and classes of workers was not seriously considered by economists."[73] The following year, he proudly boasted, "One evidence of professional integrity of the economist is the fact that it is not possible to enlist good economists to defend minimum wage laws."[74]

In the 1990s Alan Krueger of Princeton (currently Assistant Secretary of the Treasury for Economic Policy) and David Card of the University of California, Berkeley, resumed work on the minimum wage, stirring up a hornet's nest by showing again that raisng the minimum wage did not increase unemployment.[75] They too met with fierce criticism from fellow economists, some sponsored by the fast food industry. Card and Krueger were both distinguished economists. Card had won the prestigious John Bates Clark award from the American Economic Association, given to the outstanding economist under the age of forty. Moreover, their work stood up well under harsh scrutiny. Yet in the face of the controversy, Card dropped this line of research. He explained:

I've subsequently stayed away from the minimum wage literature for a number of reasons. First, it cost me a lot of friends. People that I had known for many years, for instance, some of the ones I met at my first job at the University of Chicago, became very angry or disappointed. They thought that in publishing our work we were being traitors to the cause of economics as a whole.[76]

Two Nobel laureates commented on their work in the editorial page of the *Wall Street Journal*. The milder of the two, Merton Miller, responded, "It sure plays well in the opinion polls. I tremble for my profession."[77] The second, James Buchanan, consoled his readers:

"Fortunately, only a handful of economists are willing to throw over the teaching of two centuries; we have not yet become a bevy of camp-following whores."[78] By inference, Card and Krueger did fall into that category.

Nobody need be surprised that Card went on to say that he "thought it was a good idea to move on and let others pursue the work in this area," but any career-minded economists would be well advised not to do so.[79] Lester and Card did not fail to convince their fellow economists because of errors in their work. Most economists either ignored their results or, worse yet, rejected them out of hand because they conflicted with their cherished beliefs. As Stigler's colleague Milton Friedman once wrote, "Nothing is harder than for men to face facts that threaten to undermine strongly held beliefs, to change views arrived at over a long period. And there are no such things as unambiguous facts."[80]

Another Chicago economist, Sherwin Rosen, was open about his refusal to take the study by Card and Krueger seriously. In an October 1997 interview with Craig Freedman, an economist working out of Australia, Rosen admitted:

> If someone comes up and tells me now that everything I know is wrong I tend to be defensive. I naturally believe that the claim is probably erroneous. (laughs) Given your lifetime investment. . . . That's right, given my investment, given what I've read over the years. When somebody tells me now that an increase in the minimum wage increases employment, there's just been a study out on that [presumably, the Card and Krueger study], I'm very skeptical of that claim. I don't believe it![81]

The Chicago style of economics is famous for rejecting empirical evidence out of hand. Deirdre McCloskey, a former Chicago faculty member, recounted how people who used data and called the theory into question would "be met by choruses of 'I can't believe it' or 'It doesn't make sense.' Milton Friedman's own Money Workshop at Chicago in the late 1960s and the early 1970s was a case in point."[82] Melvin Reder, another Chicago faculty member, offered further insight in the way that Chicago refuses to give ground in the face of evidence that calls the micro-foundations into question:

> Chicago economists tend strongly to appraise their own research and that of others by a standard that requires (inter alia) that the findings of empirical research be consistent with the implications of standard price theory.... The major objective is to convert non-economists to their way of thinking.... However imaginative, answers that violate any maintained hypothesis of the paradigm are penalized as evincing failure to absorb training.[83]

Charles Kindleberger, who was a distinguished economist from MIT, observed that in Chicago "Modifying the theory was the last resort, evaded as long as possible."[84] Economists frequently regard such stubborn resistance to be good science. Predictably, the troubling questions that Lester and Card raised had no effect. Economists' beloved micro-foundations and their faith in market efficiency remained invulnerable. No wonder that economists today rarely bother to publish research that might cast doubt upon the core of economic theory. In this environment, economists can continue to use their transaction-based theory without the inconvenience of dealing with work, workers, or working conditions. However, by removing these critical aspects of life from their theory, economists blind themselves—and those who defer to their advice—to the kind of inefficiencies that this book shows.

Hey, Economists, Where Are the Workers?

In the early nineteenth century, Charles Babbage, who occupied what was once Isaac Newton's Lucasian Chair of Mathematics at Cambridge, designed the world's first computer, a complex machine driven by a hand crank rather than electricity. Babbage never managed to finish constructing his remarkable invention, but recently others have built two machines based upon his original plans.

Components for something this sophisticated required great precision. In overseeing their production, Babbage had to visit many factories. He also observed the work process at sites such as the London Bank Clearing House and the *Times* of London. Based on this experience, Babbage published *On the Economy of Machinery and Manufactures*, an extraordinary book that compelled George Stigler to say that "Charles Babbage deserves full membership in the club of mathematicians who have made significant contributions to economics."[85] Babbage charged the economists of his day with excessive abstraction. In a passage that Stigler cited with approval, Babbage charged:

> Political economists have been reproached with too small a use of facts, and too large an employment of theory. If the facts are wanting, let it be remembered that the closet-philosopher is unfortunately too little acquainted with the admirable arrangements of the factory; and that no class of persons can supply so readily, and with so little sacrifice of time, the date on which all the reasonings of political economists are founded, as the merchants and manufacturers; and, unquestionably, to no class are the deduction to which they give rise so important. Nor let it be feared that erroneous deductions may be made from such recorded facts; the errors which arise from the absence of facts are far more numerous and more durable than those which result from unsound reasoning respecting true data.[86]

Despite his appreciation for Babbage's words, Stigler still remained hostile to those who would pay attention to matters of production. In this regard, he was a vociferous advocate of mainstream economic theory, which explicitly avoided matters of production. Within the contentious intellectual climate, which gave birth to modern economics half a century later, the likelihood that economists might have taken Babbage's reproach seriously and considered the actual content of the labor process was slim. Directly addressing dreadful working conditions would have undermined their determined defense of the status quo as being both efficient and just.

In addition, none of the important economists of the time had any close experience with the working class. Karl Marx wrote in detail about the appalling conditions of the workers. He was able to do so, in part, by reading the shocking reports that the British government published, and he also had extensive relationships with working-class organization.

Relatively few British economists took advantage of the opportunity to make such contacts. Nor did they read the same government documents that Marx did, although they took advantage of other official publications to inform themselves about matters of trade and finance. The United States was more cautious about making such matters public, but economists still had the option to consult with people who had blue collar jobs, even in the absence of such extensive documentation.

Intellectual ambition also played a role in the disappearance of work, workers, and working conditions. Fueled by an intense desire to make economics appear more scientific, many mainstream economists followed in the footsteps of Macleod, attempting to emulate physics, while showing how economic processes are supposed to maximize efficiency. By assuming that consumers made the sophisticated calculations necessary to maximize utility, economists were able to satisfy themselves that they were on solid scientific ground.

When this theory was taking hold in the late nineteenth century, the labor input seemed increasingly less significant in the face of massive factories and growing technological mastery. Economic theory only needed to assume that each employer would continue to hire an additional unit of labor so long as this unit added to the firm's profits.

Since economists built their whole theory around the assumption of individual rationality, one might expect a serious interest in investigating how people, including employers and workers, actually make decisions. A small group, known as behavioral economists, do follow this line of research. Drawing upon long-standing knowledge of psychologists as well as experiments of their own, the behavioral economists have reported "a range of empirical facts that are at apparent odds with assumptions of standard economic theory."[87] One might expect that economists would seriously engage with research that called their own theories into question. Such has not been the case; mainstream economics is largely unaffected by the work of behavioral economics. An article in *The Economist* matter-of-factly attempts to rationalize economists' lack of regard for behavioral economics:

> Behavioural economics . . . is best understood as a set of exceptions that modifies but leaves intact the canonical model of rational choice, not least since it is irrational to suppose that people in general behave irrationally.[88]

Ironically, this assumption of rationality does not deter many conservatives from decrying the consumption habits of the poor when defending the existing distribution of income.

The exclusion of work, workers, and working conditions was not simply an accidental oversight. It served an important purpose in defending capitalism from the accusation of exploitation. The radical shift from labor to extreme subjectivity in which unmeasurable consumer preferences became the center of economic analysis sealed labor's marginalization in the theoretical world of economic theory. Other fields, such as sociology, industrial relations, or psychology, might seriously explore questions of work, workers, or working conditions, but economics would not.

An August 8, 2008, search of the seventy-six economics journals collected electronically in the JSTOR database revealed how marginal work, workers, and working conditions have become in the economic literature. Within the articles published since January 2004, the term "working conditions" appeared in only twelve, in addition to four substantial articles in the *Review of African Political Economy*, a progressive publication that would hold little interest for most mainstream economists. Of the remaining articles, three concerned the problem of retention of teachers. Another had a footnote with the observation that people can learn about working conditions from websites. One article noted that faculty members in colleges and universities should join unions to improve working conditions. A book review considered whether globalization could improve working conditions. Two articles mentioned legislation that took working conditions into account. One article disputed that child labor abroad experienced hideous working conditions. Another cited a mid-nineteenth-century British economist who said that factory working conditions were good. Hardly an indication of serious scholarship!

My favorite entry was from Martin Feldstein, whose contempt for "spiteful egalitarians" was discussed earlier. This article was one of his many attacks on Social Security. Here, he proposed treating good working conditions as taxable income.[89] What makes this piece so intriguing is that Feldstein is an ardent anti-taxer. He teaches that business taxes are destructive for economic growth. Yet here he is willing to consider working conditions, not with workers' interest in mind, but as a source of tax revenue!

None of the articles had even a hint of serious engagement with work, workers, or working conditions. In contrast, the sociology collection, with ten fewer journals, returned 107 articles. Human resource economics would likewise provide more articles than traditional economics, but that subdiscipline is more often associated with business.

In the late nineteenth century, economists did discuss labor in terms of policy questions. Their concern for what they called "The Labor Problem" was that labor was insufficiently submissive. At the same time, questions of labor were fast disappearing from the theoretical literature, except to "prove" that labor markets were fair. Instead, economics began to elevate the status of investors' financial claims, insisting that owners of this form of property had rights equal to those of owners of real goods, such as land or factories. Even something as ephemeral as the monetary value "goodwill"— not the kind of goodwill associated with charitable behavior— became recognized as property.

In effect, economics, which one might expect to be the study of the material well-being of society, turns out to emphasize a subset of psychological processes—consumers' supposed introspection, with matters such as corporate estimates of goodwill thrown in. Because economics stubbornly treats this psychology as rational, the discipline assumes that the outcome will be efficient, even when facts on the ground indicate otherwise.

Despite the emphasis on psychology, economics carefully looks away from anything regarding the real mental and physical states of the people who do the work necessary to keep the economy going. While people commonly speak of an information economy, one might expect that the mental state of workers might have some relevance!

In short, the ideological underpinnings of economics serve to reinforce the Procrustean structure of the system, carefully ignoring the glaring inefficiencies of Procrusteanism.

The Unrealistic Realism of Procrustean Economics

Within the context of a Procrustean economy, treating workers as objects actually lends a touch of realism to mainstream economic theory. However, my crediting the theoretical treatment of the reification of labor is not so much meant as praise for economic theory but as a rebuke to the current system of production.

Within this context, business mostly treats workers as interchangeable parts, relying on the threat of job loss in order to extract the maximum possible effort. In the words of Frank Knight, "The Economic man . . . treats other human beings as if they were slot machines."[90]

From the perspective of this theory, employers hire labor with no more thought of the future than a typical consumer paying for a gallon of gas or a six-pack of beer. This simplification of the role of labor makes economics both easier and less relevant.

Indeed, employers do sometimes regard labor as disposable objects. For example, a Massachusetts state factory agent reported this exchange with a factory manager in 1855:

> I inquired of the agent of a principal factory whether it was the custom of the manufacturers to do anything for the physical, intellectual, and moral welfare of their work people. "We never do," he said. "As for myself, I regard people just as I regard my machinery. So long as they do my work

for what I choose to pay them, I keep them, getting out of them all I can. What they do or how they fare outside my wall I don't know. They must look out for themselves. When my machines get old and useless, I reject them and get new, and these people are part of my machinery."[91]

A recent biography of Charles Schwab, Andrew Carnegie's assistant, reported a similar attitude at the Homestead plant in 1897. Here was "a remarkable steel making operation," a "world leader," but one that five years earlier had been the scene of the country's bloodiest battle between labor and capital. Workers had learned to understand that they were nothing more than objects in the labor market. Schwab's biographer reported that from their perspective, Schwab's operation was "a soulless industrial monster. Men, like machinery, became items to use, write off, and replace."[92]

During the New Deal, the power of unions meant that some industries had to acknowledge a more enduring relationship with its workers. But during the height of union power, economists still taught that training workers would not necessarily be in management's best interest, because workers could use their training to bargain for higher wages elsewhere. Today, now that only a shadow of the union movement remains, the business press openly writes about disposable labor.

According to its own logic, capitalism does not use its slot machines very effectively. For example, workers' productivity would increase if business trained as many workers as possible. Yet under this system, the highest corporate priority is to show continual increases in profit to satisfy the financial interests that hold their stock. Efforts to improve workers' skills will not immediately boost short-term profits.

In addition, training may only allow workers to seek higher salaries from a different employer. As a result, what may make sense for business as a whole seems unattractive for individual firms. In short, business intentionally underinvests in workers' training, undermining long-term growth, which apologists claim to be the objective of the economy.

Another quirk of economics reinforces the inability of economists to recognize labor's potential. In order to make the theory simple enough to express with equations or with a diagram, economics typically eliminates time from consideration. Anyone familiar with a simple graph of supply and demand has seen an obvious example of this method of analysis. It starts with a situation in which supply equals demand. Then supply and/or demand shifts, causing prices to adjust to a level where supply and demand come into balance once again. The story tells nothing about how the market restores this balance, how long it will take, or how people adjust. Could this imbalance be temporary, or will further adjustments be necessary? Will the adjustments affect other parts of the economy?

Most crucially, to include time would mean that economists would have to contend with the uncertainty of the future. How could they prove that markets were efficient while taking time into account? Emphasizing consumption rather than production is useful in this regard. Consumers typically purchase finished goods. Producers, in contrast, may have to sink substantial funds in capital goods that may be unable to contribute to production for a considerable period. In the meantime, market conditions may have changed, making such investments inappropriate. Unless business has perfect foresight, market efficiency will be impossible.

Economics rarely addresses the problems associated with miscalculations by business. Most often economics merely assumes business rationality without taking into account the problem of investing for an uncertain future. In a slightly more sophisticated approach, economists can assume that some individual businesses might err, but on the whole such mistakes would not amount to much.

In contrast, despite the inattention to work, workers, and working conditions, economists tend to hold workers to a high standard of responsibility. Economists' inner Procrustes blames workers for their own misfortunes, even when business miscalculations are at fault. Workers' wages are low only because they fail to upgrade their skills—generally ignoring that workers rarely get the same educational opportunities that more affluent members of society do, especially when business "rationally" withholds training. When the economy fares poorly, workers, along with government regulation, are taken to task. Workers' unions impede efficiency. Workers' demands for better wages and working conditions are excessive, and so forth.

Practical Concerns about Working Conditions

In a sense, economists seem to have been swimming against the tide in ignoring the labor process. Management, which has the practical responsibility of running business, wants to minimize costs. Since labor is a cost of doing business, the simplest methods are to cut wages, drive workers harder, or adopt labor-saving equipment. In a competitive environment, the labor process must eventually become a matter of serious concern for business.

The obsession with reducing the wage bill actually reaches the point of irrationality—at least according to conventional economic logic. Profit maximization requires that businesses root out any unnecessary costs; however, businesses often ignore non-labor costs, concentrating their efforts on cutting back on payrolls. For example, based on a survey of sixty New England factories, Michael Piore found that employers instructed engineers to pursue the single-minded goal of developing methods to reduce labor inputs, without regard for the more rational criterion of overall cost minimization. He went on to say:

> Virtually without exception, the engineers distrusted hourly labor and admitted a tendency to substitute capital whenever they had the discretion to do so. As one engineer explained, "If the cost comparison favored labor but we were close, I would mechanize anyway."[93]

Labor-saving technology can do away with certain types of work altogether, or it can force workers to work harder or faster. To the extent that business is intent on driving workers harder, their welfare, if not their health and safety, is put at risk, as George Schultz noted earlier in this chapter.

Before the Industrial Revolution, overseeing the labor process was not nearly as challenging for managers. Those who ran factories tended to be the skilled workers, who were thoroughly steeped in the production process. After modern technology required more expensive capital goods, ownership passed into the hands of people whose major qualification was access to finance. At this point, management frequently had little or no technical knowledge. Instead, employers had to rely on the knowledge of their most skilled workers.

This deficiency of knowledge put management at a distinct disadvantage. Industrialists tried to reduce the powers of skilled workers by finding machinery that could allow unskilled laborers—often children—to perform challenging tasks. One such transformation took place in the nineteenth-century U.S. cannery industry. The California Gold Rush triggered rapid growth in the demand for canned goods. The industry expanded fifteen-fold between 1860 and 1880. Skilled tinsmiths, known as cappers, responsible for sealing the cans, were the most important workers in the industry. The perishability of the product gave them significant bargaining power. Many cannery owners had to hire a boss capper who then contracted to hire and manage related craft workers and assistants. The capitalists in the canning industry thought that the cappers used their strategic position to take unfair advantage of their employers. James D. Cox invented the first successful capping machine in 1887. He described the resentment against the cappers in the following way:

> In those days the capping all having to be done by hand, a Boss Capper took the contract to do the work, furnishing his men for the purpose, and even the owner stood in great awe of him, for of what use was it to purchase tomatoes and prepare them if, at the important moment, the Capper decided he would go on strike; or having received his pay, required more time to sober up than the boss thought necessary. He knew his importance and he used his advantage to the full, and to the too frequent annoyance and heavy loss of the canner. It was this helplessness

of the canner that made him a willing advocate of every mechanical means, and made possible the working out, through frequent failures and heavy losses, perfected mechanical means now in use. The Boss-Capper helped hasten the day of his own exit through his overbearing thoughtlessness.[94]

Many kinds of work defied such simple mechanization. More direct control of the labor process became a priority for business. Frederick Winslow Taylor introduced his concept of scientific management, based on the idea that management could and should acquire, through detailed study of work on the shop floor, the knowledge that would allow it to take control of the production process.

Taylor's project was the context of his previously cited prediction: "In the past the man has been first; in the future the system must be first." An example of the extent of Taylor's ambition to develop a comprehensive understanding of the labor process is his extensive experiments and observations just to discover better methods of shoveling.[95] Although management had no interest in training workers, Taylor used workers to train management. Through his meticulous observation of workers' performance, Taylor argued that he could teach business how to make workers perform at peak levels without any wasted motions or unnecessary moments of rest. Armed with that knowledge, employers would be in a better position to make demands on workers.

Taylor expected to play a role comparable to a person who coaches elite athletes, except that his goal was to make the workers' opponents—the bosses—come out winners. Unlike workers, elite athletes generally perform at peak levels for a short period of their lives and only at short intervals. The human body is not designed to continuously operate at maximum capacity. Therefore, to the extent that management was able to succeed in achieving Taylor's recommendations, working conditions deteriorated—at least in terms of the toll work took on workers' bodies. Management, however, has little interest in workers' physical well-being. The objective of business is to extract as much work out of their employees as possible. In effect, Taylor's role was to aid business in being able to treat workers as interchangeable parts.

Yet, Taylor saw himself as a progressive. He resented that workers resisted his efforts to speed up production. Their reluctance seemed irrational to Taylor, who believed workers were bound to benefit because they would receive increased wages in return for higher output.

Taylor never seemed to understand that the labor process is not just a matter of finding a better way of performing a job, that the labor process was part of a larger system of social relationships. This shortcoming helps to explain why, despite his gift of self-promotion, Taylor never really succeeded in revolutionizing his scientific management work for the companies that hired him.[96] Others who followed him, however, were more successful in developing the means to gain more control over labor.

This effort to make workers little more than cogs in a larger system of production was bound to be self-defeating in the long run. First, as Bill Watson showed, workers can develop counter-plans. More important, stunting workers through more obtrusive management will snuff out the potential for greater productivity—presumably the objective of scientific management.

Economists' freedom to explore such questions is limited. Since the late nineteenth century, universities regularly purged economists who were suspected of insufficient sympathy for capitalism. Fear of such reprisals was sufficient to warn most economists not to tread on unsafe territory. Recall the recriminations of Richard Lester and David Card for their work on minimum wages.

Work and working conditions are even more controversial. As might be expected, the very small number of economists with impeccable credentials who still wandered off from the mainstream expectations received equally harsh treatment.

A Brief Theoretical Intrusion of Working Conditions

William Stanley Jevons was one such exception. He showed an interest in the physical act of working and, tangentially, in the labor process. Anticipating Taylor's research on scientific management, Jevons experimented with repetitive movements in order to develop a scientific measure of the relationship between muscular fatigue and work. Jevons did not publish his results in an economic journal, but in the premier British science publication, *Nature*.[97] Even worse, from the standpoint of conventional economists, Jevons was theoretically willing to consider incorporating workers' direct utility or disutility from the job itself. He went so far as to acknowledge that work need not be unpleasant and that under certain circumstances work could actually be a source of gratification. For Jevons:

> Labour . . . is any painful exertion of mind or body undergone partly or wholly with a view to future good. It is true that labour may be both agreeable at the time and conducive to future good; but it is only agreeable in a limited amount, and most men are compelled by their wants to exert themselves longer and more severely than they would otherwise do. When a labourer is inclined to stop, he clearly feels something that is irksome, and our theory will only involve the point where the exertion has become so painful as to nearly balance all other considerations. Whatever there is that is wholesome or agreeable about labour before it reaches this point may be taken as a net profit of good to the labourer; but it does not enter into the problem.[98]

Jevons's timing was unfortunate. He began this research on work shortly before the Paris Commune was about to intensify the ideological stakes of economic theory. Economists were trying to craft an ideological justification of the status quo based on what they considered to be "scientific" economics, which could be reduced to mathematics.

For that reason, this part of Jevons's research might seem unexpected. Jevons, more than anybody else in the English-speaking world, was responsible for moving the focus of economic theory away from production in favor of consumption. Jevons himself was highly ideological, although I do not think he saw himself that way. But, even so, he was also very interested in practical matters of science and efficiency.

Downplaying labor while emphasizing transactions seemed to be an urgent priority for the defenders of the new economic theory. These economists realized that taking account of the labor process would fatally complicate the simple analysis that they were proposing. Besides, their ideology insisted that any efforts at improving economic performance, except through commercial transactions, would be sure to make matters worse. In this climate, considerations of working conditions would seriously muddy the theoretical elegance while threatening to weaken the ideological force of economics.

Economists treated employment as a voluntary transaction, but in the workplace voluntarism disappears. Instead, work proceeds according to the commands of the employers. Overbearing supervision might turn work that could otherwise be enjoyable into an ordeal. As a result, the social relations between labor and capital will affect how disagreeable work may be. Jevons's work suggests that economists should take into account workplace utility, which is not the result of a transaction such as the purchase of an object at a store.

But if economists were to take the step that Jevons suggested, they would have no way to "scientifically" measure their subject. Economists might be able to finesse the measurement of consumers' utility by presuming that they maximize their utility. Theoretically, prices offer a metric by which consumers might make their decisions. However, workplace utility would create a challenge comparable to measuring the utility of a marriage. Inside the workplace there are no monetary transactions.

Taking matters even further, close attention to working conditions threatens to create sensitivity to the lives of the most downtrodden members of the working class and the difficult and stultifying conditions on the job they face. Economists understand that because working conditions are difficult to quantify, addressing that subject could make economics appear more subjective and consequently seem less scientific.

One other factor may have made Jevons's work objectionable. The German tradition of the science of work influenced his analysis of labor.[99] Hermann Ludwig Ferdinand von Helmholtz, the great German scientist, was the major figure in this German effort to study the energetics of work. Helmholtz's concept of labor power also provided a key for the development of Karl Marx's economic theory. [100]

Not surprisingly, mainstream economists were not particularly appreciative of this part of Jevons's approach, which harkened back to his earlier discussion of a possible role for the utility of the labor process. In an 1892 letter, Alfred Marshall wrote, "I think Jevons did great harm by talking of . . . measuring disutility."[101] Marshall mocked Jevons by suggesting that considerations of the utility of labor might be appropriate only in the case of a child snacking on berries in the wild, echoing Jevons's earlier association between utility and labor. The youth could continue as long as the benefit would be worth the effort, but for a more modern product, such as "aneroid barometers," Jevons's method would not make any sense.

A group of economists from Austria launched a more influential attack, denouncing Jevons, dogmatically defending the ideological purity of their existing utility-based economics, which intentionally excluded working conditions. Economists were supposed to think in terms of consumers' introspection, not workers' production. The demand that considerations of the workplace were unacceptable soon won over the entire community of economists.[102] Jevons's "sin" was not that his analysis was imperfect, which it was. Instead, Jevons's offense was that he opened a window on the imperfection of the emerging economic consensus about economic theory.

Jevons was duly reprimanded. Today working conditions rarely intrude into economics, except to sometimes allow past or present work experience (objectified as an accumulation of human capital) to affect workers' productivity. In any case, direct concern with workers' welfare on the job never enters into the picture.

In one sense, the neglect of working conditions in economic theory is ironic. As mentioned earlier, economists are generally interested in the kind of person that a particular economy creates. For example, some economists—especially very conservative economists—insist that the discipline of work will improve people's character.

This improvement extends beyond strictly economic welfare to people's moral and ethical qualities. This belief was a major justification for the "reform" of the welfare system, which was intended to drive more people into the job market. The intended beneficiaries were supposed to be the workers, whose human capital and moral character would improve through workplace discipline. The proponents of this policy never hinted that the inflow of additional workers into the job market would force wages down.

Insofar as economics is concerned, the workplace remains what Karl Marx appropriately called "the hidden abode of production."[103] Economics can see workers entering the factory gates and the finished goods appearing on the shipping deck, but economists' view of what happens inside the factory is limited to the accountant's office, where profits and losses are calculated. There, only the shadow of work, workers, and working conditions exist in the form of a wage bill. Real-life people, whether workers or consumers, are reduced to objects that facilitate the accumulation of wealth and capital.

X-Efficiency and Ideology

Work, workers, and working conditions almost intruded into economic theory from a very unlikely direction in 1954, when Arnold Harberger, who would later become a stalwart of the University of Chicago economics department, produced an article that challenged the conventional thinking of economists, beginning:

> One of the first things we learn when we begin to study price theory is that the main effects of monopoly are to misallocate resources, to reduce aggregate welfare, and to redistribute income in favor of monopolists. In the light of this fact, it is a little curious that our empirical efforts at studying monopoly have so largely concentrated on other things.[104]

Harberger intended to show that markets were so efficient in allocating resources that any distortions created by monopoly were bound to be inconsequential—at most 0.1 percent of the Gross National Product. In 1959, Harberger returned to the same idea, suggesting that removing distortions in Chile's economy would create a relatively insignificant improvement in economic performance.[105]

The original article continues to be influential, perhaps in part because Harberger used a simple graph, displaying the effect on demand of a change in price because of monopolistic power. This picture shows increasing profits for the monopolist, decreasing costs of inputs, increasing prices for consumers, and a relatively small triangle, which represented, for Harberger, the social costs of monopoly. Even today, virtually any economist will immediately understand the meaning of the expression "Harberger triangle."

Harberger's lesson was that nobody should worry about business becoming monopolistic, because the triangles are very small, one-tenth of 1 percent, by his estimates. Harberger casually dismissed the effect of monopoly on the distribution of income:

> I have not analyzed the redistributions of income that arise when monopoly is present. . . . I leave [questions about income distribution] to my more metaphysically inclined colleagues to decide.[106]

A few years later, in 1962, the future Nobel Laureate, Robert Mundell, reflected about Harberger's triangles. He worried that if distortions did so little damage, "someone inevitably will draw the conclusion that economics has ceased to be important!"[107]

A more serious challenge to Harberger's model came from Harvey Leibenstein, a respected economics professor from Harvard University. Leibenstein argued that Harberger just looked at what would happen if a monopolist raised prices a little bit. Granted, the immediate effect of a slight price might be small; however, by restricting himself to the marginal effect of price changes, Harberger lost sight of how the reduction of competitive pressures could lead business to become sloppy, which could have major consequences. Harberger's mistake was only looking at the transactions side—what economists refer to as allocative efficiency.

In contrast, Leibenstein directed attention to the productive side of the economy, citing numerous studies of virtually identical plants producing dissimilar results. He postulated that economists needed to come to grips with the forces that account for the superior performance of some operations—forces that conventional economic models do not capture.[108]

Unpredictable outcomes should not come as a surprise. Performances in any kind of competitive activity display a degree of unpredictability. Why should firms be any different? Leibenstein took the position they were not.

Because Leibenstein could not fit his insight into a formal economic model, he called this variability of performance "X-efficiency"—an allusion to Leo Tolstoy's *War and Peace*, which contained the observation: "Two armies may be identical in every observable respect . . . yet one army, in possession of an intangible 'X-factor,' will soundly defeat the other."[109]

Leibenstein appealed to one of the three conventional effects of monopoly that Harberger dismissed—that monopolies misallocate resources. However, X-efficiency cut two ways for conventional economists. To begin with, it showed a weakness in Harberger's contention that monopolies do not reduce welfare: even if increased prices might do little harm, monopolies reduce productive efficiency. Leibenstein reminded economists that the "misallocation of resources," which Harberger mentioned at the beginning of his article, included resources used in production.

Economists did not need Leibenstein to teach them about the harm done by monopoly. A core concept of economics is that competitive pressures are the key to efficient production. Monopolistic power offers protection from competition. In the splendid words of John R. Hicks, "The best of all monopoly profits is a quiet life."[110] While economists were unlikely to welcome Mundell's nightmare of economists sinking into irrelevancy, Leibenstein's assertion of dissimilar efficiencies had even more uncomfortable implications. Virtually all schools of economics, ranging from monetarist to Keynesian, build their models and theories upon the assumption that both firms and businesses maximize.

Yet, Leibenstein's claim of dissimilar productive efficiencies implied that many firms—not just monopolies or oligopolies—do not maximize. Identical firms should produce identical outputs. In this sense, the concept of X-efficiency undermined one of the central assumptions of academic economics, threatening a fate worse than irrelevancy.

Leibenstein was an unlikely rebel. He had resigned from Berkeley after being repulsed by the campus turmoil of the 1960s. He did not intend to openly challenge conventional economics, but he made the mistake of making things difficult for economists who want to be able to reduce everything to simple equations. At the same time, he inadvertently opened the door to questions of work, workers, and working conditions.

Leibenstein's article unleashed a volley of criticism. A retrospective on his work noted:

> Between 1969 and 1980, the article was the third most frequently cited in the Social Science Citation Index. However . . . much of this citation derived from attempts to explain X-efficiency theory away: it was under almost constant attack from much of the mainstream of the profession over that same dozen years.[111]

On December 18, 2009, JSTOR registered 1,351 references to X-efficiency, including 884 since 1980, suggesting a continuing interest in the subject. Why then should an article, describing a well-known phenomenon, raise a firestorm among economists?

Stigler's Reprimand

Leibenstein's harshest critic was none other than George Stigler, who always stood ready to bully anybody who dared to stray too far from the conventional wisdom. Leibenstein was not immune from this treatment, which came in a caustically titled article, "The Xistence of X-Efficiency."

From one perspective, Stigler's vehemence in attacking X-efficiency is puzzling, because Leibenstein's article lent support to the proposition that barriers to competition—barriers that most economists abhor, such as monopolistic practices or regulation—can be wasteful. Stigler himself was a constant critic of regulation and hardly a defender of monopoly.

Stigler's main point was that these differential efficiencies were an illusion. The different firms were producing different mixes of products for sale and other non-marketed outputs, "including leisure and health."[112] Stigler did not mean the leisure and health of the workers, but that of their employers.

Stigler was undoubtedly correct that CEOs do often take actions that trade off firm profitability for their own personal utility. Contemporary research has shown that corporations underperform when their CEOs excel in golf and that the cost of corporate jets is higher when CEOs belong to country clubs far from their headquarters.[113]

Such behavior raises two questions. First, how do actions that raise managerial utility square with the idea that capitalism maximizes either output or total utility? After all, the consequences of such actions do not differ from embezzlement. Second, if the subjective side of work were relevant for employers, such considerations would be relevant for workers.

Granting that leisure can be part of output, even if that leisure is only for the employers, goes a long way toward accepting the basic thesis of this book. Quickly, after inadvertently opening the door to consideration of work, workers, and working conditions, Stigler tried to slam that door shut by concluding his paper with a warning:

> Unless one is prepared to take the mighty methodological leap into the unknown that a nonmaximizing theory requires, waste is not a useful economic concept. Waste is error within the framework of modern economic analysis, and it will not become a useful concept until we have a theory of error.[114]

In short, Stigler declared that unless economists can wrestle waste into a simple mathematical box, economists must not take such a "mighty methodological leap." Leibenstein's sin was to suggest a line of research that would require economists to look into the way that things are produced rather than confining themselves to the transactional side of the market.

Four years after Leibenstein's death, Arnold Harberger gave his presidential address to the American Economic Association on the subject of economic growth. Harberger began by downplaying the marginal perspective that was the centerpiece of his 1954 article: "Many, maybe even most, economists expected that increments of output would be explained by increments of inputs, but when we took our best shot we found that traditional inputs typically fell far short of explaining the observed output growth."[115]

Harberger gave numerous examples of the sort of productive improvements that fall through the usual net of economic analysis, many based on his experience in Latin America. In his most telling case, he wrote:

> I recall going through a clothing plant in Central America, where the owner informed me of a 20-percent reduction in real costs, following upon his installation of background music that played as the seamstresses worked. [116]

Harberger suggested two different metaphors for economic growth—yeast and mushrooms: "Yeast causes bread to expand very evenly, like a balloon being filled with air, while mushrooms have the habit of popping up, almost overnight, in a fashion that is not easy to predict."[117]

Harberger must have understood as clearly as Stigler that conventional economics is not particularly useful in hunting mushrooms, such as finding the kind of music that might make the seamstresses work harder. Yet, as Harberger realized, such unquantifiable innovations can be very productive.

The rest of Harberger's article ignored mushrooms, retreating to a conventional analysis of the yeast-like bunching of technical change within particular industries. He blamed the poor performance of the lagging industries on an inability to perceive potential cost savings together with a nod to the damage done by inflation, bad regulation, and protectionism. However, he never showed any interest in why these problems should vary among firms.

In the end, Harberger was no more prepared than Stigler to deal with work, workers, and working conditions. Interestingly, while debates about the arcane subject of X-efficiency might seem complex, in the world of team sports, people commonly speak of players' intangibles, which are something like their X-efficiency. The idea is that despite unimpressive outward appearances and statistical records, some athletes have these inexplicable intangibles. For example, in the statistics-obsessed world of baseball, Leo Durocher, a famed manager, explained why Eddie Stanky was his favorite player. Durocher told a reporter, "He can't hit; he can't run; he can't field; he can't throw. He can't do a goddam thing, Frank—but beat you."[118] Other, outwardly very impressive players are described as poison, meaning that their effect on others is destructive.

A Twisted Reflection of Working Conditions

A third potential intrusion of work, workers, and working conditions emanated from a young University of Chicago graduate student, Richard Thaler, eight years after Leibenstein's article. Unlike the hostile reaction to Jevons and Leibenstein, the discipline actually embraced this analysis.

Today, Thaler is perhaps the world's best-known behavioral economist. Here is how he explained his own work:

> I am not your usual sort of economist. I practice what has come to be called behavioral economics. We behavioralists differ from our more traditional brethren in the way we characterize agents in the economy. Traditional economics is based on imaginary creatures sometimes referred to as "Homo economicus.". . . Real people have trouble balancing their checkbooks, much less calculating how much they need to save for retirement; they sometimes binge on food, drink or high-definition televisions. . . . Behavioral economics is the study of Humans in markets.[119]

Thaler did not begin as a behavioralist. In 1974, he published a Ph.D. dissertation at the University of Chicago that found a correlation between wage rates and the probability of dying on the job and then published his results in an article with his advisor, Sherwin Rosen.[120] Based on this correlation and assuming the higher wages were a reward for accepting the risk of death, he proposed one could assume that workers were communicating through their transactions on the job market how much they thought their lives were worth. Thaler estimated that workers were demanding $200 a year (in 1967 dollars) for each 1-in-1,000 chance of dying.

This method is seriously biased downward because poor people, especially immigrants, with few alternatives, are more likely to accept low-wage, dangerous jobs. For example, a government report on workplace deaths concluded, "During 1992–2006 . . . the death rate for Hispanic workers was consistently higher than the rate for all U.S. workers, and the proportion of deaths among foreign-born Hispanic workers increased over time."[121] A different kind of study would arrive at a very different result. If, for example, economists had the capacity to plumb the minds of students who are about to graduate with MBAs from elite universities, they could investigate how much more the students would expect from hypothetical investment banking jobs with an annual 1 percent chance of workplace fatality. If such a study were somehow possible, the value of a "statistical life" would certainly be higher than estimates for a pool of potential applicants for jobs as farmworkers.

Thaler quickly realized the weakness of his results. His friends told him they would never accept anything less than $1 million in return for increasing their chances of dying by 0.1 percent. Paradoxically, the same friends would not be willing to sacrifice any income to reduce the probability of dying on the job.[122] This apparent inconsistency soon left Thaler disenchanted with his work, but his recognition that economics' central assumption of rationality was flawed moved him in the direction of behavioral economics.

Although Thaler lost confidence in his work, he was almost alone in this respect. Instead, his work resonated with the objectives of opponents of regulation, including business interests and their armies of lobbyists, who along with a number of conservative think tanks and some conservative economists, tirelessly work to weaken regulations.[123] One of the major strategies of the anti-regulators is to argue that the benefits of regulations are less than their costs.

To make that point in the case of regulations to protect human lives, anti-regulators want to find ways to diminish the importance of any deaths that regulations might prevent. To meet this need, economists constructed an influential literature to measure the value of a "statistical life."

Most people resist putting a monetary value on human life, but Thaler's idea of a "statistical life" had a twofold benefit: it gave a human life a lowball value and put scientific gloss on the anti-regulators' arguments. Once the idea of assigning a monetary value is accepted, anti-regulators could work to create even lower estimates, further minimizing the consequences of workplace fatalities, as well as deaths from consumer products.

Government agencies embraced this technique.[124] This practice is only one part of a three-pronged strategy, which also includes overestimating the costs of regulation and suggesting that money spent on regulation would do far more good in other areas, such as vaccinating children. For example, in pushing this third prong of anti-regulatory rhetoric, John D. Graham, a fervent opponent of regulation, who became President George W. Bush's head of the Office of Management and Budget's Office of Information and Regulatory Affairs, even went so far as to claim that spending money on regulations instead of vaccinating children is tantamount to "statistical murder."[125] Ironically, I know of no case when the anti-regulators came out in support of any program to actually vaccinate children, perhaps preferring to be able to recycle vaccination as a straw man to wield against all regulation.

The example of a statistical life illustrates the opportunistic ways that economists avoid looking into questions regarding work, workers, and working conditions, except where they can cherry-pick some useful results.

Thaler's career is interesting in this regard. Much like David Card, Thaler paid a price for straying from the mainstream fold. His thesis advisor, the same Sherwin Rosen who refused to take Krueger's work seriously, loved the dissertation but expressed deep disappointment that Thaler's later work in behavioral economics wasted his career on trivialities. Another University of Chicago professor, Merton Miller, the Nobel Laureate who was so critical of the work of Card and Krueger, refused to talk with Thaler.

Ironically, Thaler's behavioralism is now coming into favor in Democratic circles. Together with his co-author Cass Sunstein, Thaler has promoted the idea of "libertarian paternalism" instead of outright regulation. For example, Thaler and Sunstein suggest that business could "nudge" people to increase their rate of personal savings by requiring workers to opt out of 401(k)'s instead of opting in.[126] Such non-coercive policies are politically attractive because they seem to be doing something positive without inconveniencing business. At the same time, nudging tends to emphasize personal rather than social behavior. The irony was doubled when President Obama nominated Cass Sunstein to take the job that John Graham had held.

Thaler's experience is relevant to this book because it suggests that even in those rare cases when well-meaning economists do trespass into questions of work, workers, or working conditions—territory usually proscribed by the discipline—their work is unlikely to be helpful with respect to workers' interests. If such work will help the workers' cause, it will be rejected; however, if it can be wielded to harm labor, economists are likely to embrace it as they did Thaler's dissertation.

In this case, economists used his work by reducing the benefits of saving a worker's life to undermine efforts to improve workplace safety. If Thaler had come up with numbers that had supported greater workplace protections, he probably would have experienced ostracism earlier in his career.

Workers as Objects

The disinterest of economists in the world of work filters into the popular culture, where labor receives less interest than ordinary economic transactions. The typical newspaper has a large section devoted to business, much of it taken up with the health of the stock market. Almost no papers today keep a reporter to cover workers. Other than the occasional ideologically correct, human interest story, the only section of the paper devoted to workers is the sports page, which concentrates on working athletes. Ordinary workers—people who may have difficulty in affording the cost of attending a major league sporting contest—rarely appear in the media.

Maintaining this distance from work, workers, and working conditions seems to be a natural reaction for those whose profits depend upon pushing people as hard as possible. Their concern is to produce commodities at the lowest possible cost, no matter what the consequences might be.

Of course, compulsion of any kind is foreign to economic theory. Conventional economics describes the labor market as a thoroughly voluntary arrangement—one that does not need to traumatize workers beforehand. Yet, once a worker enters into the workplace, the employer is free to exercise despotic powers. True, some limits exist. The law prohibits physical assault. Certain types of discrimination or sexual harassment are also impermissible, but the enforcement of such rules is rare. Even laws that require the employer to maintain a safe workplace go largely unenforced.

Direct concern for workers falls outside the purview of conventional economics and, all too frequently, the public at large. Instead, the Procrusteans have managed to create an intellectual climate in which people become oblivious to the hardships of their fellow citizens.

Economists are more than willing to lend a hand in this regard. In their theory, workers once employed only exist as labor, part of what they classify as a generic factor of production, along with the equally abstract categories of land and capital—none of which could be realistically measured. In the case of labor, bodies can be counted or those numbers can be weighted by the years of education, but actual capabilities are irrelevant. Within this world, any accountant with a college degree could replace a star center on a professional basketball team without a college degree.

Within this theory, we can be confident that business will purchase the appropriate mix of land, labor, and capital and then ensure that the production process will proceed efficiently. How that happens is of no concern in terms of economic theory.

Procrusteans are more likely to react with a bitter sense of injustice when workers act as something other than a factor of production; for instance, when a union manages to win a fight for better wages. Business interests will make invidious comparisons, indignantly asking why those workers should get higher wages than some other poorly paid occupation.

Employers prefer to keep harsh working conditions hidden from the public, but the public often seems comfortable not knowing about such matters as well. There seems to be a kind of collusion on the part of business, government, the media, and the public to shroud abominable working conditions in secrecy.

The reception of Upton Sinclair's novel *The Jungle* illustrates this phenomenon. Sinclair poignantly described the horrid working conditions in the slaughterhouses—including the periodic mixing of human body parts with the animal flesh sent to the market. The book alarmed the public so much that Congress was moved to pass legislation regulating the industry. The purpose, however, was not to protect the workers' lost body parts, but rather to put consumers at ease about the safety of their meat supply. As Sinclair later remarked:

> Concerning *The Jungle*, I wrote that "I aimed at the public's heart, and by accident I hit it in the stomach." I am supposed to have helped clean up the yards and improve the country's meat supply—though this is mostly delusion. But nobody even pretends to believe that I improved the condition of the stockyard workers.[127]

Eventually, unionization improved matters in the slaughterhouses, but today, immigrants, without the benefit of protection by either unions or government regulators, perform most of the work. Conditions today are not much better than what Sinclair described. As Eric Schlosser recently reported in his immensely popular book, *Fast Food Nation*:

> The injury rate in a slaughterhouse is about three times higher than the rate in a typical American factory. Every year more than one-quarter of the meatpacking workers in this country—roughly forty thousand men and women—suffer an injury or a work-related illness that requires medical attention beyond first aid. There is strong evidence that these numbers, compiled by the Bureau of Labor Statistics, understate the number of meatpacking injuries that occur. Thousands of additional injuries and illnesses most likely go unrecorded.[128]

That people in comfortable positions would be more concerned about their stomachs than about other human beings should come as no surprise. Even so, the degree of disregard for the welfare of others, especially those who do the work upon which all of us depend, is shocking. Perhaps to do otherwise would create a painful sense of guilt.

Even people with a strong sense of humanity seem to have an easier time sympathizing with workers in far-off places than those nearby. Students in the United States have organized remarkable movements in support of workers in sweatshops in China and other low-wage countries. But the plight of the farm workers in the hot fields of California's Central Valley, which in the early 1970s generated a similar upsurge of support, no longer inspires much sympathy, even among students in California. Our language coldly objectifies these workers as field hands, suggesting that their being is reduced to a simple mechanical motion. The objectification of the people in the fields may be necessary to maintain a psychological distance. As a result, people whose plight should by any objective standard be brought to the attention of the public remain comfortably out of the sight of their more affluent brethren.

The Hidden Abode of Production

In the legend of Procrustes, travelers were unaware of the impending danger of the iron bed until it was too late, but eventually they must have realized the horror of their fate. Perhaps the Procrustean legend would have hit home for the slaughterhouse workers with severed body parts, but all too often the bed remains invisible, even to the people who are caught on it. Traumatization has not radicalized workers, but rather just made them more fearful of losing their jobs.

Perhaps a change is under way. In 2006, job satisfaction for workers under the age of twenty-five stood at only 38.6 percent, down from 55.7 percent in 1987.[129] Some corporations, such as McDonald's, Taco Bell, KFC, Staples, and Delta Airlines, are concerned enough about workers' attitudes that they have hired advertising agencies to make their jobs seem more attractive. "Building an 'employment brand' is 'absolutely critical,'" says Richard Floersch, McDonald's Human Relations chief.[130] The level of job satisfaction for all workers has fallen less dramatically to 47.7 percent in 2006, down from 61.1 percent in 1987. Even so, almost half of all workers still express satisfaction with their jobs, as do the majority of workers over fifty-five or those earning upwards of $52,000.[131]

Such satisfaction may be only relative to the alternative—the hardship and deprivation associated with unemployment. The recent economic crisis might increase the level of job satisfaction. Wages may be miserable and working conditions unpleasant or even dangerous, but without any hope of an alternative existence, such a life of unremitting toil may seem natural. A job, even a low-wage job with poor working conditions, may not seem to be a source of dissatisfaction. Given such a perspective, questions about why people should be subjected to such conditions go unasked.

When working conditions do appear in the media, it is often in the context of a spectacular disaster in which the emphasis is on the heroics of those who have come to rescue the unfortunate workers. In such cases, the media says little about any negligence that might have put workers in harm's way in the first place.

For example, in the case of the 2006 Sago mine disaster in which twelve miners died, the media largely ignored the fact that the company had a long history of safety violations. Instead, the media covered the rescue operation, often uncritically relaying misinformation provided by the company.[132] Years later, the government continued to shield the company, promoted the outlandish theory that a lightning strike penetrated deep into the earth, traveled more than a mile, and then ignited a methane deposit.

Management may well have detailed blueprints of the worksite and intricate knowledge of the equipment but know very little about the nature of what goes on in the workplace. Instead, employers concentrate on gathering information about the workplace through invasive surveillance, in part to collect statistical information to measure efficiencies. Business uses computers to record the keystrokes of people entering data or truck drivers' movements. The potential scope of such tracking expands almost daily. Fredrick Winslow Taylor would be delighted with the new Radio Frequency Identification chips that offer the potential to keep track of every employee's physical location.

Interestingly, Charles Babbage anticipated more about modern machinery than the computer, observing:

> One great advantage which we may derive from machinery is from the check which it affords against the inattention, the idleness or the dishonesty of human agents.[133]

The efforts to track and monitor workers and commodities spill over into everyday life, beyond the factory floor or the retail outlet, where the justification of guarding one's property is no longer relevant. This amalgamation of detailed personal information, which makes a mockery of the right to privacy, gives business enormous power in the marketplace. This information is most effective to the extent it does not appear to be used in a Procrustean fashion. Business even makes the claim that its detailed knowledge of personal information, such as an individual's financial situation and consumption patterns, allows it to serve the public better—as if profit were the furthest thing from the mind of corporate executives.

Even more ominously, the government is an active customer for the same data. These data are especially dangerous because the government has the ability to combine the commercial data with secret wiretaps, records of computer activity, and even library records. One of the obvious objectives of such programs is to monitor those who dare to challenge the Procrustean nature of the economy, perhaps placing government monitoring at the heart of the system of guard labor.

Control versus Cooperation

Despite the massive amount of information that business collects, real knowledge about the workplace will remain elusive without personal contact, carried out with respect. Even when management does have vital information about working conditions, as seems to be the case with the Sago mine, ignoring life-threatening risks may be profitable— partially explaining the high levels of occupational injuries, diseases, and deaths.

Given the lack of contact with those at the bottom of the chain of command, management has no grasp of the untapped potential of its employees. Instead, management demands unquestioned obedience and absolute diligence from workers at the lower reaches of the hierarchy, without realizing that many of these people have the capacity to make greater contributions to the productive effort. Consider the atypical nursing home that engaged its entire staff in an effort to protect its residents from bed sores:

> "The laundry workers helped us see that some clothes weren't fitting the residents properly and were restricting their skin," said Jeanie Langschied, a registered nurse there. The kitchen staff began putting protein powders in cookies to boost nutrition. They added buffet dining, so residents would not remain in one position for so long, compressing

fragile skin. Even the beauty shop "realized that wait times needed to decrease," Ms. Langschied said, and residents should be repositioned while getting their hair done. "It was all departments looking at everything, and it was just amazing the information that flowed through." [134]

This nursing home is the exception, not the rule. Those who live off their capital rarely understand that their own prosperity could be enhanced by engaging their workers and nurturing their capacities. To do so raises two risks. Acknowledging workers' capabilities would threaten management's claim to elevated status. More dangerously, a different management stance could embolden workers to challenge Procrusteanism.

Every once in a while, CEOs of major corporations call for improvements in the educational system. These entreaties are usually nothing more than an ideological expression of their preference for more privatization—in this case, of education. Other executives recognize that a better educated working class can pay healthy dividends. However, even here, the understanding of what education means is limited. The business vision of better education means little more than an improved ability to follow written directions or to write reports for higher management in a clearer manner. A deeper view of education—in the sense of a better ability to make critical decisions (especially with regard to working conditions)—is the furthest thing from their mind.

My students confirm this impression. Each semester I question them about their job experience. Invariably, they tell me that their employers are from the "we-don't-pay-you-to-think" school of management. Their employers just want them to shut up and do what they are told.

Seeing workers as little more than literate beasts of burden has one advantage; it serves to inflate managers' sense that their absolute authority is justified. Besides, people in high places naturally prefer to believe that their own success is due to their own hard work, not to the drudgery of others.

In this chapter I have tried to trace the connections between this comfortable view of the world and economic theory. In order to craft an ideology that justifies the current economic system, economics has gone out of its way to avoid dealing with work, workers, and working conditions. In the process, economists have generated serious misperceptions about the world that help to solidify a harsh Procrustean discipline.

Despite all the pundit talk about the need to accept Procrustean discipline, the talking heads inevitably forget to mention one factor: just as Procrustes deformed his victims, the market economy warps the creativity as well as the expectations of the people who fall under its sway. Even practicing doctors must submit their medical judgment to the authority of less trained administrators or insurance clerks, resulting in delays and denials that threaten the health and safety of patients.

CHAPTER FOUR

Everyday Life in a Procrustean World

Justifying the Neglect of Working Conditions

All too many economists refuse to consider anything they cannot derive from the discipline's utility-based micro-foundations as "scientific." Economists, however, limit their concept of utility to the useful or pleasurable effects of consuming marketed goods, thereby excluding any consideration of the labor process or any non-market factors that affect the quality of life.

The marginalization of work in economic theory is remarkable. Economists realize that in the real world the labor process is necessary for the production of the commodities that provide utility, but their theory holds that what workers do on the job is devoid of utility. Frank Knight, an early leader of the Chicago School and one of the most thoughtful economists of his day, justified the intentional neglect of what he called "sentimental" costs of work:

> We have no concern with the pains or subjective sacrifices involved in production, since it is not at all in terms of such "costs" that the entrepreneur makes his calculations on the basis of which he decides whether to

produce the good or on what scale. He takes account of sentimental costs only insofar as they influence the outlays he must make to secure the services necessary to production. That is, he is concerned only with the price measure of his costs. Their magnitude in some other aspect will not influence his decision. Pains and sentimental repugnancies are undoubtedly influences in limiting the supply of some sorts of services and raising their price, but in the aggregate they form a relatively unimportant element, and no one now contends that there is any tendency for the prices of productive services, still less of final goods, to bear any correspondence with these magnitudes. The relation between them is a separate inquiry, pertinent perhaps to an evaluation or criticism of the competitive economic order, hardly so to an explanation of its workings.[1]

As we have seen, economists presume that work is simply the absence of leisure, and that only the duration of time on the job creates a negative utility. People are free to adjust their hours of work to maximize their utility per hour of work, as if a worker had the choice to take off from work forty minutes early in order to maximize today's utility. Unemployment, even during serious depressions, reflects an increased preference for leisure over work.[2]

This strange, new conceptualization of the economy revolutionized the way economists saw human beings. No longer were workers a class of people who sold their labor to persons who owned capital. Under this new consumption-oriented interpretation of the world, classes disappear altogether. Everyone—bosses, workers, or the unemployed—only exist as consumers or investors, all of whom attempt to maximize utility. According to the logic of the theory, workers should forget about working conditions and just work hard in order to take satisfaction in the consumption that the modern economy offers.

Everything is turned on its head. The workplace disappears, and the workers—actually their wives in much of the popular literature at the time this theory first appeared—suddenly show up in the marketplace with omnipotent powers. Business meekly follows their demands, providing exactly what consumers want.

At first, this thinking emerged in academic economic theory. Then, some leading intellectuals began to push a popularized line of thinking, explicitly counseling workers not to see themselves as exploited members of the lower class. Instead, they advised workers to look beyond their immediate working conditions—no matter how horrible—and see themselves as equal participants in a consumer society.

Writing early in the twentieth century, Simon Patten, considered at the time a progressive economist, expressed this view in his book, *The New Basis of Civilization*. Patten rhapsodized, "The worker steadily and cheerfully chooses the deprivations of this week in order to secure the gratifications of a coming holiday." Patten was unusual. At least he acknowledged workers' deprivations. For Patten:

> [Workers'] zest for amusement urges them to submit to the discipline of work, and the habits formed for the sake of gratifying their tastes make the regular life necessary in industry easier and more pleasant. . . . Honesty, application, adaptability through much pain, become his assets in his new bond with society.[3]

By this intellectual sleight of hand, economics reconceptualized the mass of often surly workers into an obedient collection of contented consumers, aspiring only to shop in elite venues such as Neiman Marcus. We might say that economists hoped to transform potentially revolutionary Marxists into Neiman Marxists.

More recent economic textbooks offer a slightly different description of the relationship between labor and capital than Patten's, adding that growing productivity of labor should show up in higher wages. Higher wages, in turn, allow workers to enjoy more commodities. Textbooks continue to tell this story even though hourly wages corrected for inflation have been flat for more than thirty-five years, despite enormous increases in productivity.

One implication of this theory is that as workers' affluence increases, the utility of more leisure should become stronger relative to the accumulation of more commodities. At that point, hours of work should begin to decline—another outcome that has yet to occur. The average work week in non-agricultural occupations has increased from 38.1 in 1980 hours to 39.1 in 2005.[4] Because more women have been entering the workplace, the average number of working hours per family has grown more dramatically. Between 1979 and 2000, the typical middle-income wife in families with children has added an average of over 500 hours of work—the equivalent of more than three months of work per year.[5]

The fact that families are devoting more hours to work does not necessarily refute economic theory. Nothing can refute economic theory. Whenever facts do not follow the logic of their theory, economists can rely on their ingenuity to find explanations. They can always conjecture that preferences have changed. Perhaps, for some reason, leisure is less desirable today than it was in earlier times, thus people would choose to work longer for more commodities. Edward Prescott, a Nobel Prize–winning economist, even suggested that workers in the United States should work more hours because taxes were lowered, increasing the advantage of work.[6]

Labor's position in society is deteriorating despite higher productivity. As noted earlier, hourly wages in the United States have been stagnant for more than three decades, despite dramatically higher productivity. The preferred explanation is that many workers lack the requisite skills—such as the skills of a successful hedge fund executive.

At the same time, medical care—certainly a commodity that should have considerable utility—is becoming increasingly unaffordable. All the while, economic theory warns that tampering with the Procrustean economy threatens incalculable harm.

A Brief Rebuke from Adam Smith

Ironically, Adam Smith treated the importance of consumption far less reverentially than Patten. Smith saw the clientele of fancy shops as foolish victims of a "deception which rouses and keeps in continual motion the industry of mankind."[7] He asked:

How many people ruin themselves by laying out money on trinkets of frivolous utility? What pleases these lovers of toys is not so much the utility, as the aptness of the machines which are fitted to promote it. All their pockets are stuffed with little conveniences. They contrive new pockets, unknown in the clothes of other people, in order to carry a greater number. They walk about loaded with a multitude of baubles . . . some of which may sometimes be of some little use, but all of which might at all times be very well spared, and of which the whole utility is certainly not worth the fatigue of bearing the burden.[8]

The rich are not the only people who fall for this ruse. Smith considers the lot of "the poor man's son, whom heaven in its anger has visited with ambition, when he begins to look around him, admires the condition of the rich."[9] Smith's poor man's son behaves according to Patten's vision:

To obtain the conveniences which these afford, he submits in the first year, nay in the first month of his application, to more fatigue of body and more uneasiness of mind than he could have suffered through the whole of his life from the want of them. He studies to distinguish himself in some laborious profession. With the most unrelenting industry he labours night and day to acquire talents superior to all his competitors.[10]

Smith's imaginary worker realizes his mistake, even after he has succeeded in earning a comfortable life:

But in the languor of disease and the weariness of old age, the pleasures of the vain and empty distinctions of greatness disappear. To one, in this situation, they are no longer capable of recommending those toilsome pursuits in which they had formerly engaged him. In his heart he curses ambition, and vainly regrets the ease and the indolence of youth, pleasures which are fled for ever, and which he has foolishly sacrificed for what, when he has got it, can afford him no real satisfaction.[11]

Sadly, few of Patten's more modern workers will even get to discover the hollowness of the "deception" that Smith described. More than a few will fall prey to what Smith called "their absurd presumption in their own good fortune," expecting to enjoy a prosperous life.[12] As Mark Twain recalled in his autobiography, "We were always going to be rich next year. It is good to begin life . . . poor and prospectively rich."[13]

Like Twain's family, many workers today may live their lives deluded by the dream of the imaginary success that will bring them happiness. Most workers, however, will reject a more serious deception promoted by economic theory—that working conditions are irrelevant. Unlike economists, workers do take a keen interest in working conditions.

The Working Day

In the nineteenth century, the length of the working day was perhaps the most contentious issue for labor:

> Before World War II workers' demands for shorter hours were often advanced with greater fervor than demands for higher wages. The shorter-hours movement galvanized organized labor. It was the spark that helped found the first national labor union in the 1860s and the American Federation of Labor in the 1880s, the major issue in the steel strike of 1919, and remained important into the 1930s.[14]

Workers fought long and hard to limit the hours of work. Some workers lost their lives in the struggle, most famously in response to the executions following the Haymarket Square demonstration of 1886 and the Homestead Strike of 1892, when Carnegie increased the working day from eight to twelve hours while attempting to break the union.

Despite their general disinterest in working conditions, mainstream economists passionately opposed the demand for a shorter working day. They insisted that the length of the working day resulted from a voluntary bargain between individual workers and employers. "Coercion" by organized groups of workers (that is, unions) would be egregious. Similarly, any legislation restricting business in these transactions would be a serious violation of the laws of political economy. In such polemics, economists became strangely silent about utility maximization. As the renegade economist John Kenneth Galbraith once observed:

> Leisure is something to be regarded with misgivings, especially in the lower income brackets. Accordingly, a reduction in the standard workweek must always be considered dubious social policy inducing moral or spiritual weakness.[15]

Business leaders added that workers actually benefit from long hours because the restriction of leisure makes workers better people.

One nineteenth-century businessman asserted that the best course is to give men "plenty to do, and a long while to do it in, and you will find them physically and morally better."[16] Another told the Massachusetts Bureau of Statistics of Labor, "I worked 11, 12, 14 and 15 hours a day, and have as yet felt no bad effects from it, but rather been strengthened. It is not the hours per day that a person works that breaks him down, but the hours spent in dissipation."[17] A study of business ideology in the 1920s summarized the prevailing view at the time, which was even more damning of shorter hours:

> It may be observed at the outset that leisure and idleness are synonymous for the masses. The identification of the idea that the average man might enrich his personality by putting leisure to some constructive use was patently ridiculous. What *unthinking creature* could be ennobled by the fruits of leisure? For such as they, not to work is to loaf. Leisure is idleness.
>
> Leisure will . . . lead to an abuse of time by developing a taste for improper amusements and luxuries; it tends to increase criminality; . . . and it will eventually bring complete decay to man's capacities.[18]

Debauchery was not really a central concern for economists. If it were, they could just as easily glance up the social ladder rather than concentrating their moral scrutiny on the less fortunate. Economists might be offended by seeing a drunken worker stumbling in the streets. Better that he have a chauffeur to pluck him up before the public catches sight of his drunkenness.

Even at the height of the struggle about the length of the working day, economists did little to seriously inquire about the subject. Had they done so, they might have taken note of the corrosive consequences of long working hours. Exhaustion took a toll on workers' health. Excessive hours of work meant that workers rarely saw their families during daylight hours. Such enforced absence had a negative effect on their children. Excessive hours of work were also conducive to a psychology of despair, which people often try to control with drink, the very symptom of debauchery that long hours are supposed to hold in check. How would economists' subjective evaluation of their own welfare possibly change if they found themselves subjected to the imposition of long hours of grueling physical labor? I think any rational person knows the answer.

Consider the attitude of W. Michael Cox, chief economist for the Federal Reserve Bank of Dallas and one of the most prominent cheerleaders for markets. Dr. Cox always finds ways to put markets in the best possible light. When faced with the quandary about essential workers, such as firemen, having to work two jobs to be able to afford to live in New York City, Dr. Cox pontificated, using the language of investment advisors, "I think it's great. . . . It gives you portfolio diversification in your income."[19]

Here Dr. Cox has outdone himself, in justifying the unjustifiable, while implicitly financializing the job market. Going beyond Adam Smith who saw workers as merchants selling their labor, Dr. Cox recasts them as investors. Just as investors profit by diversifying their portfolios, workers would be well advised to hold more than one job. Sophisticated investors divide their funds among many, even hundreds of different stocks. If only the poor, benighted workers could figure out how to extend the day beyond twenty-four hours, they could do the same. I wonder how Dr. Cox would feel, however, if groggy but well-diversified firefighters arrived to save his house already so exhausted from their other job that they could not perform their duties effectively.

Extending the Years of Work

The Procrustean imperative demands that employers attempt to squeeze every possible bit of effort from everyone on their payroll. Similarly, businesses want people to be available for work for as many years as possible, so long as their efforts are a source of potential profit. The emphasis changes, depending on the prevailing business strategy.

At the dawn of the Industrial Revolution, longer hours were not the issue, because the normal working day was already fourteen hours. At the time, employers needed a steady stream of cheap, unskilled labor. Because children's wages were a pittance, employers found them ideal for many factory tasks. However, with wages so low and working conditions abhorrent, employers had difficulty obtaining a sufficient supply of children. Orphanages provided some bodies. So did some desperate and destitute parents. Even so, the supply remained insufficient for the growing demands of industry.

Intellectuals encouraged employers to push children to enter the labor force. William Temple, a contemporary of Adam Smith, called for the addition of four-year-old children to the labor force. Anticipating modern Skinnerian psychology, Temple speculated, "For by these means, we hope that the rising generation will be so habituated to constant employment that it would at length prove agreeable and entertaining to them."[20] Compared to John Locke, the philosopher of liberty and often credited as the inspiration of the U.S. Declaration of Independence, Temple was a kind of progressive. Locke called for the commencement of work at the age of three.[21]

Since people like Locke and Temple considered workers to be practically indistinguishable from animals, it is little wonder that they did not favor educating the workers' children. What is more, education might foster subversive sentiments. Yet the truth of child labor gave the lie to any justification of it and any arguments against educating working-class children.

Consider the life of Robert Blincoe, an orphan who was "given" to a factory owner and then escaped. In later life, he told his story to a journalist named John Brown, who published it in a small newspaper in 1828 and then in book form in 1832. Beatings and other sadistic punishments, together with the requirement to repetitively perform unnatural movements in an unhealthy and dangerous workplace, badly deformed Blincoe's body. Conditions were so abominable that the children at the factory were reduced to stealing food from pig troughs.[22] In the wake of the ensuing public concern about working conditions, Parliament held hearings.

Blincoe's misfortune was able to touch the public's conscience only because of a conflict between powerful interest groups. The aristocratic landlords and factory owners were at odds. Each group pretended to display its social conscience by self-righteously pointing to the abuses of the other. The manufacturers had accused the landowning classes of selfishly imposing high food prices on poor workers by using protectionism to drive up the price of grain.

The factory owners did not actually believe that the elimination of the tariff would allow workers to benefit from cheaper food. Manufacturers wanted to eliminate agricultural protection because cheap food would allow them to boost profits by reducing wages. Manufacturers also hoped to expand foreign markets. They assumed that if other nations had the chance to export grain to Great Britain, these countries would use some of their increased agricultural income to purchase British manufactured goods. In addition, potential competitors would be less inclined to try to compete with Great Britain by developing their own manufacturing if they enjoyed a prosperous agriculture.[23]

Landlords retaliated by denouncing inhuman factory conditions.[24] Blincoe's story served their campaign well. In the wake of such publicity, the British Factory Act of 1833 reduced the hours of work for British children between the ages of nine and thirteen to nine hours a day and forty-eight hours a week. Children between thirteen and sixteen were limited to a maximum of a mere sixty-nine hours.

Such episodes of concern are usually fleeting. By 1844, the mill owners won the right to hire eight-year-old children again. The concern about working hours for children also left economics unaffected. Economists were touched by the plight of the poor, unfortunate factory owners, deprived of the right to determine how long children in their employ should work.

Blincoe's experience illustrates the far-reaching destructive nature of Procrusteanism. Within the Procrustean mindset, child labor offered an opportunity to increase production. Gratuitous brutality was simply a legitimate technique for getting a recalcitrant child to work harder. Recall Nardinelli's speculation that young children actually maximized their utility agreeing to be whipped.

Neither Blincoe nor any other child received their hypothetical beating premiums. Only an ignoramus would not understand that using violence to extract excessive labor from young children limits the quality of labor over the long term. The social benefits from educating young people must surely outweigh the work that can be forced out of a five- or six-year-old child.

Although business does not push for more child labor today, a move is afoot to extend the years of work by deferring retirement. The threshold for receiving Social Security benefits in the United States is creeping upward. Propaganda in favor of old people working is mounting. The *Wall Street Journal* published a glowing front-page story about the case of Bonnie Lovellette Rooks, a janitor on the floor of a steel factory, who was a month shy of her seventy-ninth birthday. She could not afford to retire because of her medical costs and the responsibility of caring for a disabled daughter.[25] The tone of the story was not an expression of sympathy for Ms. Rooks; instead, it exuded appreciation for the potential of a stretching of working years worthy of Procrustes. Business has good reason to applaud the prolonged career of Ms. Rooks, although she has less cause to appreciate the economic conditions that left her with so much responsibility for an unaffordable medical system.

Cases like that of Ms. Rooks are certain to become more common. In a 2007 estimate, Mitra Toossie of the Bureau of Labor Statistics projected that the share of workers in the labor force fifty-five and older, would leap from 16.8 percent in 2006 to 22.7 percent by 2016, making elderly workers one of the fastest growing groups in the labor force.[26]

The BLS projections may turn out to be conservative. Corporations are rapidly cutting benefits, making private pensions increasingly rare. The recent financial crises have decimated many 401(k) accounts. As pensions shrink and medical care gets ever more expensive, the option to retire becomes less likely for millions of people.

Business understands the advantage of this new arrangement. Not only can employers shed the responsibility of providing pensions, but they can also enjoy the downward pressure on wages, further traumatizing workers in the process. Yet one is supposed to accept all of this as a result of transactions among equal parties.

Distorted Procrustean Logic

As Margaret Thatcher claimed, the economy runs according to an inexorable logic, one that cannot be defied without severe consequences. Lawrence Summers, nephew of two Nobel Prize–winning economists and a former U.S. Secretary of the Treasury, reframed Thatcher's warning that "There Is No Alternative" in the context of economic theory. Before an international audience, Summers proclaimed the necessity of following the rule of markets: "The laws of economics, it's often forgotten, are like the laws of engineering. There's only one set of laws and they work everywhere."[27]

Looking at work, workers, and working conditions objectively shatters the facade of scientific immutability as well as that of voluntarism. Imagine Summers making the same claim when the typical working day was twelve or fourteen hours. Employers would have no need to offer their workers any justification, given the severe imbalance of power. The long working day would just appear to be a natural part of the rhythm of life.

The lengths to which economists are willing to go to give "scientific" cover for increasing (and not reducing) the length of the working day and the working life is illustrated by the case of Nassau Senior. Senior attempted to invoke the science of political economy to defend factory owners from those who would be foolish enough to argue for the reduction of the hours of work. Senior was anything but an obscure economist. He was enormously influential, later becoming the first holder of the Drummond Chair at Oxford, as well as president of Section F (the social science section) of the British Association for the Advancement of Science.

Senior's "analysis" included a predictable protest against what he considered an unwarranted interference with a legitimate contract between workers and their employers. Senior went further. Using data that manufacturers had supplied him, he gave dire warnings about interfering with the labor market: "If the hours of working were reduced by one hour per day [prices remaining the same], the net profit would be destroyed—if they were reduced by one hour and a half, even the gross profit would be destroyed."[28]

One problem interfered with Senior's calculation: it was wrong. Marx had great fun in tearing apart Senior's logic.[29] Senior's blunder depended upon the assumption that all non-labor costs would remain the same, while the shortened hours of work would reduce output. Senior forgot that if the factory were spinning cotton for one hour less, it would require less cotton. The argument behind Senior's "Last Hour," as Marx dubbed it, was so absurd that no later economist defended it.

The world did not end when Parliament legislated mild restrictions on the working day. Nor did profits disappear. British industry prospered. Whereas Procrustean logic demanded that no industrialist tamper with the working day, when all faced the same requirement the outcome was benign.

Partially Suspending Procrustean Logic

Of all the contradictions that plague Procrusteanism, one stands out, undermining the central justification of the doctrine. Procrusteanism presents itself as the only way to create prosperity, yet Procrusteanism itself cannot flourish amid prosperity. Prosperity undermines efficiency in a market economy.

Economists call the period in the United States between the end of the Second World War and the late 1960s the "Golden Age." Several factors contributed to the Golden Age. The rationing of the Second World War combined with wartime prosperity let families build up savings. When the war ended, the economies that competed with the United State for markets were in ruins, and this meant that businesses in the United States enjoyed an unprecedented burst of economic demand.

The war continued something that had begun during the Great Depression. During the 1930s, intense competition forced firms to scrap outmoded plant and equipment. By 1939, U.S. firms had replaced one-half of all the manufacturing equipment that had existed in 1933. Although the total amount of investment during the Depression was relatively small, most of that investment was directed toward modernizing existing plant and equipment rather than adding new capacity. One indication of the effectiveness of this investment was that after the war, U.S. business produced as much output as a decade before with 15 percent less capital and 19 percent less labor.[30]

This prosperity of the Golden Age set off a surge in employment, severely depleting the pool of unemployed workers. As the discussion of Bill Watson's experiences in the automobile industry showed, this increase in prosperity blunted many aspects of Procrusteanism.

Workers were not alone in being relieved of competitive pressure. Good times made management complacent and overconfident. Companies with huge backlogs of orders on their books do not have to strain to cut costs. Their objective is just to pump out more goods. And why not reward themselves with larger staffs and fancier quarters? Businesses also allowed their capital stocks to age. As a result, domestic production lost its edge in the world economy. The complacency of U.S. business leaders stands in sharp contrast to its insistence on discipline for workers.[31]

This tension between competition and prosperity points to a major contradiction in conventional economic theory. Economists pride themselves in having the intellectual wherewithal to provide advice that can guide the economy into prosperity while avoiding the pitfalls of depressions or recessions; however, the same depressions or recessions are necessary to spur competition. As Joseph Schumpeter, one of the most admired twentieth-century economists, observed regarding these periodic downturns, "Cycles are not like tonsils, separable things that might be treated by themselves, but are, like the beat of the heart, of the essence of the organism that displays them."[32] I should note here that although economists regard Schumpeter as very influential, economists have for the most part merely adopted his catchy phrase "creative destruction" as evidence of market efficiency without paying much attention to some of his more challenging ideas.

The automobile industry illustrates the connections between economic conditions, class struggle, and Procrusteanism. During the early Golden Age, almost two decades before Watson's employment, labor union power was at its peak. The United Automobile Workers were demanding a say in how production should occur. Fearful of ceding any control to the unions, the big three automobile companies offered generous compensation as an alternative.

When General Motors signed its agreement with the union covering the period between 1948 and 1950, *Fortune* published an article titled "The Treaty of Detroit" that suggested, "GM may have paid a billion for peace. It got a bargain." According to *Fortune*, "General Motors has regained control over one of the crucial management functions in any line of manufacturing—long-range scheduling of production, model changes, and tool and plant investment."[33]

One estimate put the value of the industry's newfound freedom of planning at $0.15 worth of corporate profit per hour of labor. In retrospect, the industry now gives a less favorable evaluation of its strategy. After taking on the obligation to provide health care and pensions for its workers and retirees, the industry took measures to dump its responsibility. Less noticed was the most destructive aspect of Detroit's corporate strategy. Because prosperity allowed Detroit to sell its cars without much effort, the industry did little to modernize either its factories or the technologies of its products. This choice made the industry vulnerable to a wave of imports that would flood the U.S. market.

While not all dimensions of Procrusteanism disappeared during the Golden Age, this period can be characterized as the "loosening of the iron cage." By the mid-1960s, the memory of the hardships of the Great Depression had receded. Wages were increasing, substantially cutting into profits. Still, however, relatively high wages no longer seemed adequate to compensate for working in a stifling, Procrustean environment. Management still denied workers significant respect, encouraging people such as Bill Watson to mount militant challenges to Procrusteanism.

But Procrusteanism was far from dead. In response to such unruly behavior, business unleashed a counterrevolution that moved the country significantly to the right—so much so that the domestic policies of Richard Nixon were to the left of those of Bill Clinton. This right-wing counterrevolution successfully reestablished the Procrustean discipline. Although the counterrevolution modestly restored profits, it undermined the long-term prospects of the U.S. economy, already weakened by an extended period of weak investment.

The Matthew Effect

People never win even a temporary advantage against the Procrusteans without a difficult struggle. Even when pressures for social protections force the Procrusteans to yield, they will resolutely organize to turn back any reforms, convinced that their personal interests are secondary in their struggle to ensure an efficient economy. So the state of social protections displays an ebb and flow depending on the relative strength of the Procrusteans and the rest of society.

During wartime, when leaders are most in need of the support of the general population, social reforms are easier to win. Similarly, leaders become more amenable to social reforms after the system breaks down and the credibility of leaders has eroded. For example, in the wake of the Great Depression, the New Deal was intended to shore up support both for the economic system and those whom the public held responsible for the disaster.

Sometimes, conflicts among elite groups allow people to win some protections, as in the case of the controversy surrounding Robert Blincoe and the use of child labor, when two competing groups pretended to display their social conscience by self-righteously pointing to the all-too-real abuses of the other.

Similar divisions broke out before the Civil War in the United States when defenders of slavery expressed hypocritical outrage about the poor conditions of workers in Northern factories.[34] In this case, however, the accusations by the slave owners were so patently self-serving that they never gained traction. White factory workers were not about to clamor to improve their lot by demanding to be enslaved.

The most important force in spurring social reforms is ordinary people's success in organizing themselves to redress injustices. The external conditions just described may offer openings that permit better organization, but in the end the people themselves are responsible for shaping their own destiny in the face of the powerful forces arrayed against them.

Again, these victories are not eternal. For example, political and business leaders turned back much of the New Deal in the decades following the election of Ronald Reagan. This successful counterrevolution was a masterful exercise in Procrusteanism: social protections disappeared.

All the while this counterrevolution made grand promises to the general population. The reforms would soon create a more efficient economy, provide good jobs, and thereby eventually make prosperity accessible to everybody. Nothing of the kind happened. Instead, even more fruits of the counterrevolution fell into the laps of the already affluent.

The sociologist Robert Merton once wrote about the Matthew Effect, alluding to the biblical passage, "For to everyone who has will more be given, and he will have abundance but from him who has not even what he has will be taken away."[35] In this case, biblical prophecy proved far more accurate than the political promises of the Procrusteans.

Control in a Procrustean State

While the Procrusteans exercise more and more control over society, they proudly portray themselves as stout defenders of liberty. They starkly pose two alternatives for humanity: individual liberty or state control. Milton Friedman went so far as to declare, "The free market is the only mechanism that has ever been discovered for achieving participatory democracy."[36]

Underlying this market-based liberty is the power of the state—the same despotic state that the Procrusteans presumably abhor—but this state—the ideal state of the Procrusteans—is dedicated to the preservation of private property and ensuring that all citizens conform to the laws of the market.

Prosperity, presumably the primary objective of a market economy, threatens to undermine working-class discipline, as the experience of the Golden Age suggests. This contradiction between prosperity and discipline is nothing new. Consider the dire warnings expressed in an editorial of the *Commercial and Financial Chronicle* on August 3, 1929, just a couple of months before the stock market crash. Among the danger signs that the editorial listed were:

> The luxurious diversification of diet advantageous to dairy men . . . and fruit growers . . . ;luxurious dressing . . . more silk and rayon . . . ;free spending for radios, travel, amusements and sports; . . . the frills of education to thousands for whom places might better be reserved at the bench or counter or on the farm.[37]

In contrast, the miserable conditions of workers during depressions could be a cause for celebration among the Procrusteans—at least those Procrusteans who did not depend upon them as customers. For example, in December 1859, the *Chicago Press and Tribune* blamed drunkenness and laziness for 90 percent of pauperism. The only remedy was "a little wholesome hunger and a salutary fit of chattering by reason of excessive cold."[38]

Although Procrusteans appreciate when workers feel the sting of market discipline, they expect generous favors for themselves, including tax cuts, subsidies, and bailouts when their business falters. In short, although both discipline and accountability must be stringent for those who occupy the bottom rungs of society, they are unnecessary for those at the top.

True liberty is unimaginable for the Procrusteans who pride themselves as realistic students of human psychology. According to this realism, nonmarket routes to an improved society are unthinkable. People are too self-interested. Only the discipline of the marketplace can function effectively.

The Procrusteans regard any effort by the state to defend citizens from negative consequences of business activity as a violation of natural liberty. Government action that interferes with business is doubly reprehensible because it makes people less dependent on business, either as consumers or as potential workers.

The liberty that the Procrusteans propose is a particular kind of liberty. The French novelist Anatole France summed up the nature of this sort of liberty in an unforgettable passage:

> Our citizenship is another occasion for pride! For the poor it consists in supporting and maintaining the rich in their power and their idleness. At this task they must labour in the face of the majestic equality of the laws, which forbids rich and poor alike to sleep under the bridges, to beg in the streets, and to steal their bread.[39]

CHAPTER FIVE

International Procrusteanism

Pre-Procrustean Realpolitik

This short chapter shifts focus from conditions in the United States to address the scourge of Procrusteanism that is sweeping across the world. The rhetoric of international Procrusteanism, unlike its domestic version, pays little attention to the need to impose working-class discipline. Instead, international Procrusteanism focuses on the need to discipline governments so that they discipline the workforce.

International Procrusteanism represents more than just the intensification of world trade. Often described as globalization or neoliberalism, it represents a new phase in capitalist governance. International Procrusteanism allows dominant nations to avoid the expenses and responsibilities of colonial administration, in effect, contracting the job out to compliant governments. This new system has been far more effective in extracting value from these impoverished nations.

In this scheme, the brute strength of colonial imperialism recedes into the background, although the great powers stand ready to deploy force at a moment's notice when a government displays either excessive independence or weakness in administering discipline. This less overt form of imperialism helps to maintain the pleasant fiction that voluntary agreements allow everybody to benefit from opening up the world to free trade.

Mainstream economic theory teaches that international trade should be unquestionably welcomed. The likelihood of a small country having adequate mineral as well as food, energy, and manufacturing resources within its confines is very small. Such countries need some trade in order to develop, but development is not a high priority or even a welcome outcome for their powerful trading "partners."

Although both parties theoretically benefit from international exchanges, mutual benefit is unlikely to occur when an imbalance of power exists. The weaker party is likely to find its choices determined by coercion rather than the prospect of a mutually advantageous trade.

Globalization gives free rein to corporate power at the expense of workers and communities. Client governments must give way to the demands of corporate traders, who expect the right to override any domestic legislation that stands in their way. These clients have the obligation to impose harsh Procrustean discipline, one that might make an old imperial power blush.

In the new world of international relationships, imperial powers can subcontract the messy work of repression to compliant dictators, well versed in the payoffs for obedience and the penalty for resistance. In an environment that the great powers credit as representing freedom, such thugs can become fabulously wealthy at the expense of their people. For example, in 1953, *Time* published a glowing article about the kind of freedom that Procrusteans appreciate:

> One place where U.S. businessmen abroad can still flourish in a climate of high-riding free enterprise is the oil-booming republic of Venezuela. . . . Discussing the army dictatorship that has bossed Venezuela for the past five years, a banker explained recently: "You have the freedom here to do what you want to do with your money, and to me that is worth all the political freedom in the world."[1]

The great powers celebrate the compliant people who administer such states as legitimate leaders, even as great democrats, lending an air of respectability to the transactions between the great powers and the impoverished lands of the world.

International Procrusteanism provides cheap and reliable offshore workforces, which offer countries such as the United States a double dividend. Over and above low wages for companies that locate their factories abroad, the mere threat of relocation becomes an important component in the traumatization of labor. This method is far more attractive than the risky strategy of counting on the Federal Reserve to increase interest rates.

Heads of state willing to administer the policies of international Procrusteanism rarely have the public interest in mind. Instead, they tend to devote their attention to enriching themselves and their cronies. A culture of corruption is a common legacy of imperial relations. One typical outcome of such rule is a huge accumulation of national debt. The requirement to repay such debt makes independent development impossible.

When countries are not as compliant as Venezuela in the 1950s, powerful nations have a number of means of pressure at their disposal. As Venezuela later learned, they are not shy about using them.

More often than not, direct force is unnecessary. Blockades and other trade sanctions, or just the threat of sanctions or military intervention, are often sufficient to bring compliance. In those rare cases where poor countries still dare to behave defiantly, a powerful creditor, such as the United States, always acting in the name of democracy, can usually topple the recalcitrant government through covert actions, which do not involve the expense of sending in troops.

With either direct or covert imperial control, the fiction of natural market forces is hardly credible. One of the more outlandish examples comes from China, where Britain fought two wars (1839 and 1856) to force the Chinese to open their country to trade in British opium; yet the British treated opium as an illegal drug at home.

In the world of international Procrusteanism, potential wealth carries great risks. Imagine a poor country located on top of a rich oil deposit. Irresistible forces will pressure this country to open its resources through lopsided agreements in which the foreign companies enjoy the lion's share of benefits. Yet the great powers will claim to be acting in the best interest of the people in such a country, much like the employers who were willing to lengthen the hours of work to help the common people improve themselves.

Once a compliant regime is in place, all parties give the appearance of deferring to impersonal market forces. Everything is presumed to be entirely voluntary and mutually beneficial; everybody pretends that equality prevails.

Sometimes, the only chance that poor countries have is to seek the protection of some great power that is involved in a rivalry with other great powers. These protectors will seek a payback, but they may partially keep their greed in check to prevent the poor protectorate from defecting to the other side. This strategy is not without the risk that the poor countries can get drawn into wars in which they have no real stake. Since the demise of the Soviet Union, the choice of competing powers is less available to weak countries. The table is now set for the world of international Procrusteanism.

Ideological Preparations

The United States and other developed countries hold out the promise to poor countries that if they comply with the rules of international Procrusteanism, they can enjoy great prosperity. But no country has ever successfully developed on the basis of free markets. The developed countries, themselves, have gone to great lengths to control market forces, especially during their early phases of development.

Successful industrialized countries have historically accepted some market forces, and no country has ever been fully developed without some market forces. But from the earliest days of the United States, the government protected emerging industries from foreign competition. The question was the degree to which market forces had full rein.

The United States gave huge subsidies to the railroads, which were central to the modernization of the economy. Nor should one forget the enormous contribution that slave labor provided. The slaves directly created wealth for plantation owners and also indirectly for the northern bankers and traders that facilitated southern trade. Those who supplied the largely unindustrialized South with the commodities it needed also profited from the slave economy. Such matters are conveniently forgotten today. Instead market forces alone are credited with the economic successes of the United States.

The Industrial Revolution in Great Britain was also heavily reliant on nonmarket forces. The economy of Great Britain also shared in the benefits of slavery in the United States. The British cotton industry, working up the slave-grown cotton, is usually represented as the primary center of technological improvements. Besides slavery, imperial ventures in Ireland, India, and elsewhere helped to generate the wealth that financed the Industrial Revolution. In addition, the Empire provided a ready market for cotton products.

Another crucial factor that contributed mightily to the Industrial Revolution was often violent overturning of the traditional rights of the poor people in the countryside by a relatively small group of wealthy landowners who claimed ownership of land that other people had worked for generations. After tenants were thrown off their land, they had no option but to enter into the factories. This brutal process was also an important component of the agricultural revolution.

The hypocrisy of the Procrusteans is everywhere apparent in the world's poor nations, where market activities have existed for many centuries. On the teeming streets of the slums of poor countries, you are likely to see what Adam Smith once called "the pedlar principle of turning a penny whenever one was to be got, "a phenomenon he credited with initially setting capitalism in motion.[2] More recently, Sol Tax termed the same activities "penny capitalism": desperately poor people hawking cheap goods to other desperately poor people.[3] Penny capitalists can be efficient, but they are not likely to accumulate any capital. Tax's University of Chicago colleague, Nobel Prize–winner Theodore Schultz, suggested that traditional agriculture was efficient, just not very productive in terms of the market. Given the available technology, the peasants produced as much as possible, but, despite their efficiency, they were destined to be trapped in poverty. Schultz argued, something naively, that all they needed to prosper was access to capital. Instead, once capitalism gets rolling in these countries, always with the help of force and violence, as was true in the developed countries, indigenous penny capitalism collides with global capitalism and dollar diplomacy. The outcome is never in doubt, as the harried street vendors know.

The Golden Straitjacket

The ideologists of international Procrusteanism propose their own version of Margaret Thatcher's cruel pronouncement: "There is no alternative." The *New York Times* commentator Thomas Friedman has developed his own special brand of giddy promotion of the corporate-market economy, while explaining that the hardships it imposes on ordinary people are unavoidable.

Probably unintentionally echoing the *Communist Manifesto*, Friedman proposed that sovereign countries have no choice but to adopt what he calls "the Golden Straitjacket." Friedman fails to mention that though this Golden Straitjacket might be golden for those at the top of an economy and to a lesser extent for some of the more fortunate of the middle class, it is anything but golden for the masses of people. In the words of the ever-effusive Friedman:

> To fit into the Golden Straitjacket a country must either adopt, or be seen as moving toward, the following golden rules: making the private sector the primary engine of its economic growth, maintaining a low rate of inflation and price stability, shrinking the size of its state bureaucracy, maintaining as close to a balanced budget as possible, if not a surplus, eliminating and lowering tariffs on imported goods, removing restrictions on foreign investment, getting rid of quotas and domestic monopolies, increasing exports, privatizing state-owned industries and utilities, deregulating capital markets, making its currency convertible, opening its industries, stock, and bond markets to direct foreign ownership and

investment, deregulating its economy to promote as much domestic competition as possible, eliminating government corruption, subsidies and kickbacks as much as possible, opening its banking and telecommunications systems to private ownership and competition, and allowing its citizens to choose from an array of competing pension options and foreign-run pension and mutual funds. When you stitch all of these pieces together you have the Golden Straitjacket.[4]

Friedman would have done his readers a service if he had mentioned that the Golden Straitjacket does not sweep aside all subsidies, kickbacks, and corruption—only those that impede the control of multinational corporations. In fact, the multinational corporations remain largely immune from the restraints of the Golden Straitjacket.

Friedman goes on to mention that the same process that created the Golden Straitjacket unleashed what he calls the "Electronic Herd":

The Electronic Herd is made up of all the faceless stock, bond and currency traders sitting behind computer screens all over the globe, moving their money around with the click of a mouse from mutual funds to pension funds to emerging market funds, or trading from their basements on the Internet. And it consists of the big multinational corporations who now spread their factories around the world, constantly shifting them to the most efficient, low-cost producers. . . . [The leaders of the Electronic Herd] don't tell you that they feel your pain, or that they understand your grievance because of your colonial experience. They don't tell you that you are so unique, so important to stability in the region, that they won't lay a finger on you. They just have their way with you and move on. The Electronic Herd turns the whole world into a parliamentary system, in which every government lives under the fear of a no-confidence vote from the herd.[5]

Walter Wriston, as former chief executive officer of Citibank, had actually been, unlike Friedman, at the center of the Electronic Herd. A few years before Friedman, in a book tellingly titled *The Twilight of Sovereignty*, Wriston described the power that people like him enjoyed:

Today information about the diplomatic, fiscal, and monetary policies of all nations is instantly transmitted to electronic screens in hundreds of trading rooms in dozens of countries. As the screens light up with the latest statement of the president or the chairman of the Federal Reserve, traders make a judgment about the effect of the new policies on currency values and buy or sell accordingly. The entire globe is now tied together in a single electronic market moving at the speed of light. There is no place to hide.

This enormous flow of data has created a new world monetary standard, an Information Standard, which has replaced the gold standard and the Bretton Woods agreements. The electronic global market has produced what amounts to a giant vote-counting machine that conducts a running tally on what the world thinks of a government's diplomatic, fiscal, and monetary policies. That opinion is immediately reflected in the value the market places on a country's currency.

In this new world order capital will go where it is wanted and stay where it is well treated. . . . It will flee from manipulation or onerous regulation of its value or use, and no government can restrain it for long.[6]

Wriston and Friedman are correct that governments that refuse to don the Golden Straitjacket risk seeing their economy shredded. They fail to include the caveat that their own country, which wields hegemonic power, is immune from such consequences. Nor do they explain that other countries without sufficient resources and courage might not have the wherewithal to take the necessary measures to protect themselves.

However, people unfamiliar with Wriston's career might not fully appreciate the delicious irony in his promotion of the wisdom of the marketplace. Wriston had already capped his career at Citibank when this book appeared. Under his leadership, Citibank had been intent on "selling"—many used the more accurate term "pushing"[7]—as much credit as possible to Latin America, so much so that Citibank had been getting nearly 50 percent of its revenue from its loans to Latin America.

The bank made these loans without much thought about the ability of Latin America to repay them or without putting adequate reserves aside to cover potential defaults. As a result, the company became deeply enmeshed in the Latin American debt crisis. By 1991, some Citicorp debt had been reduced to junk-bond status. Public figures as diverse as Representative John Dingell and Ross Perot described Citibank as insolvent.[8]

Matters became so dire that the president of the New York branch of the Federal Reserve Bank had to fly to Saudi Arabia to arrange for Prince Alwaleed Bin Talal Alsaud to invest an additional $1.2 billion in the bank in late 1990. The Federal Reserve also had to be sure to keep interest rates down long enough to salvage the bank.[9] The Electronic Herd did not serve Citicorp very well. The bank, now rebranded as Citigroup, tottered back into insolvency in 2008, surviving only by virtue of massive government bailouts and a Federal Reserve madly pumping liquidity into the economy.

Off with the Golden Straitjacket

Little of the gold in the Golden Straitjacket that Wriston and Friedman propose will accrue to ordinary people. The regime they advocate makes progressive political processes impossible. In this new hyperactive market environment, governments are reduced to merely ratifying corporate desires, including corporate bailouts for the likes of Wriston's bank.

Many governments forced to cede power to the Golden Straitjacket are corrupt and oppressive. Because of the unpopularity of neoliberal policies, corruption is often necessary to induce leaders to impose neoliberalism on their people. Of course, Procrusteans are less outraged by corruption than by a government that responds to the wishes of its people or, even worse, allows people to give voice to their own desires.

For example, in 2005, after the French people decisively voted down a neoliberal constitution of the European Union, Friedman smugly ridiculed their choice in terms usually reserved for impoverished Third World countries. The French were unrealistic in expecting to preserve their thirty-five-hour workweek, while hardworking men and women in India were enthusiastically embracing global capitalism.[10] So much for voluntarism!

From the perspective of Friedman and Wriston, the behavior of the French regarding the length of their workday was proof that common people are incapable of understanding what is in their best interests (in contrast to the rationality ascribed to them in their role as consumers). In the end, markets, and markets alone, are capable of directing behavior in ways that ensure economic progress.

Yet Friedman and the people whose ideas he echoes would be hardpressed to find an example of a country in which a majority of the people benefited from the dismantling of social controls. None of the great economic successes—Great Britain, the United States, Germany, or Japan—were willing to rely solely on markets to fuel their economic development. Industry in the United States developed with the help of protective tariffs, subsidies, and government contracts, not to mention the slaves and the government-subsidized railroads. The Golden Straitjacket might be appropriate apparel for King Midas, but not for a free people.

I should note that even many free market economists, especially after the Asian currency crisis of 1998, now realize that the Electronic Herd is hardly a rational arbiter of human well-being. The recent financial crisis brought that lesson closer to home. Like most herds, Friedman's Electronic Herd is prone to stampeding, and when it does it is liable to trample whole economies, imposing great harm on a large share of their population.

Yet after a severe crisis, the Procrusteans dogmatically call out for more of the same: if an economy is to restore its profitability, it must make adjustments. Here again, those who pay the price for the mistakes of the Electronic Herd are the common people—especially at the workplace, where they experience lower wages, harsher working conditions, or unemployment. As wages shrink and profits soar, the economy appears to become more productive—at least to the Procrusteans.

Tightening the screws in one country sends shockwaves throughout the world. Other nations must meet the competitive challenge that

these supposedly more productive economies present, making
domestic adjustments of the Procrustean bed an international phenomenon. We can see both the recent French effort to increase the
workweek and, less dramatically, the steady, decade-long pressure
imposed on workers in the United States as examples of the force of
international Procrusteanism.

Even if we ignore the historical evidence about the fallibility of the
Electronic Herd, why would people behave differently in economic
and political venues? Are French voters really irrational in preferring
a shorter workday? If people are irrational in the political arena, why
are they presumed to be rational in the marketplace?

Are Citicorp's traders more rational than the rest of the population? If so, why does the great financial operation return to the verge
of bankruptcy? Why not put a straitjacket on Friedman's Electronic
Herd instead of on ordinary people?

The recent work in psychology and behavioral economics shows
that people—even financial traders—do not make entirely rational
decisions. Even so, economists must presume that consumers behave
as emotionless geniuses in calculating utilities to make their theories
work. Otherwise, they could not justify Procrusteanism.

Now we will explore how economics arrived at such a state by
turning to the legacy of Adam Smith.

CHAPTER SIX

Adam Smith's Historical Vision

The Wealth of Nations

It is time now to explore the intellectual roots of Procrustean economics. This chapter will explore the little-known Procrustean side of Adam Smith. Associating Adam Smith with the authoritarianism of the Procrusteans might seem somewhat incongruous. People popularly identify Smith with the invisible hand, not the invisible handcuffs. This favorable interpretation is understandable.

Virtually every contemporary school of economics finds something to admire in Smith. As Jacob Viner, a conservative University of Chicago professor, wrote, "Traces of every conceivable sort of doctrine are to be found in that most catholic book, and an economist must have peculiar theories indeed who cannot quote from *The Wealth of Nations* to support his special purpose."[1] Liberals, radicals, and even Marxists have embraced Smith because of his frequent expressions of progressive sentiments.

Adam Smith's objective was to portray the market as a realm of liberty and justice, devoid of conflict. For Smith, the market would lead toward a world in which nobody was able to take advantage of anybody else. Once market norms became common, aristocrats would no longer be able to enjoy inherited privileges; businessmen would be unable to take advantages of their connections to win favors from the government; and workers would share in the bounty of their hard work.

Smith believed that market forces would naturally erode the power of the aristocrats and well-connected businessmen. However, Smith seemed at a loss to show how market forces would make workers accept the rules of the market as just, given workers' antagonism to market forces.

Smith tried to find a way out of this morass by sweeping any hint of class conflict under the rug, portraying the market as a system of voluntary transactions. Toward this end, he turned his readers' attention away from the point of production, where employers had the authority to directly command their workers.

Smith was very effective in providing a powerful justification of the market. He had certain advantages in this project. He was a knowledgeable scholar with a sparkling writing style, and he occasionally presented a compassionate face, sprinkling his book with a few expressions of humanistic sentiments. Rather than undermining his ideological position, these sympathetic words made his ideology seem less antagonistic toward the working class.

Smith called for workers to prosper. He acknowledged that "Masters are always and every where in a sort of tacit, but constant and uniform combination, not to raise the wages of labour above their actual rate."[2]

But how serious were such sentiments? Beneath Smith's sometimes humanistic surface was a large reservoir of authoritarianism. The prosperity he wished for workers was intended only for people who worked hard and never questioned the ground rules of Procrusteanism. Smith was hardly as gracious to the many, perhaps the majority, of the working class, who protested against the system. This side of Smith has gone largely unnoticed because Smith went to great lengths to distort his picture of the world. In the process, he helped to initiate economists' long tradition of obscuring the role of work, workers, and working conditions.

The context of such passages, which gave Smith his humanitarian reputation, suggests that they were not at all at odds with his overall ideology. In fact, the humanitarian sentiments often backed up his market ideology. For example, Smith was opposed to colonialism. In the case of the European entry into the Americas, he wrote:

> The savage injustice of the Europeans rendered an event, which ought to have been beneficial to all, ruinous and destructive to several of those unfortunate countries.[3]

Smith was no more supportive of the business of the East India Company, arguing that corrupt and clumsy colonial policies were an inefficient means of extracting wealth from the periphery and that market forces alone would force these lands to do Britain's bidding.

Over time, Smith's legacy further hardened into ideology that was far more rigid and simplistic. This legacy helped economists to convince themselves that their neglect of work, workers, and working conditions represented the height of scientific analysis.

The Growing Appreciation of Adam Smith

The great lengths Smith went to obscure workers' class relationship is remarkable. Especially in his more theoretical discussions in the first part of *The Wealth of Nations*, the absence of class from his work is virtually complete. Later, in dealing with more practical matters, Smith's views occasionally crop up. These episodic treatments are consistent with what Smith said or wrote in more private settings.

Smith's reticence to address questions of class allowed him to present a kindly picture of capitalism, while parading his own progressive sentiments. At the same time, by painting such an attractive vision of capitalism as a mutually beneficial system for all participants, Smith became an important figure for the contemporary world. During the Reagan administration, more than two centuries after the publication of *Wealth of Nations*, government officials began wearing neckties with

Adam Smith's portrait, as if to justify their Procrustean policies by association with the humanistic reputation of Adam Smith.

Initially, Smith's *Wealth of Nations* did not make much of an impression. Although his earlier book, the now less-known *Theory of Moral Sentiments*, was a sensation, his more famous work seemed as if it had missed its mark. Yet unlike most ancient writers, whose importance recedes into the distant past, Smith's influence rapidly grew.

The book went through five editions, but each of the first two editions sold only 500 copies—a substantial number, but far from a roaring success.[4] In Parliament, where the members frequently quoted important political economists, Charles James Fox made the first reference to *Wealth of Nations* on November 11, 1783, six years after the book first appeared.[5] Still another ten years passed before two of Smith's friends, Alexander Wedderburn and William Petty's great-grandson and former prime minister, the Marquess of Lansdowne, mentioned the book in the House of Lords.[6]

Even in 1789 when Thomas Robert Malthus signed out the 1784 edition of *Wealth of Nations* from his college library, he was just the third person to do so.[7] Up to the year 1800, only a few Cambridge colleges had acquired the book. Emma Rothschild notes with some irony that when Adam Smith died in 1790, the influential *Annual Register* devoted but twelve lines to Smith compared with sixty-five for Major Ray, a deputy quartermaster general with an interest in barometers. The *Scots Magazine* gave Smith a scant nine lines.[8]

Only after the French Revolution of 1789 made British property owners fearful, did Smith take on an air of importance. Thereafter, the rich and powerful appreciated Smith's ideological influence. For example, Francis Horner, editor of the *Edinburgh Review*, rejected a request to prepare a set of notes for a new edition of *The Wealth of Nations*. He explained his refusal in a letter to Thomas Thomson, written on August 15, 1803:

> I should be reluctant to expose S's errors before his work had operated its full effect. We owe much at present to the superstitious worship of S's name; and we must not impair that feeling, till the victory is more com-

plete. . . . Until we can give a correct and precise theory of the origin of wealth, his popular and plausible and loose hypothesis is as good for the vulgar as any others.[9]

As one current Smith scholar observed, "There were more new editions of *The Wealth of Nations* published in the 1990s than in the 1890s, and more in the 1890s than in the 1790s."[10]

Advocates of unregulated markets praise *The Wealth of Nations* for its strong opposition to government meddling, conveniently overlooking the more interventionist stance that appears in the later chapters. In particular, they appreciate Smith's stance in the early chapters that unregulated markets are the key to promoting human progress.

Although Smith placed great faith in an ideal market society, the actual conditions he saw fell short of his ideal. As a result, Smith advocated Procrustean measures to coerce people into conforming to his vision.

While we will focus on Smith's authoritarian side, it is fair to say that he was relatively progressive for someone of his time and standing. He was still a creature of his time. Smith himself observed how earlier people had followed customs that their own society considered abhorrent. For example, Smith asked:

> Can there be greater barbarity for example, than to hurt an infant? Its helplessness, its innocence, its amiableness, call forth the compassion, even of an enemy, and not to spare that tender age is regarded as the most furious effort of an enraged and cruel conqueror. What then should we imagine must be the heart of a parent who could injure that weakness which even a furious enemy is afraid to violate? Yet the exposition, that is, the murder of new-born infants, was a practice allowed in almost all the states of Greece, even among the polite and civilized Athenians; and whenever the circumstances of the parent rendered it inconvenient to bring up the child, to abandon it to hunger, or to wild beasts was regarded without blame or censure.[11]

Just as Smith presumably did not regard Plato and Aristotle as monsters for condoning infanticide, Smith's own intolerance might be forgiven as a reflection of the society in which he lived. It is important, however, for us to keep in mind the way that powerful calls for freedom of the marketplace today still coincide with measures to withhold what might be regarded as a minimum degree of humanity.

Smith and the Production of Personality

Despite the title, *The Wealth of Nations*, Smith's chief interest was not the material fruits of economic growth but a deeper form of progress— the development of better people. George Stigler accurately captured the outlook of Adam Smith and other major early economists with his perceptive comment:

> Their concern was with the maximizing, not with the output. The struggle of men for larger incomes was good because in the process they learned independence, self-reliance, self-discipline—because, in short, they became better men. . . . The desire for better men, rather than for larger national incomes, was a main theme of classical economics.[12]

In this sense, Smith was not exactly an orthodox Procrustean. Although he agreed with the Procrusteans about the overriding importance of discipline, his highest stated priority was not the ability of the wealthy to accumulate more wealth. Some later economists, such as Alfred Marshall and John Maynard Keynes, partially followed in Smith's footsteps in this respect, but all of them wanted workers to become well-behaved and obedient employees. They share much of the vision of modern economists who consider workers' development largely irrelevant, except as it promotes the ultimate goal of increasing output.

The attitude of most of those who followed Smith reflected the class interest of capital rather than a concern for the betterment of the less fortunate. Many of them agreed that the state must refrain from giving any significant assistance to the poor, in order to prevent any weakening of their moral fiber—by which they meant the work ethic of the poor.

According to Smith, "Little else is requisite to carry a State to the highest degree of opulence . . . but peace, easy taxes and a tolerable administration of justice."[13] John Ramsay McCulloch, an influential economist of the early nineteenth century, writing with his characteristic "confident dogmatism," showed how Smith's sentiments translated into practical policy:[14]

> But whenever property is secure, industry free, and the public burdens moderate, the happiness or misery of the labouring classes depends almost wholly on themselves. Government has there done for them all that it should, and all in truth that it can do. It has given them security and freedom. But the use or abuse of these inestimable advantages is their own affair. They may be either provident or improvident, industrious or idle; and being free to choose, they are alone responsible for the consequences of their choice.[15]

Smith was more sincere than those like McCulloch, whose interest in behavioral improvement shrouded a vision of a totally Procrustean world in which everybody stands ready to do whatever is necessary for capital. His self-assured demand that ordinary people accept responsibility for their own lot and be content with what they earned from their hard work—no matter what their circumstances might be—does not require much from a person already enjoying a comfortable position and sheltered from the hardships that the poor commonly experience. On the contrary, the affluent are sure to benefit from compliant behavior on the part of the diligent poor.

Neither McCulloch nor his successors would ever admit to cruel or selfish motives. They prided themselves on a perverse benevolence. Their "tough love" was for the benefit of the poor, who, cut off from welfare support, will necessarily change their behavior, regardless of their circumstances. As a result, workers have the opportunity to pull themselves up by their bootstraps and enjoy the consumption made possible by hard work.

Smith and the Four Stages

Central to Smith's analysis was his overarching theory of historical evolution. Like other Scottish academics at the time, Smith proposed that society naturally progresses stepwise through four predetermined stages, beginning with an initial primitive stage of hunting and gathering, then progressing to herding, followed by agriculture, and finally to a commercial economy. At each stage, the typical individual personality has to adjust to the productive requirements of the economy. In the earliest stage, hunter-gatherers had to put great stock in individual courage. Survival depended on locating a food source and consuming the food. In such an environment, people would have good reason to act upon their immediate impulses, without much need to plan for the future.

With each successive stage, people's psychology has to become more future-oriented. Herders, and even more so farmers, have to nurture animals or crops in order to benefit from them later. Eventually, with the arrival of commercial society, people become even more future-oriented. Characteristics such as frugality, honesty, and hard work become just as important for survival as individual courage was in an earlier age.

Smith's approach might have led in the direction of a materialist analysis of the economy. Instead, Smith used his four stages theory to show how all previous forms of social organization ultimately led to a full-blown market society, which centered on transactions.

For Smith, as societies progress, the shackles that limit common people fall away, including cultural restraints. The superstitions that restrict primitive hunters and gatherers from developing a deeper understanding of the world disappear. Similarly, Smith expected to see the powers of the aristocrats and bureaucrats wane, giving way to the impersonal market forces that would be sure to liberate the potential of the ordinary person.[16] So, in the end, the market forms a powerful motor of individual, social, and economic betterment. Freed from the oppression of feudal lords or slave masters, the incentives of commercial society, which Smith saw as a system of natural liberty, would create both a new social structure as well as personality changes that would promote greater productivity.

Smith used the example of agriculture to illustrate how each stage of development requires a different system of organizing society. In early society, as the productive potential of agriculture increased, great chieftains, and later kings and emperors, first used slavery to extract as much wealth as they could. Yet slavery represented the height of inefficiency. Under this primitive form of economic organization, slaves, like workers on a chain gang today, could be compelled to perform certain kinds of routine work, but in performing their work they had no reason to exert themselves any more than necessary. Their efforts would merely help their owners while exhausting themselves.

The experience of slavery in the southern United States confirms Smith's speculation. The sandy soils, typical of the South, are ideal for light equipment pulled by horses, yet the plantations typically used heavy tools drawn by mules. Frederick Law Olmsted, the designer of both New York's Central Park and Golden Gate Park in San Francisco, brought this phenomenon to the attention of the world, just before the outbreak of the Civil War:

> I am shown tools that no man in his senses, with us, would allow a laborer, to whom he was paying wages, to be encumbered with; and the excessive weight and clumsiness of which, I would judge, would make work at least ten per cent. greater than those ordinarily used with us. And I am assured that, in the careless and clumsy way they must be used by the slaves, anything lighter or less rude could not be furnished them with good economy, and that such tools as we constantly give our laborers, and find our profit in giving them, would not last out a day in a Virginia corn-field—much lighter and more free from stones though it be than ours.
>
> So, too, when I ask why mules are so universally substituted for horses on the farm, the first reason given, and confessedly the most conclusive one, is that horses cannot bear the treatment that they always must get from negroes; horses are always soon foundered or crippled by them, while mules will bear cudgeling, and lose a meal or two now and then, and not be materially injured, and they do not take cold or get sick if neg-

lected or overworked. But I do not need to go further than to the window of the room in which I am writing, to see, at almost any time, treatment of cattle that would insure the immediate discharge of the driver, by almost any farmer owning them at the North.[17]

The slaves were not inherently clumsy or abusive. Their behavior was a rational response to an irrational situation. A society that consigned human beings to the status of property could not expect them to have much incentive for hard work. On a hot, muggy day, while the slave driver glanced away, a slave might be tempted to "stupidly" hurt a horse or damage a piece of equipment in order to take a brief break from unbearably hard labor.

According to Smith's account of the transition out of slavery, feudal lords later allowed serfs to produce food for themselves for part of the year, but they also had to spend a predetermined amount of the year working for their masters, almost as slaves. Serfs would work hard while producing for themselves, but they had no reason to do so while laboring on their masters' land.

After people had won the freedom to produce for themselves, the lords could still claim a share of the harvest for their own. Since workers could keep only part of what they produced, they had less incentive to work hard.

At the next stage, the lords granted people the right to all of what they produced, although the farmers still had to pay a fixed rent. Under this arrangement, farmers had a greater incentive to work hard since they could keep everything they produced, over and above what went for rent. At last, the peasants became more like capitalists. These peasants were far from being capitalists, unless they began hiring workers for wages, but their situation represented an important stage in Smith's road to capitalism.

This transition had not been completed when Smith wrote, but he believed that it was inevitable because the improvident aristocrats who owned much of the land were not likely to hold on for long.

Smith's four stages theory presents a curious anomaly. In the first three stages, the actual demands of work seem to form the core of human personality. By the fourth stage, work as such falls into the background, except for occasional reference to simple, traditional tasks. Instead, the transaction becomes the focus of Smith's commercial stage. The actual performance of work passes into obscurity, along with the outmoded traditions of the aristocracy.

The Elimination of Class in Smith's World

Extrapolating Smith's analysis from independent farmers who rented their land to workers who worked for wages requires a bit of a leap. His approach was to assume that wage earners were capitalists, except that these particular capitalists sold their labor rather than finished commodities.

Smith was too intelligent to presume that more effort alone would suffice to lift most wage earners out of poverty. To succeed, workers would also need a different kind of personality, one that stressed prudence and frugality. Wage earners who behaved appropriately could hope to improve their station in life by moving on to a different kind of work, perhaps becoming independent artisans, and then maybe employers in their own right.

A corollary of this vision would be that even if low-wage workers remained poor for a few years, over the course of their lifetimes they could comfortably enjoy the fruits of their labor. If this life cycle of labor were common, then consideration of class would be irrelevant. Poverty would be a temporary stage through which diligent young people might pass before moving up to a more prosperous life.

How realistic was Smith's vision? In a small, isolated village in which industry only consisted of artisans producing on a small scale, a market society might have worked the way Smith suggested. In such a world of micro-businesses, the ratio of workers to employers would be small. Under such conditions, young workers could reasonably expect that with diligence and a bit of luck their time as wage laborers might be relatively short. Such an economy has probably never existed.

The problem, however, is that the "normal" life cycle of labor that Smith imagined precludes a world in which large operations have become common. If only relatively few rungs at the top are open to the many at the bottom, how could the typical young worker expect to ascend the ladder of success merely through hard work and diligence? Smith grew up in Kirkcaldy, with a population of only about 1,500, which came much closer to such an imaginary village economy than anything seen today.[18] By the time Smith was writing, the town was part of the epicenter of the Industrial Revolution, with one of the largest industrial operations in the world.

The Carron Company

Smith retired to work on *The Wealth of Nations* at Kirkcaldy, which sat in the heart of the Industrial Revolution. According to T. S. Ashton, in his influential book *The Industrial Revolution*:

> In the iron industry the coke-fed blast furnaces had been growing steadily in size and number, and new areas of enterprise had been opened up. Stimulated by the demand for munitions, many new works, including those of John Wilkinson at Broseley and of John Roebuck at Carron, were set up during the war of 1756–63. In its magnitude and the variety of its products [which included the famous cannonades] the Carron Ironworks was a portent of a new type of undertaking; and the lighting of its first furnace, on Boxing Day [December 26], 1760, may serve to mark the beginning of the industrial revolution in Scotland.[19]

Ashton's reference to the "industrial revolution in Scotland" does not limit the power of his claim, because the Industrial Revolution actually began in Scotland. Besides, Smith's own universities were at the center of this new age. Following Ashton again:

It was not from Oxford or Cambridge, where the torch [of the Industrial Revolution] burnt dim, but from Glasgow and Edinburgh, that the impulse to scientific inquiry and its practical application came.[20]

Smith had close personal relationships with people at the forefront of the Industrial Revolution. James Watt, who was developing the modern steam engine, was a friend and colleague of Smith. Although Smith had left the university by the time of Watt's commercial success, one might have thought he would have followed his friend's career.

An "intimate" friend of Smith's, John Roebuck, was a doctor who, along with his two brothers, was among the seven founders of the Carron Ironworks.[21] Roebuck sent Smith a letter in 1775, which suggests the warmth of their personal relationship.[22] Roebuck is doubly relevant because of his relationship with James Watt:

> Watt [came] to believe that his engine held great promise and could be developed into a full-sized engine with outstanding economy. Black lent money to Watt so he could carry on experimenting and, what proved to be more important still, introduced him to John Roebuck of Birmingham. Roebuck had established the Carron Iron Foundry in Scotland in 1759 and leased the coalfields at Borrowstones from the Duke of Hamilton. These mines were continually flooded and more powerful and economical pumping engines are needed urgently. In 1768, Roebuck agreed to take over Watt's debts and to bear the cost of a patent in return for a two-thirds share in it.[23]

Smith never took notice of the Carron foundry in his great book, even though Kirkaldy was within easy walking distance (plus a short ferry ride to cross a river). This factory was one of the most famous, and perhaps the largest, industrial plant in the world, remembered today mostly for its cannons that helped the British navy create and maintain a great empire. The company maintained a major warehouse in Kirkcaldy proper to hold the iron rods and receive the nails in return from the busy local nail makers.

In 1772, a few years before *The Wealth of Nations* appeared, Smith's close friend, the philosopher David Hume, wrote to Smith, inquiring about how the precarious financial situation of Carron would affect his book:

> The Carron Company is reeling which is one of the greatest Calamities of the whole; as they gave Employment to near 10.000 People. Do these Events any-wise affect your Theory? Or will it occasion the Revisal of any Chapters? [24]

However, the closest Smith came to mentioning the Carron works occurred in a brief reference to a recent increase in employment in Scotland, where Carron was one of the three towns mentioned.[25]

The economic historian John H. Clapham once lamented, "It is a pity that Adam Smith did not go a few miles from Kirkcaldy to the Carron works, to see them turning and boring their cannonades, instead of to his silly pin factory—which was only a factory in the old sense of the word."[26]

Smith's contemporaries understood that the world was rapidly changing. In a conversation lamenting the end of public executions in 1783, before Smith had published the third of the five editions of his book, Samuel Johnson, an acquaintance of Smith's, remarked, "The age is running mad after innovation; and all the business of the world is to be done in a new way."[27] Benjamin Franklin and some friends engaged in a ten-day-long excursion of industrial tourism. An account left by his grand-nephew describes their admiration of the marvels of modern technology at work in the various factories and mines.[28] Smith, however, seemed unaffected by the fascination with such innovations.

Scholars who have studied Adam Smith have expressed puzzlement that the prophet of modern capitalism had so little to say about the technological developments taking hold around him. Early in the book, Smith did mention in passing "the invention of a great number of machines which facilitate and abridge labour, and enable one man to do the work of many," but he avoided any further discussion of the modern industry that was emerging around him.[29]

The usually perceptive Robert Coats, as well as E.R.A. Seligman, excused Smith's lack of material on the specifics on modern production processes by labeling Smith as an "economist . . . of the domestic period."[30] We would get no further by attributing his omissions and oversights to a lack of foresight, as Koebner once argued.[31] Charles Kindleberger's attempt to explain this defect of *The Wealth of Nations* by writing off the author as an "unworldly" professor is equally unsatisfactory.[32] Smith was not unworldly at all. He was engaged in the construction of a sophisticated ideological structure. And nothing is more revealing about this project than his famous pin factory.

Another Look at Smith's Famous Pin Factory

The first sign of Smith's pin factory appeared in a course of lectures to his students in Glasgow in 1762 and 1763, more than a decade before the publication of his great book. The discussion of the pin factory began on March 28, 1763, while he was explaining to his Glasgow students the importance of the law and government:

> They maintain the rich in the possession of their wealth against the violence and rapacity of the poor, and by that means preserve that useful inequality in the fortunes of mankind which naturally and necessarily arises from the various degrees of capacity, industry, and diligence in the different individuals.[33]

In order to justify this inequality, Smith told his students that "an ordinary day labourer . . . has more of the conveniences and luxuries than an Indian [presumably Native American] prince at the head of 1,000 naked savages."[34] But then the next day, Smith suddenly shifted gears, almost seeming to side with the violent and rapacious poor:

> The labour and time of the poor is in civilized countries sacrificed to the maintaining of the rich in ease and luxury. The landlord is maintained in idleness and luxury by the labour of his tenants. The moneyed man is

supported by his exactions from the industrious merchant and the needy who are obliged to support him in ease by a return for the use of his money. But every savage has the full enjoyment of the fruits of his own labours; there are no landlords, no usurers, no tax gatherers. . . . [T]he poor labourer . . . has all the inconveniences of the soil and season to struggle with, is continually exposed to the inclemency of the weather and the most severe labour at the same time. Thus he who as it were supports the whole frame of society and furnishes the means of the convenience and ease of all the rest is himself possessed of a very small share and is buried in obscurity. He bears on his shoulders the whole of mankind, and unable to sustain the weight of it is thrust down into the lowest parts of the earth from whence he supports the rest. In what manner then shall we account for the great share he and the lowest persons have of the conveniences of life?[35]

Smith's train of thought is confusing. First, the law is needed to constrain the fury of the poor; then the market provides for the poor very well; followed by the wretched state of the people who worked on the land—the least fortunate of the workers. For his grand finale, after decrying the "small share" of the poor, Smith curiously veers off to ask what accounts for "the great share" that these same people have. His answer should come as no surprise to a modern reader of Adam Smith: "The division of labour amongst different hands can alone account for this."[36] By March 30, Smith was confident enough about his success in finessing the challenge of class conflict that he became uncharacteristically unguarded in openly taking notice of the importance of workers' knowledge:

> But if we go into the work house of any manufacturer in the new works at Sheffield, Manchester, or Birmingham, or even some towns in Scotland, and enquire concerning the machines, they will tell you that such or such an one was invented by some common workman.[37]

Smith was too careful an ideologue to include such material in his published work without any hand-wringing about inequities and the importance of workers' knowledge. Instead, he introduced readers of *The Wealth of Nations* to his delightful picture of the division of labor in his simple pin factory:

> A workman not educated to this business (which the division of labour has rendered a distinct trade), nor acquainted with the use of the machinery employed in it (to the invention of which the same division of labour has probably given occasion), could scarce, perhaps, with his utmost industry, make one pin in a day, and certainly could not make twenty. But in the way in which this business is now carried on, not only the whole work is a peculiar trade, but it is divided into a number of branches, of which the greater part are likewise peculiar trades. One man draws out the wire, another straights it, a third cuts it, a fourth points it, a fifth grinds it at the top for receiving the head; to make the head requires two or three distinct operations; to put it on is a peculiar business, to whiten the pins is another; it is even a trade by itself to put them into the paper; and the important business of making a pin is, in this manner, divided into about eighteen distinct operations, which, in some manufactories, are all performed by distinct hands, though in others the same man will sometimes perform two or three of them. I have seen a small manufactory of this kind where ten men only were employed, and where some of them consequently performed two or three distinct operations. But though they were very poor, and therefore but indifferently accommodated with the necessary machinery, they could, when they exerted themselves, make among them about twelve pounds of pins in a day. There are in a pound upwards of four thousand pins of a middling size. Those ten persons, therefore, could make among them upwards of forty-eight thousand pins in a day. Each person, therefore, making a tenth part of forty-eight thousand pins, might be considered as making four thousand eight hundred pins in a day. But if they had all wrought separately and independently, and without any of them having been educated to this peculiar business, they certainly could not each of them have made twenty, perhaps not one pin in a day; that is, certainly, not the two hundred and fortieth, perhaps not the four thousand eight hundredth part of what they are at present capable of performing, in consequence of a proper division and combination of their different operations.[38]

Today, few people would recognize Smith's pin-making operation as a factory. It was simply a small workshop that would not have been much out of place in Smith's imaginary village. Smith himself referred to the pin factory as a "frivolous example" and later as "a very trifling manufacture."[39] But now, with the magic of the division of labor, Smith could portray society as a harmonious system of voluntary, commercial transactions. Because the economy could produce more, workers could consume more, and perhaps one day even have their own trifling enterprise.

The mere rearrangement of work created a great leap of productivity. Smith told his students that a worker might have been able to produce something between one and twenty pins per day, but with the division of labor, the output per capita soared to two thousand. By the time he published *The Wealth of Nations*, the number more than doubled to 4,800 pins.[40] Granted that the division of labor can improve productivity, how was such dramatic productivity possible? It wasn't. An early draft of *The Wealth of Nations* explains the secret of this jump in productivity. There, Smith began his description of pin production with "If the same person was to dig the metal out of the mine, separate it from the ore, forge it, split it into small rods, then spin these rods into wire. . . ."[41] In his later estimates, the workers' tasks began with wire already in their hands. No wonder they could produce so much more. Much of their work had already been completed before they began.

Even if the division of labor was responsible for a significant part of this increased productivity, further dramatic advances were unlikely to come from rearranging workers' tasks. And other than his earlier statement that "The division of labour amongst different hands can alone account for this," Smith never directly made the assertion that the division of labor alone was responsible for all technical progress. However, the absence of any other explanation (as well as his silence regarding modern technology) gives the impression he still held that belief.

A Different Division of Labor

In 1767, about four years after Smith first introduced his students to the pin factory, his friend and colleague, Adam Ferguson, published *An Essay on the History of Civil Society*.[42] Their mutual friend, Rev. Dr. Alexander Carlyle, reported on Smith's displeasure with this publication: "Smith had been weak enough to accuse him of having borrowed some of his inventions without owning them. This Ferguson denied, but owned he derived many notions from a French author, and Smith had been there before."[43]

Ferguson's reference to the French author is important. Several detailed descriptions of pin production had been published in France. Although Smith never mentioned them, he used identical numerical examples and phraseology. His reliance on different French sources could explain the different estimates of per capita pin production in his lectures and his book.

Before this incident, Ferguson had given Smith every encouragement, both in person and in print.[44] Moreover, Ferguson did not describe any pin factory. Like Smith, Ferguson does credit the division of labor with permitting increased production:

> By the separation of arts and professions, the sources of wealth are laid open; every species of material is wrought up to the greatest perfection, and every commodity is produced in the greatest abundance.[45]

Ferguson did not dwell on the technological potential of the division of labor. Instead, his book detailed the sociological implications, showing the negative consequences of the division of labor:

> In every commercial state, notwithstanding any pretension to equal rights, the exaltation of a few must depress the many. In this arrangement, we think that the extreme meanness of some classes must arise chiefly from the defect of knowledge, and of liberal education; and we refer to such classes, as to an image of what our species must have been in its rude and uncultivated state. But we forget how many circumstances, especially

in populous cities, tend to corrupt the lowest orders of men. Ignorance is the least of their failings.[46]

Besides creating class divisions, the division of labor undermines society:

The separation of professions, while it seems to promise improvement of skill, and is actually the cause why the productions of every art becomes more perfect as commerce advances; yet in its termination, and ultimate effects, serves, in some measure, to break the bands of society, to substitute form in place of ingenuity, and to withdraw individuals from the common scene of occupation, on which the sentiments of the heart, and the mind, are most happily employed.[47]

Finally, Ferguson, who had been the principal chaplain to the Black Watch brigade from 1746 to 1754, warned that the division of labor degrades the character of people who will be needed for the military.[48]

Ferguson's real sin might well have been to use the pin factory in a way that contradicted Adam Smith's libertarian vision.

Tough as Nails

Smith eventually retired to his birthplace, Kirkcaldy, to work on *The Wealth of Nations*. Although he may have relied upon secondary sources for his knowledge of the pin factory, he must have had first-hand knowledge of the production of Scottish nails. In the *Wealth of Nations*, only three paragraphs after describing the pin factory, Smith briefly turned to this industry.

The nail industry was concentrated in the neighborhood of Kirkaldy, where about 30 percent of the nation's nail producers were located. [49] Smith took note of the remarkable physical dexterity of the boys he watched making the nails, but his main point was that the division of labor was not as refined as in the pin factory.

Smith never mentioned that the great manufacturer, the Carron Company, had offered a bounty of one guinea to reward nail makers for moving their production closer to Kirkaldy. The company's purpose was to have a ready market for its iron rods that would be shaped into nails.

In addition, Smith did not inform his readers that the Carron Company entered into a bargain with the Edinburgh poorhouse to apprentice pauper boys to make nails from the age of twelve until they reached twenty-one. Finally, although Smith may not have been aware of the problem, the manager of the poorhouse received a number of alarming reports of the poor treatment of these apprentices.[50]

Similarly, Smith's picture of the pin factory was incomplete. One of his two major French sources offered an unattractive picture of the seemingly idyllic job of the pin makers:

> We also make several observations on the pin maker's trade. . . . This trade is very dirty and unhealthy. The brass rust, a greeny grey colour, affects workers differently depending on their role in the factory. The point makers are not robust, and die young of pulmonary ailments.[51]

In the end, Smith's idealized workers were not just selling their time on the job, but their lives as well. Nonetheless, for Smith, these details about the nail workers were not worthy of mention, though he spun a story about the justice and efficiency of the pin factory that still resonates strongly among market enthusiasts.

A Different Kind of Pin Factory

The first integrated pin factory was the Dockwra copper works, founded in 1692. It produced about 80 tons of copper per year, perhaps as much as half of the entire industry. The company had no less than twenty-four benches for drawing wire (for making pins). From the start. Dockwra gave attention to the possibility of new methods.[52]

Eventually, the Warmley works, founded near Bristol in 1746, surpassed Dockwra. The Warmley works came to popular attention in

1770, when Arthur Young published *A Six Months Tour Through the Southern Counties of England and Wales*. Young was a prolific observer of agriculture, as well as economic life in general. His books were widely translated in European languages. This particular book was already in its third edition by 1772. A careful study of authorities used in parliamentary debates found that MPs cited Young far more than Adam Smith.[53]

Young described the process of integrated pin production at Warmley, which he recommended as "very well worth seeing." His description began with how the molten metal was

> poured into a flat mould of stone, to make it into thin plates, about 4 feet long and three broad. The plates are then cut into 17 strips and then again, by particular machines, into many more very thin ones, and drawn out to the length of 17 feet, which are again drawn into wire, and done up in bunches of 40s value each; about 100 of which are made here every week, and each makes a hundred thousand pins. The wires are cut into them, and completed here employing a great number of girls who with little machines, worked by their feet, point and head them with great expedition; and each will do a pound and a half in a day.
>
> The heads are spun by women with a wheel, much like a common spinning wheel, and then separated from one another by a man, with another little machine like a pair of shears. They have several lapis calaminaris stones for preparing it to make the brass, of which they form a vast number of awkward looking pans and dishes for the Negroes, on the coast of Guinea. All the machines and wheels are set in motion by water, for racing, which there is a prodigious fire engine, which raises, as it is said 3000 hogsheads every minute.[54]

This system replaced the people who had turned wheels in the operation. The displaced workers represented one-sixth of the labor force.[55]

Smith's Understanding of Modern Technology

In contrast to the importance given to the division of labor, Smith showed no appreciation of the growing importance of fossil fuels in increasing productivity. The Warmley works was still largely dependent on water power, but coal was used to lift water when the natural flow was insufficient. Despite the beginnings of the Industrial Revolution that centered in Scotland, Smith offered only a few scattered references to coal in his published work. These observations mostly concern either coal as a household fuel or the process of mining, without bothering to link coal to industrial production.

In one instance, Smith discussed the government's policy of restricting exports of coal. The purpose of such legislation was to protect Britain's emerging industrial leadership, but Smith never made that connection. Instead, he merely noted: "Coals may be considered both as a material of manufacture and as an instrument of trade."[56]Possibly the closest he came to acknowledging the productive potential of modern technology was a fanciful account of a boy who invented the steam engine "to save his own labour."[57] Even though James Watt was an instrument maker in his school, Edwin Cannan, a scholarly editor of *Wealth of Nations*, reported that Smith based his account on a misreading of a three-decades-old book.[58]

Something else seems to be at work here. In his unpublished works, Smith clearly connected economic progress with the development of modern technology. In the school year of 1762–63, while lecturing to his students, he began a long discussion about the pin factory that culminated in the heightened productivity of the steam engine.[59] He used the same sequence, moving from the pin factory to the steam engine, in an early draft of *Wealth of Nations*.[60] Smith repeated almost all of the ideas in these two early discussions in *Wealth of Nations*, except for the final transition to modern technology.

Then, in a remarkable letter to Lord Carlisle, just three years after *Wealth of Nations* appeared, while explaining why the Irish could not pose much of a threat to British industry, Smith explicitly prioritized social control ahead of the emerging Industrial Revolution:

> I cannot believe that the interest of Britain would be hurt by it [free trade]. On the contrary, the Competition of Irish goods in the British market might contribute to break down in Part that monopoly which we have most absurdly granted to the greater part of our own workmen against our selves. It would, however, be a long time before this competition could be very considerable. In the present state of Ireland, centuries must pass away before the greater part of its manufactures could vie with those of England. Ireland has little Coal; the Coallieries about Lough Neagh being of little consequence to the greater part of the Country. It is ill provided with Wood; two articles essentially necessary to the progress of Great Manufactures. It wants order, police, and a regular administration of justice both to protect and to restrain the inferior ranks of people, articles more essential to the progress of Industry than both coal and wood put together.[61]

Seven days earlier, he had presented similar thoughts in a letter to Henry Dundas suggesting the importance of wood and coal for modern technology.[62] If this subject was important enough to repeat in letters to influential people, why did it not appear in the book he had just published?

Smith's reference to "the monopoly which we have most absurdly granted to the greater part of our own workmen against our selves" is also interesting. His observation anticipates the modern move toward outsourcing. But why would someone who advocated the promotion of the interests of industrious workers want to see them undercut by foreign competition?

The Primacy of Exchange

Smith's relatively primitive description of the economy is useful in suggesting that the defining characteristic of an economy is the act of exchange rather than production. This approach allows Smith to depict a world where "social distance" rather than authority was the norm.[63] Smith offered a glimpse of this world, observing, "Society may subsist among different men as among different merchants, from a sense of its utility, without any mutual love or affection."[64]

Production still existed, but exchange was central—not just because "the division of labour . . . must always be limited by the extent of the market."[65] Notice that the division of labor occurs prior to the process of production. Once the division of labor is in place, one has no need to consider production. At this point, every person—workers and capitalists alike—becomes a merchant, equally selling wares on a free and open market. In Smith's words: "Every man . . . lives by exchanging, or becomes in some measure a merchant, and the society itself grows to be what is properly a commercial society."[66]

In this world, Smith's idealized merchant-workers prosper merely by demonstrating middle-class virtues, such as punctuality and trust-worthy behavior. These merchants will compete with one another, but they must do so by following the rules at the same time as they demonstrate respect for one another.

Class antagonism, exploitation, and domination have no place in this imaginary world of exchange that Smith created. Workers existed as exchangers rather than as proletarians. Smith's merchant-workers all belong to the same community as their employers. A parallel imaginary progressive lifecycle of labor allows a large portion of the working class to become employers themselves in the not too distant future.

Smith was not alone in presenting such an idealized version of social mobility. As one historical study of British culture during Smith's day found:

> Another way eighteenth-century culture tried to instill an inner work-compulsion in the poor was to promise success for industry and dire punishment for idleness. Of course, success above a mere survival level was rarely available to members of the laboring classes, since they were seldom paid enough to allow them to rise in the world.[67]

Smith's perspective of worker-merchants becomes more credible in a world of simpler, craft-like technologies, such as the pin factory, with only a handful of workers. In the large-scale production systems that were beginning to emerge, the kind of upward mobility that Smith imagined would be impossible. Just as today, a worker consigned to menial labor in a large enterprise, such as a modern equivalent of the Carron works, among thousands of other workers, cannot expect to have a chance to become a CEO.

In conclusion, writing at a time when economists still routinely acknowledged the importance of labor in the production process, Smith gave exchange a more important role in the economy, to obscure questions of class. Workers became exchangers, no different from their employers. In this respect, the absence of the Carron works in Smith's writings was a clever rhetorical tactic. Although Smith did not go as far as modern economics in excluding work, workers, and working conditions, his recasting of workers as merchants was an important first step in the direction of modern economics.

Individualism

Smith's reluctance to discuss the Carron works makes sense in terms of his enthusiasm for individualism. Early economic systems, such as slavery or feudalism, looked at the great mass of the population as a class, while consigning the majority to function as unthinking work animals. Smith's lumping people together with work animals was a residual of this earlier tradition. Not surprisingly, the people society regarded as animals displayed few outward signs of ambitions or aspirations, at least the sort of ambitions or aspirations that would meet with the approval of Adam Smith. The system was certain to dash any hopes of conventional success for the vast majority.

At the same time, Smith welcomed a sign of a different trend emerging. Alongside dangerous mobs of poor people in urban centers, the growing individualism of small merchants and some artisans encouraged Smith. This part of society provided the positive example that was central to Smith's vision of the future. From this perspective, Smith's individualism represented at least the possibility of people breaking out of the confining class structure of traditional society. In place of a world divided along lines of class, everybody would understand their identity as individuals making commercial transactions. In this classless world, all people would have a chance to improve their lot.

Proponents of laissez-faire treated the abstract possibility of social mobility a likely reward for anyone who was willing to work hard. The mere thought of this possibility had such a liberating effect, so much so that the Spanish disciples of Smith's contemporary, Jeremy Bentham, defined themselves as "liberals"—a new word that has been subsequently redefined several times.

Smith was enthusiastic about the energy of this new individualism. Later commentators associated this energy with the burst of economic activity, commonly described as the Industrial Revolution, but, as mentioned earlier, the Industrial Revolution is absent in Smith's writings. By now, the reason for this absence is obvious. Although Smith's liberalism seemed liberating, from a different perspective it must have been disempowering to people who were toiling in the Carron works. Presenting such people as isolated individuals would have accurately conveyed their powerlessness.

Although individualism might disempower most people, Smith recognized that businesspeople knew how to wield their collective power as a class. In Smith's words:

> People of the same trade seldom meet together, even for merriment and diversion, but the conversation ends in a conspiracy against the publick, or in some contrivance to raise prices. It is impossible to prevent such meetings, by any law which either could be executed, or would be consistent with liberty and justice. But though the law cannot hinder people of the same trade from assembling together, it ought to do nothing to facilitate such assemblies.[68]

Although business was organizing for selfish purposes, larger organizational structures can also promote the public interest, giving working people's desires a greater force. Perhaps more crucial from an economic standpoint, by the twenty-first century, much truly important work requires collaborative and cooperative processes. The

Manhattan Project during the Second World War represents a striking example of the powers of collaboration, although that particular power was destructive. The government gathered some of the most skilled scientists of the day to rush through the creation of the atomic bomb. One of those scientists, Freeman Dyson, recalled how people later looked back on their experience with the Manhattan Project: "Through all the talk shone a glow of pride and nostalgia. For every one of these people the Los Alamos days had been a great experience, a time of hard work and comradeship and deep happiness."[69] To my knowledge, none of the scientists pushed very hard for recognition of their individual contributions.

Many people regard the Manhattan Project as a major scientific accomplishment. If masses of people rather than just a few elite scientists had the opportunity to participate in such collective action— with the goal of creating productive, rather than destructive outcomes—wonderful things could happen. Unfortunately, the prevailing corporate structure undermines the potential for such productive collaboration.

CHAPTER SEVEN

The Dark Side of Adam Smith

The Cauldron of Class

Although Smith's language was less antagonistic toward labor than many of his contemporaries, he was hardly a great friend of workers. For the most part, he merely suggested that once his idealized merchant-workers adopted middle-class values—what he called "a general probity of manners"—they would prosper.[1] In turn, this personal transformation would produce a stronger economy, along with better people.

Yet what Smith saw occurring around him could not give him much confidence. The rise of market-based industrialization was a juggernaut degrading a large swath of humanity in crowded cities. Smith was not at all pleased when he looked at this wretched mass of potentially dangerous workers huddled together.

These people had little in common with his idealized merchant-workers. Instead, Smith saw them as the raw material for mobs, a vision closer to Ferguson's than his own: the division of labor was creating deep class divisions rather than integrating everybody into a harmonious society. To make matters worse, this new stage of development seemed to reinforce what Smith regarded as negative remnants of the pre-commercial stage of development. In particular, Smith was aghast that urban workers, rather than seeing themselves as merchants, still adhered to the continuing, anti-commercial traditions of popular rural justice. Workers insisted that necessities should not sell above what they considered a just price—a traditional attitude that Edward P. Thompson described as the "moral economy."[2]

Smith opposed every aspect of the moral economy. He expressed disgust that these traditional cultural values made poor people feel justified in times of high prices when they would "break open granaries and force the owners to sell at what they think a reasonable price."[3] Smith condemned the government for passing laws regulating the retail corn trade in order to mollify the populace, although much of this legislation had already been repealed by 1772.[4] For Smith, such legislation was every bit as unjustified as the laws regarding religion, although, ironically, Smith himself wanted to regulate religion.

Smith claimed that people's fear of corn merchants manipulating the market was no more warranted than anxiety about witchcraft.[5] He insisted that people recognize that the corn merchants actually served a useful purpose:

> By raising the price he [the corn merchant] discourages the consumption, and puts every body more or less, but particularly the inferior ranks of people, upon thrift and good management. . . . When he foresees that provisions are likely to run short, he puts them upon short allowance. Though from excess of caution he should sometimes do this without any real necessity, yet all the inconveniences which his crew can thereby suffer are inconsiderable in comparison of the danger, misery, and ruin, to which they might sometimes be exposed by a less provident conduct.[6]

Here, writing during a time of recurrent food shortages, Smith was speculating that the experience of periods of hunger would jolt people to their senses. Such natural workings of trade and exchange should force people to change their behavior to become better aligned with the market economy. Governments certainly should not interfere with this process by regulating the grain trade—not even to prevent starvation.

The Degradation of Work; The Degradation of Workers

Despite his generous remarks concerning the abstract welfare of workers, Smith showed contempt rather than sympathy for their hardships. Although he had little regard for the small, struggling, pre-commercial independent farmers and farm workers, who were also unlikely to see themselves as merchants, Smith still held them in significantly higher esteem than unskilled urban workers. He exclaimed, "How much the lower ranks of the people in the country are really superior to those in the town, is well known to every man whom either business or curiosity has led to converse with both."[7]

In lectures to his students about the benefits of the division of labor, Smith observed:

> It is remarkable that in every commercial nation the low people are exceedingly stupid. The Dutch vulgar are eminently so. . . . The rule is general, in towns they are not so intelligent as in the country, nor in a rich country as in a poor one.[8]

Workers in a small shop, such as Smith's pin factory, who possibly worked and lived side by side with their master, might not feel as downtrodden as the urban workers, whose behavior so offended him.

Smith was disturbed that modern workers lacked the incentives and opportunities for the kind of individual initiative that more primitive people normally exercise. As a result, they succumb to the "drowsy stupidity which, in a civilized society, seems to benumb the understanding of almost all the inferior ranks of people."[9] He continued: "A man, without the proper use of the intellectual faculties of a man, is, if possible, more contemptible than even a coward, and seems to be mutilated and deformed in a still more essential part of human nature."[10]

The degradation of work had serious moral consequences that Smith found unattractive. According to Smith:

> [When a worker] comes into a great city, he is sunk in obscurity and darkness. His conduct is observed and attended to by nobody, and he is very

likely to neglect it himself, and to abandon himself to every sort of low profligacy and vice.[11]

Judging by the relatively little attention he gave to workers' "low profligacy and vice," Smith seemed more troubled by their surly class-conscious attitudes. In particular, the seething wrath of the masses of poor people packed into cities horrified Smith. He warned that "in the poor the hatred of labour and the love of present ease and enjoyment, are the passions which prompt (them) to invade property, passions much more steady in their operation, and more universal in their influence."

Smith continued:

> The affluence of the rich excites the indignation of the poor, who are often both driven by want, and prompted by envy, to invade his possessions. It is only under the shelter of the civil magistrate that the owner of . . . valuable property can sleep a single night in security. He is at all times surrounded by unknown enemies, whom, though he never provoked, he can never appease, and from whose injustice he can be protected only by the powerful arm of the civil magistrate continually held up to chastise it. . . . Where there is no property, or at least none that exceeds the value of two or three days labour, civil government is not so necessary.[12]

Smith never seemed to notice that rich people might be prospering, in part, because the state permitted and even encouraged measures to deprive people in the countryside of the means necessary to fend for themselves. Pushed into already crowded cities without adequate resources, the oversupply of labor caused low wages and appalling degradation.

Smith's own teachings suggested that a subsistence wage would be the natural outcome of such an oversupply of labor: "The natural price . . . the lowest which the sellers can commonly afford to take, and at the same time continue their business."[13]

No wonder such people continued their adherence to the moral economy!

A Central Contradiction of Market Ideology

A moment's reflection should be sufficient to realize that greater consideration of the workers might diminish the pressing need for the effort that goes into protecting the property of the rich. Instead, insofar as workers were concerned, Smith suggested that workers should count on the wonders of the market and their own hard work to secure their future.

Here, Adam Smith reflected a central contradiction of market ideology. Raw capitalism falsely promises maximum returns to the rich and powerful. In truth, some kind of social democratic regime, which takes the harsh edges off of capitalism, is perhaps more effective for extracting profits.

Though Smith seemed to have approved government taking pains to ensure that the rich could sleep in security, he never supported measures to defend the welfare of workers, either inside or outside the workplace. Recall his dogmatic antipathy to the regulation of grain prices. Instead, Smith called for somehow changing the psychology of the lower classes to reconcile them to their condition as merchant-workers, hoping perhaps that improved morale would both eliminate class conflict and increase productivity.

Smith did approve of education. His stated purpose was not so much to improve workers' lives as to provide a means to "socialize" workers and perhaps improve their productivity. However, Smith gave no hint that employers could offer a good quality of life by creating workplaces where employment could be an opportunity for fulfillment rather than an unbearable burden.

Smith never took account of the personal toll that grueling working conditions would take on the laborers in the large industrial plants that would soon become common. In the one passage where Smith did worry about the physical consequences of overwork, he attributed the problem to workers' autonomy. According to Smith, where piece rates are high, people are likely to choose overwork:

> Workmen . . . when they are liberally paid by the piece, are very apt to over-work themselves, and to ruin their health and constitution in a few

years. A carpenter in London, and in some other places, is not supposed
to last in his utmost vigour above eight years. Something of the same kind
happens in many other trades, in which the workmen are paid by the
piece.[14]

Presumably, such adverse outcomes would not occur if employers
did not pay too much. Elsewhere, working conditions appear to be
irrelevant to Smith, except to the extent that they somehow contributed to bad behavior.

Smith's obsessive concern with working-class discipline is remarkable. The core of his doctrine was that the fourth stage of development
would usher in a system of voluntary market relations. But although
Smith framed his argument in terms of volunteerism, his voluntarism
depended upon the acquiescence of people with little opportunity for
choice. Such conditions would do little to encourage workers to identify with the market economy. No wonder the working class appeared
so surly to Smith. How could he expect that people in such dire straits
would embrace the behavior that he associated with small merchants
and artisans?

In effect, then, Smith's four stages theory was working in reverse.
The transition from an agricultural to commercial society was supposed to elevate the masses. Instead it appeared to be causing degeneration within the ranks of the poor. This degeneration, however, was
in large part a rational, class-oriented response to a system that both
degraded and impoverished the urban workers whose behavior
repulsed Smith.

Because the core of Smith's doctrine was that the fourth stage of
development would usher in a system of voluntary market relations,
his obsessive concern with the need to impose working-class discipline is remarkable. But Smith's voluntarism depended upon the
acquiescence of people with little opportunity for choice. How could
Smith expect that people in such dire straits would identify with the
market economy and embrace the behavior that he associated with
small merchants and artisans.

Instead, Smith pinned his hopes on extra-market coercion.

Military Discipline, Market Discipline

Smith addressed two kinds of controls to maintain social and economic order—controls over the market and controls over the people. Smith's call for market controls are minimal compared to those that control people. This imbalance should not be surprising considering Smith's interest in molding the human personality to fit the needs of a market society.

Smith's suggested controls of personal behavior are more far-reaching than one might expect after reading the first part of the *Wealth of Nations*, where volunteerism promises a world of harmonious prosperity. People's response to the grain trade suggested that markets were not changing personal behavior the way Smith preferred.

Molding personal behavior to fit the needs of the market was not the only thing Smith had in mind. It was also crucial in terms of national defense, which Smith considered more important than opulence.[15] On at least two occasions, Smith equated opulence with effeminacy—looking back favorably at a time of "rough, manly people who had no sort of domestic luxury or effeminacy."[16] Like Ferguson, Smith was disturbed that the growing commercial society he welcomed was inhospitable to military virtue. The personal qualities that make for a strong military are different from those that are appropriate for a successful commercial society. To his credit, Smith sensed that working conditions were also part of the equation. Here Smith returned to the subject of division of labor, but his tone sounded more like Ferguson than himself, warning that "some attention of government is necessary in order to prevent the almost entire corruption and degeneracy of the great body of the people."[17]

Smith did not mean that the government should change the way business treats its workers, but rather that it had the responsibility to find a way to maintain the workers' manly vigor necessary for military service:

> The man whose whole life is spent in performing a few simple operations, of which the effects too are, perhaps, always the same, or very nearly the same, has no occasion to exert his understanding, or to exer-

cise his invention in finding out expedients for removing difficulties which never occur. He naturally loses, therefore, the habit of such exertion, and generally becomes as stupid and ignorant as it is possible for a human creature to become. The torpor of his mind renders him, not only incapable of relishing or bearing a part in any rational conversation, but of conceiving any generous, noble, or tender sentiment, and consequently of forming any just judgment concerning many even of the ordinary duties of private life. Of the great and extensive interests of his country, he is altogether incapable of judging; and unless very particular pains have been taken to render him otherwise, he is equally incapable of defending his country in war. The uniformity of his stationary life naturally corrupts the courage of his mind, and makes him regard with abhorrence the irregular, uncertain, and adventurous life of a soldier. It corrupts even the activity of his body, and renders him incapable of exerting his strength with vigour and perseverance, in any other employment than that to which he has been bred. His dexterity at his own particular trade seems, in this manner, to be acquired at the expence of his intellectual, social, and martial virtues. But in every improved and civilized society this is the state into which the labouring poor, that is, the great body of the people, must necessarily fall, unless government takes some pains to prevent it.[18]

This passage is often cited as evidence of Smith's humanitarian concerns, but the context of this critique of the division of labor throws a different light on the subject. Commercial society and national defense seem to be at odds. According to Smith's four stages theory, the market should have been turning everybody into merchants. Certainly, the merchant class had many qualities that Smith considered desirable:

Regularity, order, and prompt obedience to command are qualities which, in modern armies, are of more importance towards determining the fate of battles than the dexterity and skill of the soldiers in the use of their arms.[19]

To the extent that the market succeeded in that respect, national defense was sure to suffer. Even moderately successful people would consider their time too valuable to voluntarily devote themselves to soldiering. In Smith's words:

> Into other arts the division of labour is naturally introduced by the prudence of individuals, who find that they promote their private interest better by confining themselves to a particular trade than by exercising a great number. But it is the wisdom of the state only which can render the trade of a soldier a particular trade separate and distinct from all others. A private citizen who, in time of profound peace, and without any particular encouragement from the public, should spend the greater part of his time in military exercises, might, no doubt, both improve himself very much in them, and amuse himself very well; but he certainly would not promote his own interest.[20]

How can "the wisdom of the state" create a military if it is not in the self-interest of people to participate? Smith understood that the work demands of modern industry also required discipline, but not the healthy self-discipline Smith admired. Workers who had to submit to the harsh tedium of adapting to the unremitting rhythms of machines experienced an unnatural form of discipline—one that broke the spirit of some and made others angry and rebellious, such as when they practiced the values of the moral economy. Neither outcome was particularly favorable to the production of desirable cannon fodder. So, for Smith, almost nobody in the cities seemed suitable to provide for national defense.

The poor might seem to be likely candidates for military service, but the demands of modern industry left people with little free time.[21] The poor masses also presented an intellectual problem for Smith, who associated the degraded condition of the workers with cowardice. At the same time, Smith was fearful that these cowards might eventually rise up and threaten the wealth of the wealthy.

To remedy this situation, Smith called upon the state to transform the people, correcting their personal defects and making them into upstanding citizens. Smith did call for educating the poor, while others at the time feared that widespread literacy could make them more dangerous. However, Smith, the reputed libertarian, suggested that education be mixed with compulsion:

> The public can impose upon almost the whole body of the people the necessity of acquiring those most essential parts of education, by obliging every man to undergo an examination or probation in them before he can obtain the freedom in any corporation, or be allowed to set up any trade either in a village or town corporate.[22]

Coercion would force the poor to submit to education. The penalty would be that potential merchant-workers would be limited in the kind of merchandise (their work) that non-compliant people could bring to the market.

Smith was not advocating instructing students in the same classical literature that wealthy children studied. Instead, he advocated the creation of a martial spirit that he associated with these ancient imperial states of Greece and Rome:

> It was in this manner, by facilitating the acquisition of their military and gymnastic exercises, by encouraging it, and even by imposing upon the whole body of the people the necessity of learning those exercises, that the Greek and Roman republics maintained the martial spirit of their respective citizens.[23]

Smith's educational proposal was not intended so much to promote working people's welfare as to improve their martial spirit. This education was designed, at least in part, to improve the capacity for human annihilation rather than human flourishing.

Smith's defenders note that in his discussion of education two paragraphs earlier he discussed how familiarity with geometry and mechanics would make workers more productive, though that single mention of productivity weighs lightly compared to six references to "martial spirit."

Smith was also an avid promoter of the militia. He was a founding member of the Poker Club, the purpose of which was to further the cause of a militia rather than a standing army. By the time *The Wealth of Nations* appeared, Smith advocated a standing army—at least "one in which citizens maintain the manly virtues, a community that praises courage, a country which sympathizes with the cardinal virtue of courage."[24]

The Militia Act had authorized raising a militia, beginning in May 1757. The legislation also allowed for training on Sundays, but made no provision for paying the members. In August, a small group of village militiamen demanded a barrel of ale from an aged clergyman. Later, they demonstrated, asking for money. According to an article in *Scots Magazine*, participants said they would willingly sacrifice their lives for King and Country but "would not be obliged to quit home for sixpence a day to serve in the militia."[25]

Although one might commend these reluctant militiamen for their merchant-like calculation, Smith's reaction was harsh. He wrote to a friend, "The Lincolnshire mobs provoke our severest indignation for opposing the militia, and we hope to hear that the ringleaders are all to be hanged."[26]

Smith's military concerns reveal him as a strict disciplinarian, very much at odds with his image as a philosopher of freedom. His admirers tend to pay too much attention to the volunteerism of the first part of his book. This darker side of Smith's vision of socialization deserves more attention.

Religious Discipline

One might argue in Smith's defense that the military requires a high level of discipline. However, even in matters as personal as religion, Smith severely limited the amount of voluntarism he would tolerate. He worried about "the poison of enthusiasm and superstition; and where all the superior ranks of people were secured from it, the inferior ranks could not be much exposed to it." He called upon the state to "correct whatever was unsocial or disagreeably vigorous in the morals of all the little sects." In particular, "before [anyone] was permitted to exercise any liberal profession or before he could be received as a candidate for any honourable office or trust or profit," he should have to earn a license by proving his worthiness to the state.[27] Smith also opposed a provision that would have allowed members of the Scottish Presbyterian church to choose their own clergymen for fear that the process might unleash dangerous emotions.[28] In contrast, doctors, whose incompetence threatened only human health rather than public order, had no need for state supervision. Smith even questioned restrictions on the sale of medical degrees.

Although Smith managed to exorcise all considerations of class from his theoretical representation of the world, in practical matters, these examples show that class discipline remained a matter of utmost importance. For Smith, individual virtue rather than social influences determine people's fate. In a particularly striking passage, Smith suggested:

If we consider the general rules by which external prosperity and adversity are commonly distributed in this life, we shall find [that] every virtue naturally meets with its proper reward, with the recompense which is most fit to encourage and promote it. . . . What is the reward most proper for encouraging industry, prudence, and circumspection? Success in every business. And is it possible that in the whole of life these virtues should fail of attaining it?[29]

The truth was (and still is) that members of the lower class had little chance of succeeding in business, even with a high degree of virtue. Today, in California, you can see farm workers sweating in the fields under the 100-degree sun. Nobody can doubt that what these people are doing is difficult, but despite their hard work, their chance of material success is slight.

Yet Smith seemed bewildered about why many poor people would express their discontent. The real surprise should be that such people accept their lot in life, while others wallow in obscene luxury.

In the end, Smith was wildly successful. He was able to throw in his lot with the Procrusteans while maintaining his reputation as a philosopher of liberty.

Class Warfare

How could Smith write so glowingly about a classless economy in *The Wealth of Nations*, then turn around and explain how to conduct class warfare? The key to disentangling Smith's contradiction is that he designed his book for two different—and even contradictory—purposes.

The first part of the book celebrated the growth of the market economy. In that cleverly designed work of ideology, Smith cast the development of the market in as favorable a light as possible. Here, facts and details were not much needed, except to make an ideological point. Discussion of the Carron works would have been a diversion. In contrast, charming anecdotes, such as his portrayal of the pin factory, offered evidence to support his ideology, while making the discussion a joy to read.

In the second part, Smith was developing a handbook of practical administration. Here, too, Smith had his stories, but he necessarily had to deal with real facts—even unpleasant facts. As a result, these two parts are often inconsistent, as was the case with his negative characterization of the division of labor in discussing the military.

The first part of the book emphasizes voluntarism. Then suddenly, in the latter part of the book, the state, which heretofore was the enemy of all economic progress, becomes essential for keeping workers in line. Now the state rather than the market must administer the Procrustean bed. Students of Adam Smith's work rarely address his call for government intervention, with notable exceptions, such as Jacob Viner.[30] Instead, they emphasize the first part of the book, where the proper role of government was mostly limited to education and national defense.

Smith's advocacy of harsh discipline reflected an important element of his social thinking. A lack of discipline not only cut into

potential profits, but threatened insecurity as well. Smith was living at
a time in which the English ruling class had reason to feel insecure.
England faced three threats—regional insurrections, foreign wars,
and class war. The danger of regional insurrections seemed to be rapidly diminishing, because England had recently quashed the last serious rebellion in Scotland. Smith thought that the union with England
would integrate their economies, bringing both peace and prosperity
to Scotland. More important, Smith saw the traditional Scottish aristocracy dissipating its wealth and power through ostentatious consumption. Smith mocked that foolish behavior of the aristocracy:

> All for ourselves and nothing for other people, seems, in every age of the
> world, to have been the vile maxim of the masters of mankind. As soon,
> therefore, as they could find a method of consuming the whole value of
> their rents themselves, they had no disposition to share them with any
> other persons. For a pair of diamond buckles, perhaps, or for something as
> frivolous and useless, they exchanged the maintenance, or what is the same
> thing, the price of the maintenance of a thousand men for a year, and with
> it the whole weight and authority which it could give them . . . and thus, for
> the gratification of the most childish, the meanest, and the most sordid of
> all vanities, they gradually bartered their whole power and authority.[31]

England was also in the midst of a long series of difficult wars, but
more worrisome, England appeared to be on the verge of revolutionary insurrection on the part of workers. For Smith:

> In free countries, where the safety of government depends very much
> upon the favourable judgment which the people may form of its conduct,
> it must surely be of the highest importance that they should not be dis-
> posed to judge rashly or capriciously concerning it.[32]

Unfortunately for Smith, this "favourable judgment" among the
poor did not seem to be very common. Perhaps it is fitting that the
house in which Smith spent his last years eventually became a munic-
ipal center for troubled boys.

Labor in Smith's World

Adam Smith was full of contradictions. Despite his individualist philosophy, workers' individual qualities, other than a willingness to keep their noses to the grindstone, had no interest for him.

Ordinary people just had to earn their income by the sweat of their brow, according to the biblical injunction (Genesis 3: 19). Any role for creativity is out of the question. As Ferguson wrote, far more accurately than Smith:

> Many mechanical arts, indeed, require no capacity; they succeed best under a total suppression of sentiment and reason; and ignorance is the mother of industry as well as of superstition. Reflection and fancy are subject to err; but a habit of moving the hand, or the foot, is independent of either. Manufacturers, accordingly, prosper, where the mind is least consulted, and where the workshop may, without any great effort of imagination, be considered as an engine, the parts of which are men.[33]

Members of the working classes were limited to two options. Either they would obediently perform almost animalistic tasks in the workplace or they would become dissolute beings who submerged themselves in unruly mobs that threatened privileged members of society.

Despite Smith's denigration of workers, he knew that production still depends upon the ability to mobilize labor. Therefore, he occasionally continued in the long mercantilist tradition that attributed the value of production to labor. For example, we read in *The Wealth of Nations*:

> The real price of every thing, what every thing really costs to the man who wants to acquire it, is the toil and trouble of acquiring it. What every thing is really worth to the man who has acquired it, and who wants to dispose of it or exchange it for something else, is the toil and trouble which it can save to himself, and which it can impose upon other people. What is bought with money or with goods is purchased by labour.[34]

Smith's labor theory of value treats workers as interchangeable parts. He went further than modern economic theory, which regards work as nothing more than the loss of the potential utility of leisure. Smith presumed that the psychology of any worker was indistinguishable from the others. In his words:

> Equal quantities of labour, at all times and places, may be said to be of equal value to the labourer; in his ordinary state of health, strength and spirits; in the ordinary degree of his skill and dexterity, he must always lay down the same portion of his ease, his liberty, and his happiness.[35]

Given this perspective, no one should be surprised that Smith paid little attention to working conditions, with one exception: he alluded to working conditions by mentioning that without strict supervision workers might slack off. The workers he used to make his point in this case were not manual workers laboring under difficult conditions. Instead Smith turned to the lax performance of college professors—workers with whom Smith was acquainted.

> It is in the interest of every man to live as much at his ease as he can; and if his emoluments are to be precisely the same, whether he does or does not perform some very laborious duty, it is certainly his interest, at least as interest is vulgarly understood, either to neglect it altogether, or, if he is subject to some authority which will not suffer him to do this, to perform it in as careless and slovenly a manner as that authority will permit. If he is naturally active and a lover of labour, it is his interest to employ that activity in any way from which he can derive some advantage, rather than in the performance of his duty, from which he can derive none.[36]

Neither Smith nor most later economists gave much consideration to exactly what the toil and trouble actually meant for the masses of workers who made life comfortable for people who had the leisure to reflect upon such matters.

As his book progressed, Smith shifted his approach, abandoning this idea of labor-based value. Smith had good reason for this. He was attempting to put the relations between labor and capital in the best possible light. This objective explains why Smith would go to such lengths to obscure the role of technology and large-scale production. Similarly, Smith avoided criticizing government policies to rig the labor market by holding down wages.[37] Such regulations would give the lie to Smith's vision of the market where people met as equals.

In the end, Smith succeeded, giving considerable support to future generations who wished to exclude work, workers, and working conditions from economics.

The Degradation of Adam Smith's Legacy

Although labor was important for the political economists who followed Smith, their idea of labor was not a reflection of workers' individual skills and knowledge. Instead, their conception of labor was reduced to an abstraction—much like the eternal lament that good help is hard to find.

The concern with labor is understandable. Technology was not yet particularly advanced. Management's main task was to mobilize labor. However, the realism of basing economics on the labor process created a significant contradiction that Smith missed. How could an analysis that treated labor with such disrespect turn around and then give labor great credit as a productive force? Beginning around 1830, this contradiction came to a head.

One of the most vehement opponents of a labor-based theory of production was Samuel Read, who advocated giving capitalists the place of honor in production. Read's work was probably more in tune with the underlying thrust of Smith's writings than with David Ricardo's then influential labor-based approach.

Read feared that basing value on labor might provide workers with grounds for demanding higher wages. His goal was to provide objective proof that any attempt to use economic theory to justify higher wages was fallacious. According to Read:

The labourers have been flattered and persuaded, that they produce all, whilst the capitalists on the other hand, have combined and established laws of preference and favour which really tread upon the rights of the labourers. . . . The labourers must be informed, and made to understand that they do not produce all, whenever they seek the assistance of capital; the capitalists lending that assistance must be equally instructed that no individual can have a right to exclude or interdict others from coming forward or to attempt to enhance their gains by means which are unjust or injurious to their neighbours.[38]

For Read, the capitalists provide the essential means of production, such as machines and material, but more important, value itself reflects the preferences of consumers rather than the work of laborers. This masterpiece of intellectual legerdemain eventually became the centerpiece of economics, although few of the economists who were answering Marx a half century later acknowledged Read as their forerunner.

Read's theory provided stronger grounds to regard the context of work as a matter of indifference. As for workers, they should merely content themselves with the consumption that their work makes possible—the idea that Simon Patten echoed almost a century later.

Although Ricardo used a labor-based theory of value, his intentions could give little comfort to workers because he was showing how wages could be reduced. In particular, Ricardo was calling for the elimination of the protection of domestic agriculture, which made labor more expensive and thus lowered profits. And for Ricardo: "Nothing contributes so much to the prosperity and happiness of a country as high profits." Then he added:

There is no other way of keeping profits up but by keeping wages down. In this view of the law of profits, it will at once be seen how important it is that so essential a necessity as corn, which so powerfully affects wages, should be at a low price; and how injurious it must be to the community generally, that, by prohibitions against importation, we should be driven to the cultivation of our poorer lands to feed our augmenting population.[39]

By contrast, Smith himself, despite his authoritarian streak, at least wished success for those workers who accepted the rules of the game:

> No society can surely be flourishing and happy, of which the far greater part of the members are poor and miserable. It is but equity, besides, that they who feed, cloath and lodge the whole body of the people, should have such a share of the produce of their own labour as to be themselves tolerably well fed, cloathed and lodged.[40]

Such sentiments may have given Smith more of a reputation as a humanitarian than he deserved, but this part of Smith's legacy quickly disappeared.

The Making of a Pseudo-Science

Before Adam Smith, the prevailing metaphors for society were largely biological, picturing society as a body in which each part made a special contribution to the whole. Each "caste" (class) had its predestined role to play and none could prosper without the other. Just as a foot could never replace a brain, a peasant could never expect to rise to the level of an aristocrat.

Breaking with the biological metaphor had an obvious attraction for the socially rising portion of the middle class. This group had already partially escaped the confines of feudal castes and now longed for the opportunity to rise further, but an aristocratic elite still occupied many of the high positions in society and looked down with contempt at the pretensions of the rising middle class. This aspiring group, in turn, was naturally somewhat antagonistic to and/or jealous of the inherited privileges of the British gentry.

The social context of Smith's theory of history is relevant here, in the sense that he used his four stages theory to explain how social forces exert powerful influences on people. Once the fourth stage arrives, making the aristocracy superfluous, the resulting social forces would make people more individualistic.

At the same time, physics appeared to offer an ideal metaphor to replace biology. The crowning achievement of physics at the time of Adam Smith was Isaac Newton's work on planetary motion. Long before he embarked on his study of political economy, Smith concluded an essay, *The Principles which Lead and Direct Philosophical Enquiries; Illustrated by the History of Astronomy*, by praising Newton's system "as the greatest discovery that was ever made by man."[41]

One appeal of the method of physics was that one object (person) could easily substitute for another, regardless of class origins. Ignoring for the moment the fact that the force of gravity meant that no single body can move in isolation from others, Newton's method seemed capable of analyzing the world as discrete units, which acted independently of one another. Extending the physics metaphor to society, people also interacted as individual atoms. An appeal to the work of Newton even lent a touch of theological support for economics since the great physicist wanted to demonstrate the rationality of God's handiwork.[42]

Smith initiated an approach to political economy that seemed to conveniently combine class interests with scientific legitimacy— exactly what Macleod was aiming for a century later with his coining of the expression "economics." Backed up by both science and theology, Smith could argue that within the context of the market, middle-class people who prospered must have done so because of their own hard work.

Smith's Newtonian economics naturally appealed to the middle class in a modern commercial society, especially after the French Revolution. Smith was never as explicit in making the ties between economic theory and physics as Macleod and the other economists discussed previously. Yet, by building his theory around a network of commercial transactions, Smith did lay the foundation for his successors. These later economists did change the basis of value from the simple adding up of wages, profits, and rents to the abstraction of utility, which was even further removed from production.

In the words of one scholar of political economy, physics permitted British economists to study "man as an individual and as a social being in the same way that the physicist studies other matters, and here again to apply the Newtonian method with a view to determining the smallest possible number of general simple laws which, once discovered, will enable all the detail of phenomena to be explained by a synthetic and deductive method."[43]

Later economists pushed the physics analogy further, presuming that adopting the method of physics promised a scientific method for prediction.[44] In stable times, such predictions could be relatively accurate, but they give an unwarranted confidence to those who accepted the expertise of economists, leaving them unprepared to dangers that lay ahead.

At least until after the Second World War, the Newtonian heritage never took root as strongly in the economics practiced in Continental Europe. Even today, attitudes toward the poor are still colder in the Anglo-Saxon countries than in Continental Europe.[45] An increasing number of economists in Europe did follow the English style, but many still attempted to understand the economy in a way that took account of the social context in which people lived.

Summing Up

Looking back to Adam Smith serves a useful purpose. Although many people today have unconsciously absorbed parts of Smith's perspective, seeing how Smith's thinking evolved can allow one to take a more objective view of his mindset, especially when considering the intellectual climate of the time.

Smith's discussion of the division of labor seemed as if it might allow him to describe the economy with simple laws, without acknowledging the conflict between labor and capital, but on closer examination this approach was a dead end. For Smith, progress, fueled by the division of labor, comes from a master organizing passive workers into separate tasks.

Once the master has created the division of labor in the workshop, nothing more can be done because Smith ignored both technical change and increasing workers' potential (other than the acquisition of the necessary manual dexterity for the job). Smith's repeated denigrations of workers suggests that he probably agreed with Ferguson's judgment that the mechanical arts "require no capacity; they succeed best under a total suppression of sentiment and reason."

As a result, Smith suggested that progress was only possible by extending the market, which could allow a more refined division of labor. But then how would a market grow? Britain was rapidly increasing its markets by expanding its empire. Smith denied the value of this method of increasing the division of labor because it depended on the state rather than the market, invalidating his voluntaristic scheme. Instead, he presumed that each nation would choose to specialize—Britain in manufacturing and the colonies in raw material production.

Yet, according to Smith's theory, agriculture, unlike manufacturing, does not offer many opportunities for much of a division of labor. One might expect that colonies would be ill advised to specialize in raw materials. In fact, much of Britain's dispute with the North American colonies revolved around the mother country's efforts to force the colonists to accept Britain's monopoly in manufacturing.

Smith sidestepped this limitation of a division of labor approach by deftly shifting the role of production into the background, as the economy came to be pictured as a system of commercial transactions, which were measurable in terms of market prices. Accordingly, Smith altered his theory of value from one based on the labor used in production to a simple sum of the transactions involved in the payment of wages, profits, and rents.

Work, workers, and working conditions disappeared from view. At the same time, Smith was able to avoid any hint that the rise of modern industry demanded stronger and more repressive forms of control.

This transaction-based representation of the world homogenized people by recasting almost everybody—merchants, capitalists, or workers—as merchants, except those who existed with minimal transactions in the market. Smith's marginalized group included the aristocracy and those who directly worked, along with "churchmen, lawyers, physicians, men of letters of all kinds: players, buffoons, musicians, opera-singers, opera dancers, &c."[46] Smith classified such people as unproductive labor. After all, everyone is supposed to act as a merchant.

The following chapter will turn to the construction of the Gross Domestic Product (GDP). At first glance, this shift might seem abrupt, but, in reality, the GDP frames the economy just as Adam Smith did. Adding up commercial transactions—even imaginary transactions—while excluding work, workers, and working conditions.

CHAPTER EIGHT

Keeping Score

The Gross Domestic Product

The concept of the Gross Domestic Product might seem unrelated to Procrusteanism. However, in imitation of Procrusteanism, it emphasizes commercial values while ignoring a plethora of human costs and benefits, including work, workers, and working conditions.

An old adage suggests the relevance of this defect of the GDP: "What gets measured, gets managed." In other words, so long as the public accepts the GDP as a reasonable measure of economic performance, Procrustean policies can flourish with little or no concern for those things missing from it, such as work, workers, and working conditions.

The individualistic perspective of Adam Smith, as well as that of later economists, provided a convenient ideological framework for explaining the economy, but little useful policy guidance, except for people who dogmatically insist that nothing interfere with the function of markets. For the purpose of making policy, economists needed a measure of the wealth of nations, something Adam Smith never offered, despite the title of his book.

For centuries, economists had been groping for a measure that could give them a handle on the performance of the national economy. William Petty, writing in the seventeenth century, was trying to win favor from the king by promoting a war with France. To make his case, Petty suggested that victory would be easy because his data showed that Britain was more powerful than its rival. In the process, Petty pioneered in the calculation of national statistics.

Because governments did not publish any statistics, Petty had to resort to guesswork. His method of improvisation occasionally invited satire, including a rousing treatment by Jonathan Swift in his *Modest Proposal*, as well as in *Gulliver's Travels*. Guy Routh, a modern economist, humorously described Petty's crude methods:

> In comparing wealth of Holland and Zealand to that of France, he takes guesses by two other people, does not like the results and ends up with a guess of his own. He estimates the population of France from a book that says that it has 27,000 parishes and another book that says that it would be extraordinary if a parish had 600 people. So he supposes the average to be 500 and arrives at a population of 13 1/2 million. And so it goes.[1]

Despite his fanciful predictions and wild guesses, Sir William managed to set economics on the course it was to follow for the next three centuries. Although Petty's successors had a far superior statistical database with which to work, even as late as the First World War, economists still had to rely on guesses and vague estimates to gauge the size of the economy.[2] During the early part of the Great Depression, the Department of Commerce called upon Simon Kuznets to begin what became a decades-long effort to create a better measure of the economy. Kuznets was a meticulous researcher, who later won the Nobel Prize for his efforts. Kuznets's pioneering estimation of the national income eventually led to his work on the GDP (then called the Gross National Product), which followed the path laid out by Adam Smith—emphasizing exchange rather than production.

If we use exchange as the basis for our calculation, a tree has no value until it is sold for producing lumber. In addition, the fact that wealth and power are concentrated in the hands of a few is unimportant. And, questions of the quality of life are irrelevant. This last point is especially important as far as working conditions are concerned.

Kuznets clearly saw the limits of his work. In his first report to Congress in 1934, he publicly expressed his reservations about the national accounts that he helped to create. Data limitations made Kuznets construct his estimates from commercial transactions.[3] He wrote:

> The present study's measures of national income, like all such studies, estimates the value of commodities and direct services sector market prices. But market valuation of commodities, especially of direct services, depends upon the personal distribution of income within the nation. Thus in a nation with a rich upper-class, the personal services to the rich are likely to be valued at a much higher level than the very same services in another nation, characterized by a more equal personal distribution of income.[4]

As a result of limiting the measure to commercial transactions, work done within the household was not included in the calculations. A few later economists, discussed below, recognized this shortcoming, but none understood that any effort to estimate economic welfare would also have to take into account what goes on in the workplace. As Kuznets recognized:

> No income measurement undertakes to estimate the reverse side of your income, that is, the intensity and unpleasantness of effort going into the earning of income. The welfare of the nation can, therefore, scarcely be inferred from the measurement of national income as defined above.[5]

The Gross Domestic Product Goes to War

Because Kuznets wanted to create a more inclusive measure of economic well-being, he broke with the Department of Commerce. After the outbreak of the Second World War, the government called Kuznets back to service. The military was worried that it could undermine the war effort if it consumed too much, starving the domestic economy. In the words of one of Kuznets's former students: "To ask for too little was to prolong the conflict; to ask for too much was to inflate costs without producing significantly more."[6] With the stakes so high, Kuznets's reservations about the GDP as a measure of welfare had to be put aside for the moment.

Kuznets and a former student, Robert Nathan, rose to the challenge, showing that the military could siphon more from the domestic economy than the military command had estimated. Based on this analysis, the government ramped up military spending to nearly 45 percent of the GDP.

Unlike Petty, whose calculations the military did not seem to appreciate, Kuznets's work was held in high regard. John Kenneth Galbraith later told Nobel Laureate Robert Fogel that people in Washington commonly said that Kuznets and Nathan were the equal of several divisions of soldiers.[7] Given the war, the narrow purpose of the GDP was understandable. The goal was not to create a measure of welfare but to learn how much military spending the economy could bear.

Even during the war, however, Kuznets continued to acknowledge the limits of his project, warning, "Exclusion of the products of family economy, characteristic of virtually all national income estimates, seriously limits their validity as measures of all scarce and disposable goods produced by the nation."[8] His later *National Product in Wartime* was still more explicit in cautioning his readers that the methods developed for the wartime economy were inappropriate during times of peace:

> National product cannot be measured for the years of a major war as it is in peacetime because the customary long-run assumptions concerning the goals of economic activity are not basic. Is provision of goods to ultimate consumers in fact the sole purpose that guides and should be used to evaluate economic activity? When the very life of a social system is at stake the everyday purposes of economic activity are overshadowed. Yet

since from the longer-run viewpoint they are dominant, we retain the peacetime goal-provision of goods to consumers.[9]

Just as the authorities ignored Kuznets's recommendation that unpaid household labor be included, so too was his advice regarding the treatment of the military.

As the measurement of the GDP became more refined in later decades, Kuznets was celebrated as a pioneer in working with economic data. Unfortunately, his reservations about the statistic were largely forgotten.

For example, in their influential introductory economic textbook, Paul Samuelson and William Nordhaus confidently informed their students, "Without it [the GDP] macroeconomics would be adrift in a sea of unorganized data."[10] The problem is that the GDP still leaves economics adrift insofar as matters of work, workers, and working conditions are concerned, reinforcing the damage done by conventional economic theory.

The GDP doubly serves the business community, by reinforcing the illusory promise of market efficiency and supplying useful transactional information for business. In addition, putting a precise number on the GDP provides an undeserved scientific veneer to economics at the same time that it lends confirmation to the exclusion by economists of work, workers, and working conditions from consideration.

Married Maids

Because the GDP statistic is now available for a relatively long period of time, it is helpful in getting a feel for movements in commercial economic activity, especially during times when the economic structure is relatively stable. But as far as Kuznets's objective of creating a measure of well-being, the statistic falls short. Even if economists could perfectly measure the nation's GDP, welfare would depend upon its distribution. If the bulk of the economy belonged to a single individual and the rest of society lived in misery, an increasing GDP might simply improve welfare for that one fortunate individual.

The economists who work in generating this statistic have great professional expertise. However, many dimensions of economic performance are ignored. The distinguished economic historian Stanley Lebergott commented, perhaps only half facetiously:

> The arbitrary . . . definition of the national product . . . does not derive from any measurement of wealth or illth [a word that economists use for things that create bad effects]; nor is it limited to the production of goods or useful products. It measures merely the value of certain market transactions. . . . The baby has contributed more to the gaiety of nations than have all the nightclub comics in history. We include the comic in the labor force . . . as we include [his] wages in the national income but set no value on the endearing talents provided by the baby.[11]

Counting the joy that babies contribute might seem farfetched, but it reminds us that many non-commercial activities are vital. Of course, business would be delighted to commercialize them, which could increase profits, as well as the GDP.

Years before Kuznets began his work, Alfred Marshall's successor, Arthur Cecil Pigou, offered a famous example of how shifting the boundaries between commerce and direct social relations affects what would become the Gross National Product a couple of decades later. Pigou noted that a maid's activities properly belong in that measure because maids earn wages; however, if a man marries his maid, her now unpaid labor would disappear from the view of the economists, even though she continues to do the same work as before.[12] Introductory textbooks still use the paradox of the married maids.

What Else the Gross Domestic Product Ignores

Although the married maids would not have a noticeable effect on the GDP, housework would. In 1968, when the Gross National Product was $864 billion, one estimate of the market value of the goods and services produced in the U.S. households was $212 billion.[13] Such figures of household production are by necessity imprecise. For example, Robert Eisner estimated that the value of household production ranged from 20 to 50 percent of the measured Gross National Product.[14] Based on Canadian data, including the value of unpaid household work would increase the GDP from somewhere between 35 and 55 percent.[15] One factor that creates such wide divergence is the choice of the measure used. We could count what women might earn working for wages for an equivalent amount of time or, alternatively, the cost of hiring someone else to do the work—something comparable to the imaginary rent that homeowners pay to themselves.

As women have entered the labor force in large numbers and have taken jobs providing goods and services that they used to provide to their households themselves, the GDP rises, despite the fact that social welfare might not have changed and even might have declined. For example, if women work in restaurants or in plants manufacturing ready-to-microwave dinners instead of cooking meals at home, they would be functioning like the unmarried maids.

The share of women in the labor force is rapidly approaching that of men; by 2007–8, the husband was the sole worker in only 19.5 percent of married-couple families.[16] The surge of women into the labor force has created a substantial increase in commercial transactions,[17] increasing the GDP and creating the illusion of an enormous burst of economic activity.

Prior to the mass entry of women into paid labor, earlier data had suggested a long-term increase in the relative importance of unpaid housework. James Tobin and William Nordhaus estimated that the ratio of nonmarket to market consumption had increased by 14 percent between 1929 and 1965.[18] What explains this apparent trend?

Despite the labor-saving household appliances, household tasks have frequently become more complex. Budgeting and shopping are good examples.[19] Household work might also be becoming more demanding because of the stresses resulting from the Procrustean regimen.[20]

As we saw above, it is possible to estimate the value of work done within the household. However, several factors work against this. First and foremost, the purpose of the GDP statistic is to support the interests of the commercial sector, as opposed to those of the public at large. Like Lebergott's babies, household work contributes to the quality of life, but does not necessarily produce profits for business interests.

Business concerns itself with the growth of markets, not the quality of life. Because household work often substitutes for the potential purchase of commercial goods or services, it represents a barrier to the expansion of markets.

Obviously, work in the home is an important component of economic activity. Though the goods and services markets deliver count as evidence of their effectiveness, what people have to do to produce these goods and services does not enter into the evaluation of efficiency. Who does the work, how they do it, and what it does to them goes unnoticed in this statistic. Work only counts insofar as it shows up in a transaction on the labor market.

The GDP statistic suffers from other challenges. Calculating how the GDP evolves over time creates a difficult challenge. To do so requires that we compare the same product at different dates, even when the nature of the product is rapidly changing. Today we use CD or MP3 players and not records. If a record and a CD have the same price, has GDP remained unchanged? If the CD is cheaper than the record, has the GDP declined? The statisticians have to estimate the contribution of new products to the economy. To do so, they must disentangle the many qualities of the new version of the good from its price. This calculation is a matter of judgment, not science.

Even without considerations of technical change, questions of quality complicate the calculation. Most people would agree that a dinner at an expensive restaurant with excellent service represents a greater contribution to welfare than a meal from a drive-through fast-food restaurant. This difference would hold even if the quality of the food were comparable at both establishments.

Yet in other kinds of retail commerce, no account is taken of lower-quality service. Instead, government statisticians treat a lower price at a big box store as an unalloyed benefit for consumers, despite the fact that the poorer quality might accompany the lower price. Deteriorating service is more common than economists concede, for example, the endless phone mazes that now await a consumer who needs to contact a company for service and the lack of help for a shopper in a big box store.

Equally difficult challenges stand in the way of any attempt to compare the GDPs of different countries. In one country wages might be lower, but workers might have excellent public housing, convenient public transportation, and national health care. Accounting for such differences in national economies is virtually impossible.

Inadequate reporting also contaminates measurement of the GDP. Unreported cash transactions escape calculation. Massive tax avoidance distorts the data. For example, multinational corporations can reduce their reported domestic profits by inflating the costs of inputs from their foreign affiliates and deflating the revenue from their exports. Suppose a U.S. company produces a car made only from domestically produced components, with the exception of an imported steering wheel. To reduce taxes, the company claims the steering wheel cost $1,000 more than its actual price. Because of this deception, contribution of this car to the GDP will be $1,000 less than it would be with honest accounting.

The GDP assumes that all commercial activities serve people's needs, making no distinction between commercial transactions that add to well-being and those that diminish it, as would be the case with tainted food. In terms of evaluating well-being, merely summing up commercial transactions is not particularly informative.

Here we see the influence of economic theory on how we regard our lives. Underlying the calculations of the GDP is the assumption that people are informed consumers who purchase the commodities that will give them the most satisfaction (utility). That assumption may not be true. For instance, pharmaceutical companies sometimes market medicines successfully, despite dangerous side effects, even when generic products, which are both cheap and safe, are available. The purchase of the generic medicine would lower the GDP.

Besides uninformed or irrational purchases, the GDP includes indirect purchases that consumers unintentionally make. Thr GDP also includes unnecessary packaging, while ignoring the inconvenience of plowing through layers of plastic to finally arrive at the purchased commodity. Also, corporations spend billions of dollars on advertising to make people buy things they otherwise would not. Advertising expenses then become part of the cost of the goods, which are then counted into the GDP. Parenthetically, although the alleged objective of the economy is to maximize utility, much of advertising is designed to create dissatisfaction with one's existing possessions, thereby annihilating utility.

Finally, people rationally make some purchases because they must do so as a requirement for their work. They must purchase specific attire for their workplace they might not otherwise wear, such as a necktie. Some companies permit people to dress casually on Fridays, allowing employees to demonstrate the disutility of neckties.

In the case of this undesired clothing, the expense represents a cost rather than a benefit. Other workers must partake in activities not of their own choosing to further their careers. Some workers even undergo plastic surgery for that purpose, again adding to the GDP.

Take this logic a step further. Suppose a person purchases a car just to commute many miles to work. Unlike a vacation or an addition to a house, this car has no attraction for its owner except as a means of commuting to work. Surveys indicate that people regard commuting as the least pleasant activity of the day.

Imagine, however, that our commuter has purchased some special touches that make the commute more bearable, for example, a top-of-the-line stereo system. Theoretically, the stereo belongs in the GDP, although the rest of the car may not belong in a statistic intended to measure welfare.

Even without the challenge of the stereo adjustment, the car raises a host of other measurement problems. What about the extent to which the car creates pollution or congestion or contributes to global warming? Economists refer to such matters as externalities, meaning that they remain external to the price system—and therefore invisible as far as the GDP is concerned.

What about traffic accidents that the commute might cause? In this case, the GDP will benefit. The work done in the body shop or the hospital will appear as an increase in the GDP.

Finally, the measurement of the GDP is more difficult than when Kuznets began his work. Then, the economy consisted largely of tangible products, such as machines, food, and housing. In the contemporary world, much of the economy is subjective. For example, intellectual property—a subject rarely considered in Kuznets's era—has major economic effects, even though it cannot be measured. Accounting gimmicks and fictions and indirect measurements must be used to account for such things.

Yet, despite all this, economists and the business press often take the GDP as the agreed-upon measure of overall economic performance, although the even less informative Dow Jones average is reported more often.

Alternatives to the Gross Domestic Product

In recent years, a few economists have attempted to remedy some of the deficiencies of the GDP. Tobin and Nordhaus proposed in a 1972 study that the value of leisure and household work be included in the GDP, while some costs, such as commuting, be deducted. In 1988, Robert Eisner also made valuable suggestions about an improved system of accounts.[21] His most incisive comments concerned the proper measurement of capital and investment. Anwar Shaikh and Ertugrul Ahmet Tonak reviewed some other efforts to refine the system of national accounts and then attempted to develop a calculation using insights from Marxist economics.[22] Their measure purposely avoided the inclusion of "non-economic" activities, such as those carried out within the household.

More recently, a small think tank, Redefining Progress, has worked to create a more comprehensive measure called the Genuine Progress Indicator. The Genuine Progress Indicator includes many activities that the GDP neglects, such as housework and volunteer work, while excluding many expenses that do not add to social welfare. This calculation also attempts to take into account the depreciation of natural resources.

The Genuine Progress Indicator calculations reported that the $11 trillion GDP of the time overestimated social welfare by $7 trillion.[23] Without debating the fine points of the Genuine Progress Indicator, the disparity between its $4 trillion estimate and the $11 trillion GDP demonstrates the subjectivity of any statistical formula for estimating human welfare.

Remarkably, in China, where the environmental costs of the economy are obvious, the government calculates a parallel GDP number that deducts the effects of depletion and pollution, resulting in a 3 percent lower rate of growth.[24] A 3 percent rate of growth is sufficient to double the size of the economy in less than twenty-five years.

By the 1960s and 1970s, the shortcomings of the GDP as a proxy for well-being were becoming especially obvious to economists who were studying the more impoverished regions of the world. Experts explored a number of alternatives that emphasized more direct measures of welfare, such as infant mortality and nutrition, rather than solely counting commercial activity.

Despite commendable efforts to make the calculation of the GDP more inclusive, one important factor has completely fallen from view: the conditions under which people work. Tobin and Nordhaus correctly included leisure in their calculations, but no economists have considered working conditions.

This oversight might make sense so long as the GDP is understood as just a measure of commercial activity. But the neglect of working conditions is unforgivable whenever people use the GDP as an indicator of social well-being. People devote a good part of their existence to work, especially if we include the long commutes that are a major part of the normal working day for millions of workers. Working conditions affect not only the quality of life for workers, but that of their families and friends.

An Alternative Approach: Eudaimonia

An earlier European tradition understood economics to be a much broader subject. This more expansive understanding of economics followed Aristotle, who regarded *eudaimonia,* often translated as "human flourishing," as the highest objective of society, although such flourishing was to be the exclusive domain of those who were not intended to be ruled by others. The leaders of this European tradition enjoyed a classical education, the foundation for traditional intellectual training in Europe.[25]

Alongside this Aristotelian school of economics, a small group of French intellectuals, known as the Physiocrats, embarked on a course that largely anticipated the work of their younger contemporary, Adam Smith. Not surprisingly, the Anglo-Saxon economists who followed Smith tended to identify continental economics with the Physiocrats, while ignoring the Aristotelian approach.

Although the European tradition continued, especially in Germany and Italy, the Anglo-Saxon approach gained more and more influence in Europe. The influence of the United States, which had been a relative backwater in terms of economic theory before the First World War, grew along with the power of the postwar U.S. economy. Then, beginning in the 1920s, the Rockefeller Foundation began giving fellowships to young European social scientists. Economists and statisticians represented more than 35 percent of the researchers whose total grants between 1924 and 1934 came to more than $2 million.[26] Soon thereafter, a massive exodus of economists from Europe increased the prestige of U.S. economics.

The English economists had good reason to reject Aristotle, who denigrated commercial relations. An anonymous writer published a pamphlet in 1686, "The Character and Qualifications of an Honest Loyal Merchant." The thrust of this work was that a merchant's activities created prosperity and culture in the kingdom, despite "whatever low conceits Aristotle or some other pedants may have had of merchandize in old times, when its dignity was not known, and when it was but huckstering and pedlary."[27]

Although many European economists acknowledged that the British approach was more like a science, for a long time the continental economists refused to follow the British project of creating an economic theory that could emulate science. They realized that to do so would mean losing sight of too many important aspects of life. Luigino Bruni quotes both an Italian and a French author from 1829 and 1837 who explained their reluctance to adopt the British style. He then summarized their stance:

> Therefore, these two authors agree in acknowledging that the English school was more scientific, but this target has been obtained thanks to the elimination of important dimensions from the field of political economy, such as the relationships between wealth and ethics, wealth and happiness.[28]

This Anglo-Saxon/European split also surfaced outside of economic theory. For example, about the same time that Taylor was about to begin his famous efforts to control the labor process, France and Germany became the center of a much broader study of the science of work. In Europe, where the Aristotelian tradition had taken hold, "the science of work was based on the premise that greater productivity would lead to social happiness—and not, as in the American, import Taylorism, or later Fordism, on the view that unhappiness had to be compensated through external, non-work-related material rewards."[29] In other words, the Europeans thought that a better understanding of work could improve everybody's lot, even that of the workers.

At times the European approach to the science of work actually had positive effects in the workplace. For example, "In Germany on the eve of the First World War, railway maintenance shops provided couches for older workers to rest on, while Ford and General Motors were firing workers for sitting or even leaning against a machine when not working."[30]

An American student of working class life recalled similar differences between working conditions in Germany and the United States:

> When I was in Germany, Professor Roscher of Leipzig, told me of German workmen who, after living in America, returned to Germany, preferring

the long hours and low wages there rather than stand the strain at which they were required to work in America. When in Chicago, I found that some American workmen sympathized with this view. At the carpenters' union headquarters, when I spoke warmly of the union victory in securing the eight hours' day, I was surprised to have one of the carpenters remark, "Yes; but if we won seven hours, half of us would be dead."[31]

Partially because economists lost sight of working conditions, what really makes an economy productive largely fell from view.

Measuring Eudaimonia

As the British tradition of political economy displaced the older European tradition, virtually all traces of eudaimonia disappeared from economics—at least until recently. Even so, you can still find remnants of the Aristotelian worldview in Smith and some later economists, but these traces of eudaimonia fall outside of the core of their writings, or at least what their followers took to be the core.

Recently, Nobel Laureate Amartya Sen took what seemed to be a novel approach to understanding economic measurements of human welfare. He showed how the GDP was uncorrelated with more direct measures of human welfare, such as life expectancy and child mortality. To make his point, Sen juxtaposed pairings of countries or regions in which the quality of life in supposedly poorer areas substantially exceeded that of their wealthier counterparts. For example, he observed:

Countries such as Sri Lanka, pre-reform China, Costa Rica, or the Indian state of Kerala . . . have had very rapid reductions in mortality rates, without much economic growth. This is a process that does not wait for dramatic increases in per-capita levels of real income, and it works through priority being given to providing social services (particularly health care and basic education) that reduce mortality and enhance the quality of life.[32]

Sen proposed a different dimension, what he called capabilities, as the real measure of human welfare. Sen's capabilities defy easy definition. His explanations were necessarily vague, yet they pointed in an important direction that conventional economics overlooks. In his words, "Capability is . . . a kind of freedom: the substantive freedom to achieve alternative functioning combinations or, less formally put, the freedom to achieve various lifestyles."[33]

One study described Sen's approach more succinctly: "The focus . . . is on what people can do or become, not what they have."[34] In any case, for Sen, material goods were not an end in themselves, but rather a means to enhance capabilities. In conclusion, Sen is absolutely correct that the GDP is a poor indicator of society's success in developing capabilities.

Sen's approach seemed novel—at least within the Anglo-Saxon tradition of economics—but certainly not to those familiar with the literature concerning eudaimonia. Sen was ideally positioned to bring eudaimonia back into the conversation. Besides being an accomplished Cambridge economist, he had already devoted considerable attention to philosophy, a subject with little appeal for most economists. In addition, Sen enjoyed a classical Indian education. With the advantage of his broad background, he was able to see what should have been obvious—that traditionally measured economic growth is not the only way to improve the quality of life.

Drawing on the Physical Quality of Life Index proposed by economists David Morris and James Grant of the Overseas Development Council, a classmate of Sen's at Cambridge, Mahbub ul Haq, developed the United Nations' Human Development Index. The design of this index was intended to capture some of the elements of human welfare missing from the GDP. Although the World Bank publishes its World Development Indicators, it also ranks countries by their per capita GDP. In addition, the World Bank still retains the GDP as part of the calculation of its Human Development Index.

Signs of concern about eudaimonia are starting to pop up elsewhere. The tiny mountain kingdom of Bhutan, nestled between India and China, has embarked on the most ambitious study of all, attempting to develop its measure of the Gross National Happiness. The fruits of this project will not appeal to many conventional economists, especially since nobody has yet dared to quantify this objective.[35]

More troubling for Bhutan's efforts to improve its Gross National Happiness, the country has recently introduced television, which seems to have released a plague of anti-social behavior associated with efforts to achieve a more Western version of happiness.[36]

The idea that people are now considering how the organization of the economy contributes to or detracts from happiness is certainly a worthy project, especially in comparison to some of the arid economics that passes for important scholarship today. Although the efforts of Bhutan may lack what modern economists would consider scientific scholarship, they might remind the larger world about the disconnect between the conventional GDP and the quality of life—in effect, telling the world that the Patten perspective of working hard just to obtain more consumer goods is not rational.

The Politics of the Gross Domestic Product

The United States ranks relatively high according to the Human Development Index, but not nearly as high as one might expect. According to the 2004 Index, Norway ranked number one, followed by Sweden, Australia, Canada, the Netherlands, Belgium, and Iceland. The United States ranked a modest eighth.[37]

At a press conference following the publication of the World Bank's 2001 edition of *World Development Indicators* on April 30, 2001, a questioner asked James Wolfensohn, then president of the bank:

> One thing that struck me was that out of all of the countries, there was one particular country that shone in all indicators: education, health, social spending, and that country happens to be Cuba, and it's the only country that does not take advice from the World Bank and IMF. . . . Do you stand by those statistics, and if so, what is the reason for Cuba being so outstanding?

MR. WOLFENSOHN: Well, we don't cook the statistics, and we put them out so that you can read them. I think Cuba has done—and everybody would acknowledge—a great job on education and health. And if you judge the country by education and health, they've done a terrific job. So I have no hesitation in acknowledging that they've done a good job, and it doesn't embarrass me to do it. It wasn't with our advice, but it wasn't without our advice either. I mean, we just have nothing to do with them in the present sense, and they should be congratulated on what they've done.[38]

But the World Bank had indeed cooked the statistics. Earlier, both the Reagan and Bush administrations had applied pressure to modify the index to include not just literacy as a measure of educational success but also to add years of schooling as a component. This modification improved the standing of the United States and slightly lowered Cuba's. Even so, Cuba's ranking still remained quite high.

The Cuban incident serves as a warning that efforts to improve upon the conventional GDP can raise sensitive issues. Breaking through the illusion of the GDP could help to set society on a path of creating an economy that works for people.

The Economics of Happiness

Most people would expect that an increase in a society's income would bring about a corresponding increase in happiness, but such is not the case. Instead, students of the subject have learned that "once a country has over $15,000 per head, its level of happiness appears to be independent of its income per head."[39] Basically, once a growing economy has passed through the $15,000 threshold, the standards by which its people measure their condition also increase. Germans and Nigerians seem to be equally happy. A similar equality holds for Cubans and Americans, although the United States government might want to call for a revision of that calculation.[40] What explains why increasing prosperity does not bring about happiness? For the typical individual, economic success does seem to provide happiness. At least, the more income that individuals have relative to others, the happier they are. H. L. Mencken once summed up this phenomenon by defining wealth as "any income that is at least $100 more a year than the income of one's wife's sister's husband."[41]

However, if everybody's income increases proportionately, nobody becomes happier. As Gore Vidal is reputed to have said, "It is not enough to succeed; others must fail."

German happiness does not exceed that of Nigeria because Germans have higher material expectations than Nigerians do. These expectations rapidly shift as people experience a higher standard of living. Although people in Germany might be getting more material goods, they might not feel much happier so long as they are not doing any better than their friends and neighbors.

Economic growth can shuffle the rankings of monetary success within a community, but for each person who moves up the ladder, someone else moves down. Individuals that ascend may be happier, but those who lose ground in their ranking will be less happy. Such a shuffle in the rankings can lower happiness because downward shifts in expectations are sluggish, and upward shifts are rapid.

For example, if the German standard of living fell to a Nigerian level, Germans would not be indifferent. Similarly, if the Nigerians were brought up to a German standard and then fell back to their earlier level, their happiness would also fall well below where it stands today.

As a result, people's subjective interpretation of prosperity becomes an ever-receding goal. For example, in 1986 the Roper polling organization asked Americans how much income they would need to fulfill all their dreams. The answer was $50,000. By 1994 the "dreams-fulfilling" level of income had doubled from $50,000 to $102,000.[42] After his years on a desert island, Robinson Crusoe understood the basic problem:

> It put me to reflecting, how little repining there would be among mankind, at any condition of life, if people would rather compare their condition with those

that are worse, in order to be thankful, than be always comparing them with those which are better, to assist their murmurings and complainings.[43]

Unfortunately, real people rarely share Crusoe's insight. Instead, people experience what psychologists call the hedonic treadmill, although a hamster wheel might be a better metaphor. The more people get, the more they want. As a result, the extra happiness, which is supposed to be the reward for hard work and success, will continue to prove elusive.

In effect, then, the whole Procrustean game is a ruse. People are expected to keep their nose to the grindstone, because, as Simon Patten explained, the payoff comes in the form of consumption, which provides utility, which, in turn, translates into happiness.

Adam Smith recognized the problem with the Patten perspective a quarter millennium ago, when he disparaged consumptionism as a "deception which rouses and keeps in continual motion the industry of mankind." Smith, however, proposed that the hard work required to increase consumption would create better, if not happier people. In fact, if people actually did become happy, the obsessive need for more consumption would diminish and the GDP would suffer.

In recent years, a number of established economists have begun to explore the subject of happiness. For example, between 1991 and 1995, EconLit, a bibliographic service for economics, reported only four papers analyzing data on self-reported life satisfaction or happiness. A decade later, from 2001 to 2005, that number had risen to more than one hundred. [44]

Daniel Kahneman, Princeton psychologist and Nobel Laureate in Economics, along with Alan Krueger, currently Assistant Secretary of the Treasury for economic policy, and two other colleagues proposed to create "National Well-Being Accounts."[45] Detailed surveys asking people to report on their satisfaction with specific aspects of their life, such as work, are central to their approach.

This work of Kahneman and his colleagues is intended as a complement to the estimation of the GDP rather than a replacement. Such calculations do not pretend to measure the output of the econ-

omy. Nor do they attempt to take account of environmental degradation, as some of the modifications of the GDP propose to do.
Instead, the survey approach directly tries to ascertain a subjective
measure of happiness.

Not surprisingly, these surveys find that activities that are
non-economic, such as intimate relations, socializing after work, dinner, relaxing, lunch, and exercising, ranked highest in terms of satisfaction. Equally unsurprising, the activities that ranked lowest were
the evening commute, working, and the morning commute.[46]This
last result helps to put the above-mentioned surveys of job satisfaction in context.

Such survey results also suggest that economists may have been
wise to have avoided any analysis of happiness or working conditions
for so long. Traveling along this road inevitably devastates the benev-
olent pretenses of Procrusteanism. The long hours of work and the
long commutes are preventing the creation of the kind of human communities that make for a better life. At the same time, happiness
research undermines economists' scientific pretenses.

One dimension of a society's capacity to improve people's capabilities, or even happiness, would have to be the complex network of
social relations that provides a healthy framework for human existence. Class distinctions that consign the majority of the population to
the degradations common among the lower orders of society prevent
the full development of social relations for a large body of people. But
economics is predicated on treating people as isolated individuals
making their own decisions to maximize their welfare.

Of course, you can define economic statistics any number of ways
for any number of purposes, but the popular use of the GDP with its
narrow emphasis on commercial activities distracts people from the
real issues that enrich life. Since the GDP is wholly inadequate as a
measure of human welfare, as Sen brilliantly demonstrated, why do
economists still take this statistic so seriously? The reason is not hard
to fathom. Economists generally learn to see the world through the
eyes of the marketplace. Since economic growth is taken to mean an
increase in commercial transactions, it must be good.

Concluding Remark

Under the cover of a growing GDP, the unshakeable Procrustean ideology of economics confidently insists that market forces alone will ensure the maximum benefit for society, and that one need only worry about ignorant meddlers who might attempt to interfere with the magic of the marketplace. The evidence for this belief consists mostly of dense mathematical theorems based on unrealistic assumptions and elaborate statistical analyses, backed up by distorted measures of economic success.

However, the GDP is a seriously flawed measure that obscures the nature of Procrusteanism by sweeping workers, working conditions, and the promised happiness from more work under a great statistical rug. The GDP ignores everything, other than formal education, that expands human capabilities, including that which can allow people to develop their productive potential. In short, the GDP helps to obscure that self-actualization is a major source of productivity as well as happiness.

Even worse, the general acceptance of the GDP as a measure of economic success focuses policy on Procrustean measures, while turning attention from the need to build a better society.

Within this perspective, the recent interest in the economics of happiness is a welcome development, especially if it forces people to look more deeply into the root causes of unhappiness—a class-ridden society that makes a healthy sense of community all but impossible.

The next chapter will explore the destructiveness of Procrusteanism in more detail.

CHAPTER NINE

The Destructive Nature of Procrusteanism

Social Relations of Work

One of Karl Marx's deepest insights was to understand that capital is a social relation and not just a thing. People who are unfamiliar with Marx's analysis may be perplexed by the idea that capital is a social relationship, that a factory is not merely a building populated with various machines but also a reflection of the relationship between those who own the factory and those who work in it. People who study the evolution of technology, however, understand how social relations shape technology.

David Noble provided one of the most in-depth analyses of the interplay between technology and the social relationship between employers and workers in his outstanding history of the development of computer numerically controlled machine tools at General Electric. The chief purpose of this new technology was to wrest control of the shop from the skilled workers who had accumulated vast reservoirs of expertise.[1]

Traditionally, skilled machinists would first operate their equipment manually while shaping a piece of metal. Employers hated the power that the machinists' knowledge gave them and tried repeatedly to break it. Frederick Taylor's first job was in a machine shop, and after he became foreman, he tried to use his system of time and motion studies to wrest control away from the workers. The work the machinists did, however, was too complex and the men too strongly organized, and he was unable to do this. After the Second World War, however, scientific developments begun in the military gave employers the means to finally achieve control over their workplaces. Two possibilities presented themselves. In one process, monitoring machines would record the workers' moves and then a playback device allowed the machine to automatically repeat the same procedure on new materials, as long as desired. In a second scheme, instead of reliance on the machinists' skills for setting the machine's pattern, the responsibility shifted to software programmers, divorced from the shop floor, who programmed the complex removal of metal to form a part that marks the machinists' craft onto a tape that could then be attached to the machine, which would than automatically do what the worker had previously done.

General Electric believed that "the innate properties of the new material technology would themselves guarantee increased production of high-quality engine parts."[2] But turning these highly skilled workers into mere "button pushers" proved far more difficult than the company had imagined. The new equipment required skilled intervention.

The company's openly confrontational approach proved counterproductive. Without the workers' cooperation, the company's experiment proved to be a disaster. General Electric had no chance of eliminating the inevitable bugs in an entirely new system without the cooperation of workers.

After a prolonged period of turmoil and lowered productivity, General Electric finally realized its dependence on workers' expertise. Rather than openly acknowledging this dependence, the company resorted to subterfuge. Management pretended to bow to the workers' demands by changing course and giving them more or less free control of much of the shop floor. Meanwhile, the company paid close attention to what the workers did to learn how to make their skills expendable.

In the end, General Electric was correct in believing that numerically controlled machines had a future, even though the company's antagonistic stance toward labor made the transition costly. However, the eventual higher productivity of numerically controlled machines was secondary; the driving force behind the introduction of this technology was to gain advantages over the workers.

In a rational society, such efforts would be unnecessary. Everybody would have a stake in developing more efficient technology, since all could share in its benefits. The capture of workers' knowledge has a long history, dating back at least as far as William Petty's History of the Trades Project. Petty was in some respects more advanced than the management of General Electric because he understood that knowledge creation was a collective activity.

Not surprisingly, Charles Babbage offered one of the more sophisticated analyses of knowledge capture. Note that, as a prisoner of his time and class, Babbage blamed workers' failure to share their information on their "erroneous" distrust of capital:

> A most erroneous and unfortunate opinion prevails amongst workmen in many manufacturing countries, that their own interest and that of their employers are at variance. The consequences are,— that valuable machinery is sometimes neglected, and even privately injured,— that new improvements, introduced by the master, not receive a fair trial,— and that the talents and observations of the workmen are not directed to the improvement of the processes in which they are employed. [3]

Babbage got things backwards. A more cooperative system of social relations—one not based on class—could offer a better quality of life for employers as well as workers. Class division is so destructive that even the winners turn out to be losers.

Bureaucratic Control

Bureaucracy is one of the chief organs of Procrusteanism. The scale of bureaucratic control has grown alongside the rapidly expanding scope of the giant corporation.

Just compare Alfred Marshall's description of the early firm with the state of the contemporary mega-corporation. In the early twentieth century, Marshall was witnessing the end of an age in which business owners could still have a detailed command of their operations. In Marshall's words:

> The master's eye is everywhere; there is no shirking by his foremen or work-men, no divided responsibility, no sending half-understood messages.[4]

In Stephen Hymer's more forceful expression, by the mid-twentieth century, the employer during the early stages of capitalism ideally "saw everything, knew everything, and decided. . . . everything." But then, Marshall's employer had relatively little to know compared with the expanded span of a modern corporation, which employs many thousands of workers serving markets around the world. As Hymer put the matter:

> The Marshallian capitalist ruled his factory from an office on the second floor. At the turn of the century, the president of a large national corporation was lodged in a higher building, perhaps on the seventh floor, with greater perspective and power. In today's giant corporation, managers rule from the top of skyscrapers; on a clear day, they can almost see the world.[5]

In reality, their vision is largely filtered through abstract account sheets rather than the actual functioning of the world. An excessive layering of bureaucracy clouds their vision even further. For example, by the 1980s, Ford had built twelve layers of organization between the factory floor and the chairman's office. Any child who has played the game of telephone could predict the quality of the resulting communication.

General Motors was no better. John DeLorean, head of the Chevrolet division and known as a flamboyant and innovative executive at General Motors until he got involved in a drug deal to finance his floundering automobile company, reported a similar organizational maze. A plant manager had to go through five layers of management to reach DeLorean's office. A worker on the shop floor did not have immediate access to the plant manager, and DeLorean himself probably had to jump through a few hoops before he could see the chairman.[6]

Although DeLorean attempted to reduce the number of layers within Chevrolet, he was dismayed by the increasing centralization of the company:

> As I progressed in the corporation, I watched GM's operations slowly become centralized. The divisions were stripped of their decision-making power. Operations were more and more being made on The Fourteenth Floor.[7]

In 2007, almost thirty-five years after DeLorean left General Motors, the automobile industry had still not improved its channels of communication. Here is how *Business Week* described the organizational structure at Ford:

> In the royal hierarchy at Ford, an elaborate system of employment grades clearly established an employee's rank in the pecking order. The grades also had the unintentional effect of quashing ideas and keeping information tightly controlled. When [Mark] Fields, now president of Ford Americas, first arrived at the company from IBM in 1989, he couldn't make a lunch date with an executive who held a higher grade. People asked him what his grade was "as a condition of including me or socializing with me," Fields recalls. And he was discouraged from airing problems at meetings unless his boss approved first.
>
> Ford . . . is today: a balkanized mess. It has four parallel operating units worldwide, each with its own costly bureaucracy, factories, and product development staff. . . . Examples of Ford losing opportunities

because of its byzantine corporate structure abound. A recent example involves Sync, a system that allows voice-command control of a cell phone and MP3 player. It was a big success at last January's North American International Auto Show. Ford developed it with Microsoft Corp. last year and will start rolling it out this fall. Although Volvo and Land Rover are also dying to offer Sync, neither will get the system because the electrical architectures of the Swedish and British cars are incompatible with Ford's.[8]

Even as the major U.S. automobile companies stumbled into bankruptcy, little changed. Steven Rattner, the financier the government charged with overseeing the bailout of General Motors, reported:

> The cultural deficiencies were . . . stunning. At GM's Renaissance Center headquarters, the top brass were sequestered on the uppermost floor, behind locked and guarded glass doors. Executives housed on that floor had elevator cards that allowed them to descend to their private garage without stopping at any of the intervening floors (no mixing with the drones).[9]

Despite the inhospitable climate for communication, poor design, outsized executive salaries, and outrageous fuel consumption, blame for the dire straits of the U.S. automobile corporations fell largely on workers. How dare they demand decent wages, pensions, and medical care!

In a sense, labor might bear some responsibility for the decline of the automobile industry. Had the United Automobile Workers not agreed to the Treaty of Detroit and demanded more control on the shop floor, the automobile industry might have turned out to be much healthier.

The problem of bureaucratic control is not limited to the automobile industry. More than fifteen years ago, in a moment of Cold War triumphalism, Peter Huber compared the corporate command structure of U.S. megacorporations with the overthrown planning system of the Soviet Union:

As market forces and the rise of the information age ultimately forced the unbundling of the Soviet Union, so they are forcing America's largest economic organizations to break up into more efficient pieces. If you've grown accustomed to a sheltered life inside a really large corporation, take pity on the unemployed apparatchiks at the Kremlin. The next Kremlin to fall may be our own.[10]

Huber was correct to predict change, but its direction was not what he expected. The U.S. Kremlin is more powerful than ever. While many corporations spun off or shut down divisions, the trend in the concentration of the corporate sector continued unabated. Huber is still correct that the byzantine management structure remains a certain recipe for failure.

Financial Control

By the time Huber was writing, the locus of corporate control was shifting from the CEO's office to Wall Street and owners of private equity funds. The power exercised by outside financial interests has further insulated the decision makers at the top from the people who are doing the work on the ground. Adding this new layer of control on top of an already dysfunctional bureaucratic control makes disaster even more certain.

Like bureaucratic control, financial control takes a top-down view of the world. The masses of workers at the bottom of the hierarchy exist almost as pure abstractions, except to the extent that wages cut into profits. Yet, in a sense, financial and bureaucratic controls are polar opposites. Bureaucracies tend to be lethargic, wedded to past procedures. In contrast, finance moves with lightning speed. In the world of finance, the past means nothing compared to a chance to turn a quick profit.

With the rise of financial control, the stock market has become the crucial arbiter of corporate management. Financial markets use the current stock price as indicators of success. Because money can exit industry in seconds, management cannot afford to let stock prices sag, even for a relatively short period. In addition, CEO compensation largely depends upon stock prices.

Hedge funds, pension funds, and a handful of extremely wealthy shareholders make strong demands on corporate leadership, removing CEOs who do not meet their expectations of financial success. Corporate executives cannot appear to resist these expectations, even when these are unreasonable.

Even more directly, financial organizations take over firms under the pretext that they can "add value" by reorganizing the business. Generally, the objective is to repackage the company in order to sell it to unsuspecting investors, but only after charging large fees and loading the company with so much debt that it is vulnerable to failure. All too often when companies find themselves in this position, they try to save themselves by squeezing more out of their workers in terms of wages, workload, and safety.

Corporate executives were once insulated from such pressure. But by the late twentieth century, the stock market became a prime concern for CEOs. According to a former U.S. Treasury secretary, "It is not uncommon for the chief executive officers of major U.S. corporations to spend a week or more each quarter telling their corporate story to security analysts."[11] The analysts' predictions of quarterly earnings reports are a major determinant of stock prices, and stock prices determine the fate of the CEOs. CEOs who can hold on to their positions by satisfying the financial markets can command more money, while protecting their managerial reputations.

Given the pressing financial imperatives, management must focus on the next quarterly earnings target, rather than measures that would make the company more productive in the long run. As a result, financial pressure often makes business reluctant to put money into expensive investments in physical capital or training workers, which could increase future productivity.

Even companies not directly under siege by financial interests often behave more like a financial than an industrial operation. For example, in July 2007, Exxon reported the fourth-largest quarterly earnings that any corporation has ever earned—$10.26 billion. One might have expected that such enormous profits would be a cause for celebration. However, because this amount was slightly lower than the $10.26 billion for the second quarter of 2006, Wall Street pummeled Exxon's shares, knocking them down 4.9 percent. To please shareholders, Exxon had been spending more on buying back its stock than on capital expenditures.[12]

Finance represents another threat to the economy. Just as Procrusteanism makes real handcuffs become invisible, it makes imaginary wealth seem real. Once the recent economic meltdown began, trillions of dollars of wealth seemed to disappear overnight. People had invested in houses and securities under the illusion that their wealth was growing, even though the market values were to a great extent imaginary. Had people paid more attention to the real productive wealth-producing activities that form the foundation of any economy, they might have been more skeptical about the prospects of those investments. Here again, the efforts of economists to render work and workers invisible contributed to the disastrous aftermath of the bursting of the bubble.

The Toxic Mix of Bureaucracy and Finance

When financial interests demand immediate increases in profits, corporations can mislead investors by manipulating their earnings reports, but sooner or later this deception will be uncovered. In the short run, management might be able to improve stock prices by currying favor with financial markets, convincing security analysts that their stock deserves a high price. Eventually, however, management has to create real profits. In any case, the efforts to inform or mislead investors or stock analysts will be a waste of time that might have been spent on something productive.

In its effort to jump-start improvements in profits, business also suffers the consequences of clumsy bureaucratic structures. Those at the top of such structures can have no real idea of what happens on the ground floor. As financial pressures began to grow in the early 1980s, flattening the command structure became a popular managerial mantra, but flattening did not mean a shrinking of the distance between top management and the bulk of the workforce. Instead, layers of middle management disappeared, while the central office imposed goals and quotas on lower-level managers without real knowledge about feasibility.

Regardless of such structural changes, corporations eventually resort to a meat ax approach as a quick fix to improving profits. In one egregious example, Circuit City dismissed 3,400 people, about 8 percent of its workforce, in April 2007, not because they were doing a bad job and not because the company was eliminating their positions. Instead, executives said the workers (who earned $10 to $20 an hour)were being paid too much and that the company would replace them with new employees who would earn less. It was the second such layoff at Circuit City in the last five years, and it offered an unusually clear window on the ruthlessness of corporate efficiency.[13]

Two years later, Circuit City declared bankruptcy.

Although few companies are as clumsy as Circuit City, ultimately, when faced with often impossible demands, CEOs have few options, except to pass the responsibility on to their subordinates, who then must put pressure on still lower-level employees to meet the looming financial expectations.

One common practice is to create some method to rank the workers and even entire divisions according to a quota, then to eliminate those with a low rank. CEOs proudly announce to the investment community that they are energetically clearing out the deadwood from their corporations, generally unconcerned with the long-term consequences of their actions.

Management by numbers ignores both human costs and the destruction of human potential. Arbitrary quotas might be effective in imposing a superficial focus on corporate goals, but they create counterproductive stress. Even worse, they encourage people to develop strategies to maximize their own position rather than contribute to the business. They also stifle the fostering of creativity and innovation.

Work such as research and development, which does not produce immediate profits but is important for the future survival of the firm, becomes vulnerable.

Finally, managers under intense pressure cut corners to ensure that they make their quotas. They may neglect safety in an effort to avoid falling behind, or they may force people to work uncompensated overtime.

Management by numbers prevents communication between those who sit at the peak of the bureaucracy and those who bear the everyday responsibility, with the ultimate burden falling on the workers, who have virtually no opportunity for redress or to explain how to achieve corporate goals without creating as much hardship for them.

At the same time that giant corporations have attempted to flatten their management structures, they have been making their corporate structure ever more complex by a ravenous takeover and merger wave, not only merging with competitors, but combining across industries. As a result, the distance between top management and ordinary workers continues to become more tangled. Familiarity with work, workers, or working conditions becomes virtually impossible.

Yet, without the slightest hint of irony, the same corporate executives who devise unwieldy bureaucratic structures rail against government bureaucracy (with the exception of the Federal Reserve), calling on government to behave more like business. Perhaps they should look at Huber's article.

Of course, the most serious costs of financial control are the financial crises that cripple the economy from time to time.

How Rigid Control Paralyzes Creativity

Even a casual consideration of the modern economy should be enough to eradicate any remnant of Smith's quasi-humanistic vision of markets. Certainly, markets do not offer nearly as much opportunity as Smith would have us believe, especially for workers. Instead, the nature of markets is to demand unquestioning discipline amid the rhetorical celebration of freedom.

Framing the world in absolutes is not a good practice. Freedom is good, but untrammeled chaos is not. Nor is strict discipline a guarantee of success, but cooperation has the potential to produce far superior outcomes than hierarchical control. While too many cooks may spoil the broth, putting a bad cook in charge is not likely to produce an appetizing meal.

Strict hierarchies have a tendency to destroy individual initiative. A perhaps apocryphal story about a famous military episode illustrates the self-defeating nature of strict hierarchies. In 1707, four British warships were returning home after a successful campaign against the French at Gibraltar. A common sailor approached the admiral, Sir Cloudesley Shovell, to tell him that the ships were in danger. Despite the official navigators' calculations, the sailor, who lived on the nearby Scilly Isles, knew that the ships were not in the open sea because he recognized the familiar smell of the land. For his trouble, the sailor was hanged for insubordination. Because of the navigators' mistake and the admiral's discipline, 6,000 men lost their lives.

Procrusteanism does not usually create such dramatic consequences. Most of the damage done by rigid hierarchies comes from the steady accumulation of a series of small errors over an extended period of time. Managers, oblivious to the negative consequences, might believe that their system is a model of efficiency, especially if workers behave obediently. Toyota offers an interesting counterexample.

Toyota treats its workers just as ruthlessly as any successful business.[14] It has a reputation for driving employees hard and even, in a few cases, causing death by overwork. Nonetheless, Toyota still offered its workers a modicum of respect, perhaps a residual of Japan's pre-market traditions. Reports told of cars covered with Post-it notes containing suggestions from workers, many of which proved valuable:

> Toyota implements a million new ideas a year, and most of them come from ordinary workers. . . . Most of these ideas are small—making parts on a shelf easier to reach, say—and not all of them work. But cumulatively, every day, Toyota knows a little more, and does things a little better, than it did the day before.[15]

In the United States, an employer offering $50 rewards for work-ers' suggestions is unusual enough to merit an article in the *Wall Street Journal*.[16] Such token payments are less important than the implicit concession that workers are intelligent beings with much to offer. For a hardened Procrustean, that cost is generally too much to pay.

Motivated workers do much more than just suggest better options for managers. Their expertise can make a significant difference in the production process. For example, in coal-fired electrical plants, where fuel makes up a disproportionate share of the cost of production, a skilled operator can increase fuel efficiency by as much as 3 percent.[17]

A major study on productivity in U.S. industry compared the con-tributions of workers in the Italian textile industry with their counter-parts in the United States:

> In Italy we observed highly trained loom operators working together with fabric designers to exploit the technical possibilities of the loom and to dream up new products. In the United States we heard a prominent textile manufacturer boast that only the top manager in the plant knew how to set up new looms and that the operators, "guys down from the hills who are good at fixing cars," did not need any special training to work on them.

The report concluded:

> By defining jobs narrowly and making each job relatively easy to learn, American industry pursued flexibility through interchangeability of workers with limited skills and experience rather than the cultivation of multiskilled workers. Employees could be hired and fired with the ups and downs of the business cycle without much loss of efficiency. The result was a progressively narrowing of worker responsibility and input and the tendency of management to treat workers as a cost to be con-trolled, not an asset to be developed.[18]

This description of practices in the United States is in line with Smith's version of the division of labor: management more or less distributes workers to their appointed task and within any particular job each worker is identical to the others. These workers are expected to follow orders and do nothing else.

The Obsession with Rigid Control

Procrusteanism protects itself by reinforcing class divisions that benefit capital at the expense of labor. The disrespect that management shows workers is replicated within the managerial hierarchy. The many layers of hierarchy further complicate the dissemination of information about potential opportunities.

Individual capitalists might profit by making their own hierarchies less rigid, yet management identifies so strongly with Procrusteanism that it becomes unable to recognize its own self-interest. The self-identification with power and authority makes any relaxation of Procrusteanism threatening.

The Toyota example suggests that taking workers seriously enough to listen to their suggestions might pay healthy dividends, even for a Procrustean firm. The problem is that Procrusteanism creates a system of social relationships that prevents management from seeing workers as anything more than living implements. From foreman on the shop floor to the highest levels of management, people take comfort in their own status relative to those below them.

Fear that cooperation might prove more efficient than hierarchy can make management tighten its traditional techniques of control. A dramatic example illustrates the obsessive lure of absolute managerial control. Shoshana Zuboff, a professor at the Harvard Business School, reported on her experience as a consultant for paper factories during the 1980s when computer controls were first being introduced in the industry. In one factory, which she called Tiger Creek Mill, everybody initially had access to the new computer system—even the workers on the production line. Workers could see the same information on costs and prices as management. At first, the workers used their newfound information to make profitable modifications in the production process.

Economic theory and business logic would have us expect that management would reward these workers for their contribution to the profitability of the corporation. Instead, management, horrified by the possibility that workers were going to make managerial control at least partially irrelevant, quickly cut off the workers' access to the system.[19]

Such sharing of information should be a high priority in any organization in which information is supposed to be a central input. Besides, sharing can stimulate productivity in other ways. Stanford professor Jeffrey Pfeffer made the case that sharing information can improve the level of trust in the workplace:

> Sharing information with another party signifies trust. That trust is likely to be reciprocated. Conversely, when a company keeps secrets from its employees it signals it does not trust its employees to keep secrets or to use the withheld information effectively. Those feelings of distrust and disdain are also likely to be reciprocated. . . . Decentralizing decision making also signals trust and a belief in employees' competence, again engaging the norm of reciprocity.[20]

Sociologist Richard Sennett reported on his own experience, witnessing the importance of trust firsthand:

> I witnessed the strength and weakness of informal trust in two industrial accidents separated by thirty years. In the first, in an old-style factory, a fire burst out, and the circuit of fire nozzles turned out to be broken. Line workers knew each other well enough to decide who could do what. The managers squawked out orders, but in the emergency nobody paid attention to them; damage to the plant was soon brought under control by a strong informal network. Thirty years later I happened to be in a Silicon Valley plant when the air-conditioning system began sucking in rather than expelling noxious gases, an unforeseen design disaster in this high-tech building. The work teams did not hold together. Many people dangerously stampeded for the exits, while others, more courageous, were at a loss as to how to organize themselves. In the aftermath, the managers, many of whom had responded well, realized that this plant of

thirty-two hundred people was, as one said, only "superficially organized on paper." [21]

Unfortunately, as the Tiger Creek incident suggested, control seems to have more allure than profits. The exercise of power and control becomes a major source of enjoyment in itself, over and above providing a defense of existing privileges, just as it did in the automobile factory where Bill Watson worked.

Sennett recognized the importance of a deeper level of trust than management sharing information. The trust he encountered was not workers trusting management, but trusting each other—finding collective power.

Think back to Jacob Riis's image of the stonemason hammering away until the extraneous rock is ready to fall off. Permitting too much trust and too much respect threatens the whole edifice of Procrusteanism. Many employers reason that it is better to forgo some immediate profits than risk the irruption of a whole new system of social relations.

A hint of the potential of collective power comes from the open-source movement, where thousands of programmers voluntarily contribute to the growing mass of software. Some people have the responsibility of coordinating these inputs but nobody really commands the programmers, who are all volunteers. Yet the open-source movement manages to produce software that is generally superior to the products of the mammoth Microsoft empire.

I have been unable to find how many people work on Microsoft's Internet Explorer. To give some idea of Microsoft's scale of operation, the company added 11,200 employees in 2008.[22] The tiny Mozilla Foundation, with a mere 175 employees as of late 2008, coordinates a number of important software projects, including the web browser Firefox, which most experts regard as superior to Microsoft's Internet Explorer.[23] Microsoft has many more projects than Mozilla, but the manpower devoted to its browser must be many times more than Mozilla employs. Microsoft ends up following Mozilla's lead in many important respects.

So, in the end, crude techniques of control might be able to force outward compliance, but ultimately they are unable to harness people's full potential. Frederick Law Olmsted made the same point regarding slavery, but he never connected his insight to what was going on in the Northern states. The more general lesson is that nobody can make another person work effectively, even at the point of a bayonet—especially if that work requires any skill or discretion.

Floggings Will Continue until Morale Improves

The study of human relations specializes in understanding how business can extract the maximum effort from workers. This field suggests that business fails in its efforts to maximize profits by not fostering relationships built around respect and trust. Despite the research in this field, business still insists on managing by threat and intimidation, rather than nurturing workers.

Researchers in human relations offer a different perspective, understanding employment as a potentially ongoing relationship. This field is not concerned with radical reforms, only with using less overtly Procrustean methods to extract profits. For example, in a symposium on human relations and economics, published in the American Economic Association's *Journal of Economic Perspectives*, Jeffrey Pfeffer addressed the mysterious disconnect between economic theory and well-understood human relations practices, which promised to make business perform better—not so much from the perspective of workers, but for business itself:

> Comprehensive evidence from studies in numerous industries and countries establishes this point and also helps us identify high-performance management practices. Third, in spite of the fact that much of what is required to build engaged and successful organizations is at once well known and not always costly to implement, many, maybe most, organizations have failed to take appropriate actions, thereby, in some sense, "leaving money on the table."[24]

The kind of antagonism in the auto plant that Watson described is a perfect example of the more obvious kind of losses that business experiences because of short-sighted understanding of its relationship with workers. Elsewhere, Pfeffer pointed out, "The dominant economic theories are also filled with language not apt to produce trust and cooperation, to put it mildly."[25]

After listing a number of prominent examples of economists to prove his point, Pfeffer turned to another widely circulated literature that indicates that in real life economists tend to behave more selfishly than most people. Based on this material, he concludes:

> It is scarcely surprising that training that stresses self-interested behavior, rampant opportunism, and conflicts of interest would produce less collaborative behavior on the part of those exposed to the training and the language used to express these ideas.[26]

Another contribution to the symposium, titled "Paying Respect," explains how respect, as well as monetary incentives, can encourage workers to perform better. Economists, however, have difficulty taking account of respect because "respect cannot easily be traded in a market."[27]

This mild critique of Procrusteanism makes economists uncomfortable because it raises questions about their basic assumptions about human behavior. For example, two economists, one of whom, Edward P. Lazear, was then serving as the chief economist in the administration of George W. Bush, also participated in this symposium on human relations. Their contribution is interesting because it mostly ignores the contributions of the human relations theorists. Instead, they complained, "The issues studied by human resources specialists were of interest to economists, but the approach taken by the non-economists lacked the formal framework to which economists have grown accustomed."[28] Recall that this formal framework explicitly excluded the labor process, emphasizing commercial transactions instead.

These economists suggested financial economics as the "model for personnel economics." They claimed that just as finance lacked a formal approach until a few decades ago, personnel economics will benefit from economic formalism.[29] Ironically, the article appeared just as the teachings of financial economics was about to push the economy over a cliff.

Earlier, Lazear justified why mainstream economists found past human resource management unpalatable: "It was loose, unfocused, and ad hoc, and lacked the general rigorous framework to which economists were accustomed."[30] Lazear was correct about the absence of a "rigorous framework" in management theory, but forcing the study of human resource management into a Procrustean bed of theoretical rigor drains the subject of any relevance, except as an academic exercise. So, rather than taking seriously the complexity of the human relations literature, Lazear and his coauthor proposed that economists should go ahead and apply their theoretical tools to this subject. In effect, however, their suggestion all but removes the "human" from "human relations." This formal framework is part of the problem, not a solution.

Economics contributes to the almost universal application of Procrustean management strategies. Professors repeatedly teach students of economics, beginning in introductory classes and continuing through graduate studies, how firms can maximize profits. Unfortunately, the models used to convey this message do not often include the way that business has to make decisions as events unfold in real time—or, in the rare cases when they do, the models exclude the kinds of uncertainty that business faces.

Even more pertinent to this book, these models demonstrate how business should add or subtract labor according to market conditions, with scant attention to long-run consequences. Such models probably depict business behavior somewhat accurately, in the sense that business does tend to buy labor like it does with inanimate inputs. But unlike machines or other inputs, workers have the potential to grow and develop. Driving workers harder rather than building long-term capabilities might produce short-term benefits, but it is at a significant long-term cost.

The workers themselves bear the immediate brunt of these costs. Over time, overwork takes a toll on the system as a whole, damaging the capitalists' prospects. However, individual employers have no incentive to lighten the load on their own employees, whom they will replace once they are no longer capable of keeping pace. Here is another example of the self-destructive nature of the system.

Objectifying labor also serves an important psychological purpose for the Procrusteans. The comfort of the prosperous does not depend on the sacrifices of hard-working people who abide by the rules of the game. Instead, the key to prosperity is the knowledge and skill of management. As a result, workers do not deserve to share much of the prosperity. Authoritarian measures—whether directly applied or waiting in the background—become unavoidable to enforce the discipline of this system.

The Subtle Resistance of Control

Earlier, we discussed the widespread perception by economists and employers that workers are objects. The diary of Ralph Miliband, a poor refugee in London during the Second World War who later became an influential academic and the father of a recent British foreign secretary, casts some light on the cultural response to this inhuman attitude. Miliband recorded a "curious combination of kindness, cunning, ignorance, feigned servility and subordination, actual contempt which this particular part of the unskilled working class had for their masters."[31] As a result, even if people in authority expect absolute obedience from the "living objects" they employ, they may only be able to elicit a superficial obedience, which may be nothing more than the appearance of compliance, especially when people are denied trust and respect.

Part of the problem that employers face is that effectively framing their orders is almost impossible. To ensure that a subordinate carries out orders, the employer faces the virtually impossible challenge of conveying them in a clear, complete, and unambiguous manner. Yet commands, even if formalized in a contract framed by expensive lawyers, almost inevitably contain a certain ambiguity.

Anyone involved in a construction job understands the difficulty involved. A cost-plus arrangement gives the contractor no incentive to be efficient. Costs can spiral out of control. A contract for a fixed amount creates an incentive to cut corners, since the contractor will get the money no matter how shoddy the work is—so long as it passes the scrutiny of a building inspector. Nobody could specify the particulars of the job precisely enough to make sure the outcome will be satisfactory for all concerned. Even for people with sufficient knowledge of the project, the time required to make the specifications detailed enough to remove ambiguity would be excessive.

A large literature of legal and economic scholarship has wrestled with what is known as "the principal/agent problem," exploring ways to structure authority so that underlings feel that their interests coincide with that of their superiors. No one has discovered a formal way to align incentives. If a job were so simple that management could drain its commands of the last drop of ambiguity, then that job would seem to be ideal for a robot rather than for a living, breathing human being. The resulting ambiguity of commands gives subordinates a degree of latitude to exercise their wills, often to the detriment of those who are supposed to be in control.

One of my favorite works of literature revolves around this dilemma. Jaroslav Hasek's 1912 novel *The Good Soldier Sveijk* is the charming story of a Bohemian soldier caught up in the turmoil of the First World War. Most of the humor of the book arises from Sveijk's practice of seizing upon ambiguity or hyperbole in the orders that his superiors give him. By taking his orders literally, he is usually able to do whatever he wants. When challenged to explain his absurd behavior, Sveijk unflinchingly boasts of being a lunatic, much to the consternation of his superiors and to the delight of generations of readers. After all, how can employers expect competence from machines, even "living machines"?

Sveijk-like behavior is not restricted to the world of fiction. The same defect that drove Sveijk's officers to distraction plagues the typical authoritarian relationship. Recall how slave owners had to use heavy equipment because their unfree workers were prone to "accidents."

While a fictional Sveijk might play the fool, surreptitiously challenging management can be a source of pride, especially when management treats workers disrespectfully. Early in his career, David Packard, a co-founder of Hewlett-Packard, learned something about this almost instinctual desire to subvert control:

> In the late 1930s, when I was working for General Electric . . . the company was making a big thing of plant security. . . . GE was especially zealous about guarding its tool and parts bins to make sure employees didn't steal anything. Faced with this obvious display of distrust, many employees set out to prove it justified, walking out with tools and parts whenever they could. . . . When HP got under way, the GE memories were still strong and I determined that our parts bins and storerooms should always be open. . . . Keeping storerooms and parts bins open was advantageous to HP in two important ways. From a practical standpoint, the easy access to parts and tools helped product designers and others who wanted to work out new ideas at home or on weekends. A second reason, less tangible but important, is that the open bins and storerooms were a symbol of trust, a trust that is central to the way HP does business.[32]

Unfortunately, few managers are as sophisticated as Packard.

Real Life Sveijk

An engineer, Stanley Mathewson, reported a classic description of an automobile worker's finding a loophole in a job description worthy of the good soldier Sveijk:

> A Mexican in a large automobile factory was given the final tightening to the nuts on automobile-engine cylinder heads. There are a dozen or more nuts around this part. The engines passed the Mexican rapidly on a conveyer. His instructions were to test all the nuts and if he found one or two loose to tighten them, but if three or more were loose he was not expected to have time to tighten them.

[A supervisor who was puzzled that so many defective engines were passing along the line] discovered that the Mexican was unscrewing a third nut whenever he found two already loose.[33]

Loosening one nut required less effort than tightening two. A famous railroad manager and disciple of Frederick Winslow Taylor, Harrington Emerson, related a similar incident:

A railroad track foreman and gang were recently seen burying under some ashes and dirt a thirty-foot steel rail. It was less trouble to bury it than to pick it up and place it where it could be saved.[34]

During his reelection campaign in 2004, Vice President Richard Cheney, now a strict disciplinarian, recalled his own Sveijk-like past. As a young man in the early 1960s, Cheney worked as a lineman for a power company in Wyoming. Because copper wire was expensive, the linemen were instructed to return all unused pieces three feet or longer. Rather than deal with the paperwork that resulted from following orders, Cheney said, he and his colleagues found a solution: putting "shorteners" on the wire—that is, cutting it into short pieces and tossing the leftovers at the end of the workday.[35]

Workers adopt other creative methods of subverting management's authority. In one case, pilots at Eastern Airlines reversed the classic strategy of pressuring employers with a slowdown. Instead, they flew at higher speeds, which burned more fuel. Although passengers might have found the shortened flight time convenient, the extra fuel cost undermined corporate profitability.

Work to Rule

Business sometimes unintentionally encourages Sveijk-like behavior by concocting elaborate official policies. The management does not expect people to take these orders seriously; to do so would be too time-consuming. The real purpose of these policies is to allow management to avoid responsibility. In the event of a bad outcome, management can blame irresponsible workers who failed to obey strict company policy. This practice is especially useful in the case of serious accidents and fatalities on the job.

When workers fear repercussions from overt protests, they sometimes follow these orders to the letter, which generally causes a slowdown, eating into profits. For example, during a dispute with Verizon, workers adopted a "work-to-rule" strategy. According to one account of the workers' behavior:

> Technicians delayed the start of their days with a 20-minute truck safety check each morning. The check involved two technicians, one to operate the truck and another to inspect turn signals, brake lights, and hydraulic lifts. "Some mornings at the Watertown garage, you'd see 100 bucket trucks with their lifts spinning in the air," said Dave Reardon, business agent for IBEW Local 2222. "It drove managers crazy." "State and federal regulations require that we put out the proper signage—signs, cones, flags—when we work in manholes and near highways," said Steve Carney, a field tech and a steward in CWA Local 1103. "We refused to take trucks out that did not have the right signage."[36]

Taking a page from Sveijk:

> A CWA [Communications Workers of America] fact sheet told workers how to work to rule: "Never go by memory, check your reference material" and "Never use your own judgment—ask!" This tactic was a powerful weapon for "outside" workers, the ones who maintain the underground infrastructure and install and repair lines and equipment. These technicians had leeway to determine how best to complete a job. During regular times they often disregarded company rules in order to get a job done quickly. But during the work-to-rule campaign, they followed Department of Transportation regulations, for example, to the letter. [37]

While such behavior might infuriate management, you can be sure that had an accident occurred during "normal" times, the company would have held the employee responsible for not following company policy.

The work-to-rule strategy is not limited to organized labor. Sometimes individuals or small groups of workers informally adopt work-to-rule behavior out of sheer frustration. Harley Shaiken uses the example of a machine shop:

> A familiar sight in most shops is an engineer walking in with a stack of blueprints to ask the worker if a particular job is feasible. The machinist carefully studies the prints, looks at the engineer, and says, "Well, it can be tried like this but it will never work." Grabbing a pencil, the machinist marks up the print and, in effect, redesigns the job based on years of experience....
>
> [In one shop, when] management initiated a campaign to strictly enforce lunch periods and wash-up time, the judgment of some machinists began to fade. About this time a foreman dashed up to the shop with a "hot" job.... Anxious to get the job done quickly, the foreman insisted that the machinist run the lathe at a high speed and plunge the drill through the part. Under normal circumstances the machinist would have tried to talk the foreman out of this approach but now he was only too happy to oblige what were, after all direct orders. The part not only turned out to be scrap, but part of the lathe turned blue from the friction generated by the high speed. The disciplinary campaign was short-lived.[38]

Joan Greenbaum tells of a group of disgruntled British typists, who demonstrated their displeasure with their bosses by exactly transcribing dictation tapes. If the executives said, "Oh no, typist," they typed "Oh no, typist." They carefully transcribed all the sounds that the tapes recorded—"um," "eh" included.[39] Byzantine bureaucratic structures amplify Sveijk-like behavior because orders move down from one layer to the next, creating more space for would-be Sveijks. As Richard Sennett noted:

> As orders pass down through the chain of command, each agent "translates" the order into action. This allows the agents considerable discre-

tion. With a childlike innocence, [Frederick Winslow] Taylor fretted that his precepts—so clear, so "scientific"—became smudged and messed in the corporations for whom he consulted. Reality failed him. [40]

Procrusteans can construct sophisticated command structures, but without the empathy of the people below, their systems may create enormous waste, even though they may be rational from the perspective of those in control.

Waste

A French scientist, Sadi Carnot (1796–1832), analyzed the nature of an ideal engine, one without friction or any loss of energy. He realized that such a mechanism, now known as a Carnot engine, would be impossible. Nonetheless, an understanding of an ideal machine does have a value. Comparing the performance of a real machine with an ideal one provides a measure of efficiency.

In the more complex world of human performance, coaches often take advantage of films of their athletes' movements, searching for telltale signs of wasted efforts. The slightest hitch can dissipate energy or throw off the rhythm of the whole movement. For athletes competing at the highest levels, eliminating minute defects can spell the difference between success and failure.

Unlike the engineers or coaches, laissez-faire enthusiasts insist that market principles automatically maximize productive efficiency. The system would work better by eliminating government interference or unions, but otherwise nothing else is needed. Economists have their complex systems of equations that "prove" this market efficiency. Unfortunately, a careful analysis of these "proofs" reveals that they depend upon hopelessly unrealistic assumptions. A casual tour of the world quickly reveals that the economic performance of markets is less than stellar. As always, the chorus of free marketers will respond that the problem is that marketization has not gone far enough.

Why are our schools leaving so many poor children uneducated?

Here is a waste of monumental proportions because education is the key to unlocking the potential of the upcoming generation. The Procrusteans inevitably offer their market-based solution: privatize the schools and run them according to market principles without the interference of unions.

What about offering the schools better funding? Absolutely not! President George W. Bush, himself a product of an elite and expensive system of private education, callously compared providing more public educational spending to "pumping more gas into a flooded engine."[41] Privatized schools promise to produce as-yet-unproven market efficiencies that will somehow magically lower educational costs.

One obvious cost-cutting strategy is to relieve the educational system from the responsibility of educating those children who are most expensive to teach—the physically handicapped and those who are most deeply scarred by poverty. Would a rational society regard such measures as efficiency?

More Waste

Modern technology, based on what has so far been an adequate supply of cheap energy, has advanced to the point where relatively few people are required to manufacture the goods people consume. The shrinkage in manufacturing employment follows a pattern similar to the earlier trend in agriculture, in which technological advances made a large portion of the farm population redundant.

Such technological improvements should make possible more leisure or free up labor to produce goods and services that improve the quality of life. But instead, leisure has become scarcer. Part of the problem is that business employs an increasing portion of the workforce in activities that do little or nothing to promote human welfare but which consume great quantities of working time. Often, this work actually detracts from human well-being. For example, unwelcome advertising and marketing intrude into many parts of our existence. The U.S.

Department of Labor estimates that sales managers, along with people engaged in advertising, marketing, promotions, and public relations held about 638,000 jobs in 2008. These jobs are expected to grow faster than the average growth in employment, although the development of online commerce should be expected to reduce their numbers.[42] Many other forms of wasteful sales and advertising activities fall through the government's statistical net. For example, a good number of young people probably get paid under the table to wave signs at passing motorists urging them to buy something from a particular merchant.

Spammers certainly fall outside of government surveys of marketing personnel. Business devotes considerable time and energy to defeating spammers, who often use brilliant technical schemes. These corporate expenses appear in government data as part of the normal costs of doing business, although they are really part of a web of unauthorized marketing. Business's defensive actions force the spammers to devise even more ingenious methods of avoiding filters, causing still more resources to be dissipated.

Advertising is doubly wasteful from the standpoint of economic theory. The purpose of the market economy, according to its advocates, is to produce utility, but much advertising is designed to destroy utility by making people dissatisfied with their own possessions in order to induce people to buy something new.

Duplication of facilities also represents a form of marketing. For example, four competing gas stations were on a corner a few blocks from where I grew up. A single station would have easily supplied all the existing traffic. The extra effort required to construct and maintain the three superfluous stations represented a substantial waste. But since each company wanted to have a share of the market, the profit motive demanded this wasteful duplication. The mathematical economist Harold Hotelling even produced a theorem demonstrating why such locational strategies were rational for the individual businesses.[43]

One might argue that society lacks the expertise to decide which of the four operations should remain, but even if the wrong choice is made, the elimination of duplication surely offers sufficient savings to compensate for any errors of judgment.

An increasing share of the workforce devotes itself to mere paper shuffling, such as the buying and selling of stocks, bonds, or options. In order to make that work possible, a host of other people must supply those workers with energy, buildings, information technologies, and paper.

The federal government estimates that in 2008 real estate brokers held about 123,000 jobs and real estate sales agents, 394,000. Although, helping people relocate may provide a useful service, are almost half a million people necessary? Much of this industry assists real estate speculation, which makes housing less affordable. Given the vast improvements in informational technologies, certainly a good deal of the labor associated with the real estate business is wasted. Nonetheless, the U.S. Department of Labor expects employment in this industry to grow faster than overall employment during the next decade.[44]

Finally, much of the labor in the economy is dissipated in producing consumer goods that do not add to people's happiness. Diverting efforts wasted in unproductive activities could offer great dividends. Some of the time saved could be used for leisure that could enhance workers potential, especially if society signaled to people how their skills could be rewarded. In addition, the resources currently used unproductively could be used to benefit society in ways that markets neglect, such as building schools and environmental remediation.

Guard Labor

Another kind of waste results from the efforts to control access to goods and services. Capitalists are only able to earn money to the extent that they can prevent people from using their products without paying. They must find ways to deny non-customers access to their goods, so they must devote considerable effort just to protect their property rights. Economist James O'Connor coined the term "guard labor" to describe this form of protection of property. To illustrate the nature of guard labor, he offered a description of a job I once had to explain what he meant:

Consider the labor of the ticket seller at a movie house. The seller's task is merely to transfer the right to sit in the theater to the movie-goer in exchange for the price of a ticket. But it may not be immediately obvious that it is not the lack of a ticket that keeps you out of the theater.... The ticket is actually torn up and discarded by a husky young man who stands between the box office and the seat that I want. Marx writes that "it is plain that commodities cannot go to market and make exchanges of their own account. We must, therefore, have recourse to their guardians, who are also their owners."[45]

Theaters often have layers of guards. One person may sell the tickets while another tears them up. With the advent of modern technology, a new generation of guards works to prevent people from accessing the show outside the theater—in the form of digital media for music, movies, and the like. Hordes of lawyers and technicians labor to create laws or develop new technologies to prevent the digital leakage of these commodities to people who might avoid paying for them.

Unlike the operator of the movie theater, some providers of goods and services allow the consumer access to the product before payment. In such cases, the guardians must make sure that consumers complete the transaction by paying their bills. This activity also employs many people. Then, in order to make sure all this guard labor works effectively, another layer of guardians must oversee the accounts.

In addition to the direct performance of guard labor, millions of auxiliary workers labor to provide the resources necessary to support guard labor. These workers build and maintain the offices, produce the telecommunications infrastructure, and supply the other goods and services that the guards require. In addition, these workers have their own complement of guards to oversee their work.

Retail stores employ sophisticated surveillance systems to deter theft. Other forms of guard labor are less obvious. Look at the shelves where stores encase their commodities in multiple layers of packaging. This packaging might help to protect the product from damage, but for the most part it does nothing to make the product more useful. In part, the packaging is intended to entice consumers to buy the product. More often than not, the overriding function is to deter theft.

Consumers also assist in guarding the commodity by putting up with the nuisance of cutting through a series of plastic or cardboard containers in order to extract the commodity. Next, the consumer must dispose of the wasted materials. A long chain of guard labor associated with the packaging extends from the production of the raw materials to those who finally haul away the garbage.

Much white-collar work consists of nothing more than guard labor. Even some blue-collar work that appears to be directly providing services is actually guard labor. Years ago, gas station attendants pumped gas. In exceptional cases, some people needed assistance in filling their tanks, but most people did not. The attendant, who was supposed to be a service worker, was actually performing guard labor to make sure the customers paid.

Eventually, this deception fell apart. Once modern technology allowed one person to lock and unlock the pumps at a distance, one guard could supervise several pumps. People began to pump the gas on their own, revealing the previous attendants' chief function as guards.

The rise in guard labor represents a significant drain on economic potential. The United States Department of Labor predicts that by 2012, the nation will have more private security guards than high school teachers.[46] Although such comparisons do not constitute proof of inefficiency, they do indicate a distorted set of priorities.

Guard Labor in the Workplace

Where the commodity in question is the employees' working time, the direct supervision of labor represents an obvious form of guard labor. Rather than empower workers to take on more responsibility, employers restrict workers' autonomy by relying instead on guard labor (supervisors).

This form of guard labor has a distinct Procrustean dimension, but the degree of Procrusteanism is indeterminate. Employers have a choice. They can either empower workers to take on more responsibility or they can restrict employees' autonomy, relying instead on discipline to enforce their commands.

The nature of guard labor reflects larger social conditions. For example, according to historical accounts of the decisive Battle of Salamis in 480 B.C., the Athenian navy with 360 ships under sail defeated 1,000 Persian ships. The Persians used slave rowers who required squads of armed overseers. Their weapons were intended for the control of the rowers rather than for fighting enemies. As a result, the Athenians, with free men at the oars, had a distinct advantage since they had more space for archers and infantrymen on deck.[47] Despite the traditional celebration of the Athenian roots of Western democratic society, the United States is coming to resemble Persia (or Sparta) more than Athens.

The growing costs of guard labor offer a revealing window into the self-defeating nature of Procrusteanism. In 1890, U.S. supervisors made up a mere 0.8 percent of the labor force. By 1979, just before the time when corporations began their efforts to flatten their hierarchical bureaucratic structures, the share of supervisors in the labor force had risen to 11.7 percent. By 2002, that number had risen by more than a third to 15.7 percent.[48] In addition, many millions of workers supply the material resources necessary for the supervisors to carry out their work, including the modern technology used to spy on workers.

The rising share of guard labor is not a necessary consequence of modernization. The workers producing labor-saving advanced spy technology are not included in the statistics for guard labor, although they should be. However, this estimate does include prisoners and the unemployed, whose fate serves to warn existing providers of labor power to keep their noses to the grindstone. These two factors partially offset each other.

Significant differences exist among modern societies. In particular, the United States uses a far higher share of supervisory workers than any other advanced capitalist economy, employing 14.9 percent of its labor force in some sort of supervisory position. England, with 13.4 percent, is not far behind. In comparison, Sweden, with its more egalitarian society, has only 4.4 percent of its labor force working as supervisors.[49] The share of guard labor appears to be closely related to the extent of inequality.[50] The shameful increase in inequality in the United States over the last thirty-five years, approaching a degree akin to that found in impoverished Third World countries, tears at the social fabric. The ensuing conflict spills over into the workplace, intensifying the demand for guard labor. As a result, even teachers have to perform their share of guard labor.

Over and above the time and resources devoted to the direct exercise of authority, the Procrustean economy requires additional resources to maintain the authority of guard labor. This aspect of guard labor is probably most transparent in the military. For example, part of the training of soldiers includes marching around in formation. The ability to perform in this way does nothing to improve the soldiers' ability to fight.

Nothing would make soldiers more vulnerable in a battle than to march in formation. Instead, marching according to the officers' commands merely habituates the troops to take orders without a moment's reflection. Once responding to command becomes instinctual, soldiers in the heat of battle will instantaneously follow orders regardless of the consequences for their own well-being.

Procrusteans welcome this same kind of mindless obedience. Frederic Natusch Maude, a British officer and later an influential theoretician of military tactics, understood how military training would suit industrialists:

> The sense of duty (the essence of a man's whole teaching in the ranks) [has become] the very corner-stone of modern industrial efficiency. I submit that if no Army existed they would have to create one, simply as a schoolroom for the factory.[51]

Here are the impressions of a U.S. engineer of a scene at Toyota, which seems to follow Maude's advice:

> A large group of company employees were lined up, military-style, shouting company slogans. They were all dressed in Toyota company uni-

forms of one-piece jumpers and soft-brimmed hats. The hat was the same style used by Japanese soldiers during the Second World War, and it was standard issue for all employees at the company. One employee stood at the front directing the drill. He would shout out a slogan and the group would shout back in unison. This display of group obedience reminded me of old films of the Japanese military. "But why here?" I wondered. "Why would a company need to engage in military drills?"[52]

The point of the observer, who had been working for a Toyota-related firm, was that the system dissipated enormous energy in enforcing dysfunctional hierarchies.

The reliance on guard labor is counterproductive because it does not just enforce discipline. It also blocks workers' development. That Toyota profited as much as it did in engaging its workers is a testimony to what could be accomplished without the irrational incentives of capitalism.

Samuel Gompers, the first president of the American Federation of Labor, gave another example of the possibility of a system that transcended markets. Gompers recalled that in his youth, late in the nineteenth century when he worked as a cigar maker, one of the workers would be selected to read books, including those of Karl Marx, out loud. This reading cost the employers nothing except the expense of providing a chair. Instead, the others would pay the readers by crediting them with making some of their cigar production.[53] This environment provided a rich education to people who would have otherwise had no opportunity for further formal education.

This arrangement proved incompatible with an advanced capitalist economy. Later, as the cigar industry replaced adult male workers with unskilled young girls, the organization of work took a giant step backwards. Gompers complained to a committee of the United States Senate that the cigar industry had instituted harsh authority relations to diminish the autonomy of the young cigar workers. The employers prohibited the girls employed as cigar strippers from conversing with each other under pain of fine or dismissal.[54]

Prisons

The metaphor of guard labor becomes literal for many of the workers in the employ of the government. Between 1982 and 2001, employment in the criminal justice system in the United States rose from 1.2 million to 2.3 million people.[55] The figures have risen considerably since then.

The prison clientele has also multiplied. In a flourish of Procrusteanism, by 2003 the number of prisoners had reached more than six times the level in 1972. As of year-end 2006, more than 2.2 million people in the United States were in federal or state prisons or in local jails, representing a population larger than that of seventeen states. An additional five million adults were under probation or parole jurisdiction.[56] Between 1982 and 2001, the cost of the criminal justice system in the United States soared from $37.8 billion to $167 billion, representing about $600 per American. In California, the state has built twenty-three prisons in the last twenty-five years, in contrast to a single new campus for the University of California and another campus for the larger state university system. Prisons now claim a greater share of the state budget than higher education, and the disparity keeps becoming more extreme. Prison guards presently earn more than assistant professors.

Although a criminal justice system is necessary, the U. S. system is absurdly excessive. The incarceration rate in the United States is five to eight times as high as in Canada or Western Europe. Perhaps symbolic of the end of the Cold War, the United States has now displaced Russia as the world's leading incarcerator.[57]

Prisons represent an important ingredient in a Procrustean economy. Besides serving as a vital component of guard labor in protecting private property, the criminal justice system threatens members of the working class who might resist the discipline of the market. What might pass for an immature prank for a wealthy college student will be punished as a serious offense for a member of the working class. Perhaps nothing symbolizes the class nature of the criminal justice system as much as the differential penalties for powdered cocaine and crack cocaine. A gram of crack cocaine (stereotypically associated with dangerous black youths) draws a far harsher sentence than an equal amount of powdered cocaine (commonly thought to be the misguided recreation of the more affluent). More often than not, the courts require nothing more of privileged young people than to enter some sort of clinic.

The intended lesson of the prison-industrial complex is that working-class people are expected to work hard and toe the line. No deviations will be tolerated. Only if they get rich will society permit them to do more or less what they choose.

Less Obvious Forms of Guard Labor

Business meetings offer an interesting analogue to the military marches. The ostensible purpose of meetings is to improve efficiency, but anybody who attends a few soon realizes that they are mostly pointless. Simon Ramo, the ninety-six-year-old co-founder of TRW Inc. (a conglomerate that Northrop Grumman acquired for its defense business in 2002), estimated that he had attended more than 40,000 meetings—an average of two or three per workday. Ramo guessed that about 30,000 of these meetings could have been shorter or eliminated altogether without any loss to the company—even ignoring the extra productivity that the company could enjoy allowing people to work rather than attend meetings.[58] Since he probably called many of these meetings himself, he may be giving too much credit to them. Yet the frequency of meetings continues to rise. The average executive participated in twice as many meetings in the 1980s as in the 1960s.[59]

Much of the time spent in meetings is more ceremonial than functional. People come face to face with their superiors. Each of the underlings sees how others fall in line and realizes that to express any dissent can jeopardize a career. Meetings thus function as a means to impose discipline on white-collar workers, much like the soldiers' marches.

At issue here is the dissipation of productive potential in the effort to maintain authority relationships. Such efforts prop up authority, consume time, energy, and resources, but even more costly consequences are at stake.

Although managers who call meetings might justify them in terms of improving morale, meetings negatively affect workers. Survey data indicate that frequent meetings reduce participants' sense of well-being.[60] Besides, authoritarian relations themselves snuff out valuable creativity. A system more devoted to meeting the needs of people and less intent on solidifying hierarchy would encourage more autonomy and voluntary collaboration.

Unfortunately, the human and economic costs of guard labor usually pass unnoticed. However, despite the outpouring of economic rhetoric praising the productive merits of markets, in a Procrustean world, authority always trumps efficiency. A more rational system would both nurture and draw upon the expertise of the entire workforce rather than relying on a system of command and control.

By any rational standard, guard labor should be in decline. Rapid progress in information technologies should have the effect of reducing the number of people keeping track of others, but instead, business has largely taken advantage of information technologies to intensify the Procrustean workplace. At least some of the efforts of scientists and engineers who develop such technologies should be included as guard labor. The same logic holds for the workers who build the computers and maintain the buildings that support this technology.

Some forms of guard labor become so familiar that people might not recognize it. Consider the ubiquitous cash register. The original purpose of the cash register was to help storeowners deter employee theft. Since the register kept a record of each transaction that the employee rang up, clerks were more likely to deposit customers' payments. Warren Buffett's partner, Charles Munger, once proposed, "The cash register did more for human morality than the Congregational Church."[61]

The registers were not foolproof, however, since employees still had the option of not ringing up the sale and then pocketing the money for themselves. To make the clerk more likely to record the sale, employers turned to 99-cent pricing, which became common soon after the introduction of the cash register. With 99-cent pricing, customers would be less likely to pay the exact price. The clerk, in turn, would need to open the cash register to get a coin, which could only be done by ringing up the sale.[62] Stores with multiple clerks could purchase machines with cabinets with separate cash drawers and a distinctive bell tone for each clerk.

In contrast to Munger's Congregational Church, the direction of the collection plate is reversed in the case of the penny. Business offers the customer a penny to monitor the potential sins of the clerk. Similarly, customers in some fast-food restaurants can receive free meals if the clerk fails to give them a receipt, which serves the same supervisory function as the penny.[63] Since the clerks themselves belong to the ranks of guard labor, guarding commodities rather than other workers, the customers become the guards of the guards.

With more modern technology, such as surveillance and radio frequency devices, requiring clerks to give a penny change is no longer as necessary as it once was. As a result, some economists and politicians have recommended eliminating the penny so that the government could save the expense of producing the coins. In addition, clerks would no longer have to spend as much time counting up change.

Business would not be likely to pass these savings on to the public. Instead, without the penny, merchants will probably round prices up to the nearest nickel. According to one estimate, this rounding would cost the public $600 million per year, suggesting the scale of even unnoticed guard labor.[64]

What the Fed Hath Wrought

Let us return to the sado-monetarist policies of the Federal Reserve system discussed in chapter 2. Remember that the policies initiated by Paul Volcker in the 1980s and continued by Alan Greenspan aimed to traumatize working people, making them too fearful to demand better wages and conditions. To flesh out this point requires discussing the nature of monetary policy.

When the economy seems healthy, monetary policy makers often get a considerable credit. Lavish praise, such as Bob Woodward bestowed on Alan Greenspan, is not unprecedented. For example, in 1988, Milton Friedman and his co-author, Anna Schwartz, famously blamed the Great Depression on the Federal Reserve, yet the public credited the Fed for the prosperous years of the 1920s. As Friedman and Schwartz observed:

> As the decade wore on, the [Federal Reserve] System took—and perhaps even more was given—credit for the generally stable conditions that prevailed, and high hopes were placed in the potency of monetary policy as then administered.[65]

The leaders at the Fed recognized the danger of the excessive speculation during the late 1920s. They thought that they could target speculation without damaging the economy as a whole. They only learned how wrong they were when the Great Depression hit.

Fifteen years after Friedman's book appeared, he wrote on the editorial page of the *Wall Street Journal*:

> The Fed has consistently . . . claimed credit for good results and blamed forces beyond its control . . . for any bad outcomes. And this avoidance of accountability has paid spectacular dividends. No major institution in the U.S. has so poor a record of performance over so long a period as the Federal Reserve, yet so high a public recognition.[66]

Fifteen years later, Friedman repeated much of this same statement in another opinion piece in the same paper.[67]

The severity of the Great Depression may have been surprising, but the downturn should have been expected. The market economy often fails to accommodate the desires of policymakers; instead, it tends to move by unpredictable fits and starts. Interludes of uninterrupted growth seem to promise a new normality, but they are never permanent.

When the economy stumbles, not just workers, but the economy as a whole suffers. Even the business community has to pay a steep price.

In a severe downturn such as the Great Depression, the glorification of the wonders of the marketplace itself does not seem so credible. A large part of the business community, normally hostile toward government intervention, welcomed Roosevelt's efforts to use the powers of the state to generate an economic recovery.

During this period, economists became disoriented. The economy was not behaving the way mainstream economic theory had assumed. John Maynard Keynes temporarily refocused economic theory by developing what to conventional economists seemed a revolutionary theory. He showed why market forces were unable to produce enough investment to keep the economy healthy.[68] In the United States, economists wrongly interpreted Keynes as simply advocating more government spending. The New Deal was seen as validation of this narrow interpretation of Keynes's theory.

Although Keynes's work had captured the imagination of the bulk of economists by the end of the Second World War, within a few decades the economy slowed down. In that environment, Keynes's ideas fell out of favor. Robert Lucas, a conservative University of Chicago economist and future Nobel Laureate, smugly declared Keynes's theory to be dead.[69] Ironically, once the economy began to unravel in 2007, Lucas admitted to a reporter, "I guess everyone is a Keynesian in a foxhole."[70]

The most popular school of economics in the period following Lucas's declaration was called monetarism—a theory that held that a modest but steady growth of the money supply was the most effective way to keep the economy running at maximum efficiency. The chief attraction of monetary policy was that it minimized the role of government intervention in the economy while appearing technocratic, even scientific. For the monetarists, all that was needed for a strong economy was to give the Federal Reserve the right to manipulate the economy in the way that the monetarists advised and keep the government out of the way.

A good number of economists followed Milton Friedman in advocating a policy that puts the economy on a monetary autopilot. Accordingly, monetary rules were to be set in stone, denying monetary authorities any discretion.

The Fed did briefly follow a monetarist formula when Paul Volcker was driving the economy into a depression. After the recession threatened to spin out of control, Volcker took his foot off the breaks. Since then, the Fed has left Friedman's abstract monetarism on the shelf.

Neither Friedman's nor Volker's nor Greenspan's policies are capable of creating a stable economy. When coupled with the goal of controlling labor, they are certain to do great damage.

The Hopelessness of Monetary Engineering

Friedman and Schwartz explained that the mistakes of the Fed on the eve of the Depression were due to the death of the agency's chairman, Benjamin Strong, which deprived the Fed of a strong leader who might have met the challenges of the late 1920s. Obviously, the problem went far deeper than an individual personality.

The Fed still makes serious mistakes as Friedman had noted time and again. Yet many of the governors and bank presidents of the Fed are very skilled people. In addition, the Fed employs an enormous number of economists—an estimated 495 full-time staff economists as of 2002, besides contracting with a couple hundred influential outside economists.[71] No single person is capable of making the Fed guide the economy to perpetual prosperity.

The task of the Federal Reserve is complicated because its regulation of the money supply takes a while to work its way through the economy, especially when the Fed is trying to stimulate the economy. Just think about the way changing the mix of hot and cold water in a shower only affects the temperature after a delay. Until then, the preexisting mix of hot and cold water is still working its way through the pipes.

In the case of the economy, the typical delay for stimulation is about six months. In part because of the long lags between cause and effect, the Federal Reserve often causes the economy to speed up when, in retrospect, slowing down would be appropriate and vice versa.

Although the Federal Reserve may not be able to calculate the appropriate time to do so, it is more than capable of putting the brakes on economic activity. When the Federal Reserve tightens monetary conditions, or even if business believes that it is on the verge of tightening, management may fear that many other firms will be laying off workers in the near future. Worries about weak economic conditions make business even less likely to invest.

One danger is that either markets or the Fed itself can overreact, turning the desired slowdown into a major recession, or possiby a depression. Friedman and Schwartz are not alone in blaming the Fed for causing the Great Depression when it tried to rein in speculative activity.

In contrast to the threat of overkill in slowing the economy down, the Fed's powers to stimulate economic activity are limited. Interest rates can be a factor in determining investment, but confidence about the future is far more important.

Business realizes the difficulty that the Fed faces in trying to revive the economy through monetary policy. Without confidence about the likelihood of the Fed engineering a recovery, business will hesitate to invest. New investments in plant and equipment generally bring in profits only after a relatively long delay, increasing the probability of a miscalculation. After coming out of a depression or recession, business is likely to be gun-shy about investment.

Economists use the metaphor of a string to suggest the asymmetrical nature of the power of the Fed. Yanking on a string (tightening the money supply) has an obvious effect; pushing on a string (making money more available) may not. Often, in order to create enough confidence to start a recovery, the Federal Reserve pushes so hard on its string that it sets off a period of wild speculation. Confidence mutates into overconfidence. Sometimes, however, the crisis becomes so severe that monetary policy is important.

In any case, all too often the Federal Reserve tends to create the exact phenomenon that it is supposed to eliminate: economic instability. Efforts to control labor while trying to create a steady rate of economic growth make serious mistakes even more likely. The processes set in motion then have had far-reaching consequences.

The Inadvertent Traumatization of Business

The traumatization of labor under Greenspan made the crisis that occurred late in the administration of George W. Bush more severe. With wages held back for decades, many households tried to maintain a growing standard of living by relying on unsustainable debt burdens. This debt became the plaything of finance, which was registering enormous profits. However, these profits could not find profitable outlets, so business turned to speculation rather than to investment in productive capital. This strategy meant that the future economy would be equipped with a less effective capital stock.

The traumatization of labor also contributed to Alan Greenspan's policy response to the dot-com and housing bubbles. Confident that he did not have to worry about wage inflation, Greenspan sat back and watched the bubbles inflate. When this bubble burst in 2000, Greenspan defended his performance in managing the economy by contending that, even with his army of economists, recognizing the dangers of financial speculation is impossible to identify in advance.[72] About that time, the chairman was fueling a real estate bubble that was about to crash only a few years later. Soon thereafter, Greenspan launched a similar defense.[73]

We have made the case that the Fed's effort to hold wages in check lowered the long-term rate of economic growth. And once this was coupled with the difficulties any monetary authority would have with the time lag for policies to become effective and business uncertainty about future costs and technological conditions, the risks of using monetary policy to control labor increase substantially. Engineering a healthy economy is tricky enough, but when efforts to fight against labor are thrown into the mix, the difficulties are compounded.

We cannot precisely calculate the toll of sado-monetarism. Over and above the direct economic costs of lost production, traumatization campaigns erode the quality of labor. Workers lose the opportunity to develop on-the-job skills to the limited extent that such opportunities are possible in a Procrustean workplace. Prolonged unemployment causes so much damage to some workers' self-esteem that they effectively become unemployable.

While precision is impossible, we can conclude with confidence that the cost of recent monetary policy has been substantial. With the collapse of the subprime mortgage bubble, trillions of dollars quickly evaporated in the United States alone. The long-term costs in terms of lost economic growth are likely to be even greater. Ignoring all the personal hardships associated with the downturn, suppose that efforts to control labor caused a tiny share of the crisis. In that case, one might question whether the bloodlust of the Federal Reserve actually served the real interests of its business clients.

The Irony of Asset Prices

In contrast to the harsh medicine used to "cure" increasing wages, the Fed treats financial assets with kid gloves. Several reasons might explain why the Fed has been loath to limit speculative excesses. First, the obsession with transactions distorts economic policy. Although the Fed's mandate is to control inflation, the government's measurement of official inflation rates only looks at the prices of products sold on the market—not financial assets. With that mindset, during the late Greenspan era the Fed's successful traumatization of labor made inflation seem an unlikely threat. At the time, the speculative buildup of asset prices seemed to be a sign of economic health.

The economics profession echoed the Federal Reserve in not displaying much appetite for checking speculative behavior. Both economists and the Fed typically seemed to confuse speculative excess with financial innovations that supposedly promoted efficiency. This misguided association of rising asset prices with a strong economy might seem natural for the financially minded people who run and advise the Fed. But with all the regulatory tools at its command, the Federal Reserve, with its army of economists, would have been able to discover other mechanisms to rein in speculation without traumatizing labor. Direct regulation of dangerous and deceptive financial practices would have been a better tool for managing excessive speculation than manipulation of the money supply. The Fed, however, has another, class-based agenda, and it is unlikely to apply the same kind of treatment to wealthy speculators that they impose on workers.

The Absence of Normal Discipline

Firms at the highest reaches of the economy are largely immune from the Procrustean pressures that plague the rest of society. Management has no need to justify its actions because it is accountable to nobody, except the stockholders—and, all too often, managers take advantage of their stockholders as well. The vast majority of individual stockholders—the presumptive owners of the corporations—are almost as powerless as ordinary workers in terms of corporate governance.

Even higher on the economic pyramid rest the financial markets. There, the movers and shakers of the financial world enjoy the maximum possible amount of flexibility. These speculators can drive industries, or even nation-states, one way or another, according to their whims. The maneuvers of the financial sector, however, add a strong dose of irrationality to the influence of greed. Everyone else must adapt to their bets.

In this stratosphere of big business, survival depends less on efficient methods of production than on access to people of power and influence. Probably the best investment that big business can make is in purchasing the compliance of powerful politicians:

> The timber industry spent $8 million in campaign contributions to preserve a logging road subsidy worth $458 million—the return on their investment was 5,725 percent. Glaxo Wellcome invested $1.2 million in campaign contributions to get a 19-month patent extension on Zantac worth $1 billion—their net return: 83,333 percent. The tobacco industry spent $30 million for a tax break worth $50 billion—the return on their investment: 167,000 percent. For a paltry $5 million in campaign contributions, the broadcasting industry was able to secure free digital

TV licenses, a giveaway of public property worth $70 billion—that's an incredible 1,400,000 percent return on their investment.[74]

Those who celebrate the wonders of the free market are usually silent about this sort of voluntary transaction between business and political leaders. As the great corporations accumulate increasing power, they enjoy unimaginable freedom.

Here, ironically, Adam Smith again enters into the picture. While Procrusteans are quick to quote chapter and verse of Adam Smith, the chapters they almost exclusively quote are from the first part of his book about voluntary exchanges or from his scattered references to the problems associated with government policies.

In fact, Smith had many uncomplimentary things to say about business, especially the kind of business that is rampant today. A not atypical example reads, "The interest of the dealers, however, in any particular branch of trade or manufactures, is always in some respects different from, and even opposite to, that of the publick."[75] Or one might prefer:

> The directors of such companies, however, being the managers rather of other people's money than of their own, it cannot well be expected, that they should watch over it with the same anxious vigilance with which the partners in a private copartnery frequently watch over their own. Negligence and profusion, therefore, must always prevail, more or less, in the management of the affairs of such a company.[76]

The real world of greed and speculation seems far removed from Smith's imagined voluntarism in the first chapters of his book. Instead, what exists is a whirlwind of irrationality that leaves a trail of human tragedy in its wake—a toll that makes the crude brutality of Procrustes seem quite modest by comparison.

In this speculative hubbub, the people who make the entire system work—the people who just follow orders producing the goods and services on which everybody depends—largely go ignored, except when management finds the need to impose more discipline.

Out of Control

In the long run, even the mightiest corporations face a different kind of threat. When business excessively disturbs natural forces, it risks creating destructive reactions that can engulf even the most powerful. After all, the laws of nature are more powerful than the artificial laws of economic theory. So, while the Procrusteans might believe that their rule is natural, nature pays little heed to the profit imperative.

For decades, much of the business community stubbornly denied the existence of global warming, although today some sectors, such as insurance, are starting to recognize the devastation that this phenomenon can bring to their balance sheets. The costs of meeting the challenge of global warming will be staggering. Global warming is only one of a large number of serious challenges that lie ahead, including the disappearance of cheap oil, the increasing pervasiveness of toxic chemicals, and the alarming scarcity of fresh water around the world. In addition, the explosion of poverty and a transportation system that makes long-distance travel commonplace create an ideal setting for pandemics, for which the world is ill-prepared.[77]

To meet these challenges, and others we have not yet imagined, will require great skill and creativity. Just as nations have historically scoured the land to find soldiers when serious dangers threatened their existence, so too must society now enlist as much brainpower as it can muster if humanity is going to successfully face the future. Society must go out of its way to nurture people.

Unfortunately, the present Procrustean system based on command and control inhibits the development of the very skills upon which our future depends. Thinking back to the way in which the managers at Tiger Creek thwarted the technological potential of the information technology, we must decide between an obsolete system of control that could spell disaster and a fantastic opportunity for success.

The Procrusteans never tire of describing how the market provides magnificent new technologies that offer splendid opportunities to improve the quality of life. In reality, academia and government-sponsored research are the driving forces for the development of technology—not the business sector. Even if the corporate sector had developed all of modern technology, profit-minded businesses are still not suited to handle urgent and complex challenges.

Deep down, many people have serious reservations about capitalism. Just consider for a moment what societies do when they face a serious security threat. During the two world wars, did the government trust the fortunes of the society to the free market? No; the federal government took control of the economy so that it could direct the business sector.

The government made the decision to suspend much of the market without much of protest. It was accepted that ordinary business procedures were not capable of meeting the challenge of supplying both the civilian sector and the massive military demands.

In contrast, during the invasion of Iraq, the government privatized much of the effort. Symbolically, the president at the time was the first MBA to hold that office. Despite the relatively small scale of this incursion, this experience should stand as convincing proof of the necessity of a non-business approach to emergencies.

If the Iraq invasion does not dispel faith in the ability of private markets to respond to complex emergencies, then the privatized effort to respond to the devastation of Hurricane Katrina in the Gulf states certainly should. Wal-Mart proved that it could deliver supplies, but by and large the vast majority of private contractors proved more adept at looting the Treasury than complying with the terms of their contracts.

The profit motive becomes abhorrent under emergency conditions. People who profit by charging exorbitant rates for bottled water or electricity generators during emergencies appear to be immoral creatures rather than intelligent entrepreneurs meeting a social need.

CHAPTER TEN

Where Do We Go from Here?

The Procrustean Language

Presently, two conflicting trends are colliding. On the one hand, those in control are successfully accumulating more power, solidifying the hold of Procrusteanism. On the other hand, the application of these new powers is producing dismal results, except for the most privileged sectors of society. Once people come to recognize the growing gap between economic performance and the potential productivity of society, the destructive nature of Procrusteanism will, hopefully, become self-evident.

Even so, the ideology of the status quo is so thoroughly ingrained that little progress—or even little hope of progress—appears on the horizon. We can only hope that Frederic Jameson was wrong when he observed that within contemporary society "it is easier to imagine the end of the world than to imagine the end of capitalism."[1] One precondition of moving in a progressive direction is to carefully reframe the imagery of the economy. The problem is that the Procrustean world has created a special language, one that intentionally clouds the harsh reality in which people find themselves, in effect, making the handcuffs invisible and questions of class unthinkable.

The key concepts of this rhetorical façade are freedom and equality. Recall how leaders as far afield as George W. Bush and Edmund Burke, who had little in common except a deep antipathy toward anything progressive, play upon the themes of freedom and equality. But the typical refrains of freedom and equality have a peculiar ideological twist—one that echoes Anatole France's remark about how the law forbids both rich and poor from begging on the street.

This warped understanding of freedom is not necessarily hypocrisy, but rather what psychologists call "cognitive dissonance," meaning the ability to maintain two conflicting ideas at the same time without acknowledging the contradiction. People in power often have, or at least develop, an inflated view of themselves, which can make contradictory ideas easier to accommodate.

Late in life, almost two centuries ago, John Adams eloquently wrote to Thomas Jefferson, in words that can be interpreted as describing this Procrustean mindset that speaks of freedom while abusing the authority of the state:

> Power always thinks it has a great soul and vast views beyond the comprehension of the weak; and that it is doing God's service when it is violating all his laws. Our passions, ambition, avarice, love, resentment, etc., possess so much metaphysical subtlety, and so much overpowering eloquence, that they insinuate themselves into the understanding and the conscience, and convert both to their party; and I may be deceived as much as any of them, when I say, that Power must never be trusted without a check.[2]

Unlike Adams, I am not sure which of God's laws the Procrusteans violate, but I do know that they are more than willing to violate other laws with impunity whenever anyone effectively challenges their system of control. In such cases, the rhetoric of liberty and democracy quickly gives way to violent repression, typically justified in the name of protecting freedom. If people could break through the veil of indoctrination, they would clearly recognize that the current system is neither efficient nor productive of human welfare.

Perhaps they might even catch a glimpse of the potential for a better society within the harsh confines of the present one—something akin to sensing the power of the partially revealed *Bearded Slave*, struggling to free himself from the rock in which he is embedded. They might even be likely to rise up. In that case, violent repression would be ineffective in preventing people from casting off their invisible handcuffs. Sooner or later, people will look back at the present phase of capitalism with the same disdain that surrounds earlier stages of economic development, such as feudalism and slavery—as a flawed system, inappropriate for a developed society.

Unfortunately, so long as the Procrustean theology goes unchallenged, business will be able to continue to pretend that the economy is a realm of freedom. For example, anything that interferes with workers' ability to arrive at voluntary agreements is supposed to represent an unjustified intrusion into a perfectly harmonious arrangement. Given this perspective, unions have absolutely no justification, even if every single worker would prefer to have union representation to redress labor's unequal bargaining position. Instead, in this fantasy world, freedom means that no union could prevent a high school dropout from having the opportunity to sit down and come to an amicable arrangement with a corporate behemoth, such as Wal-Mart—as if such personal encounters actually exist in the real world.

The Procrustean language, however, in painting employers in this charitable light, also betrays the underlying imbalance of power. Employers are said to "give" jobs to workers who are reduced to "taking" jobs. This language suggests that the transaction between employer and employee represents an act of benevolence on the part of the job giver rather than a bargain among equals. Framed this way, the generous giver of jobs—an almost feudal figure—certainly occupies a superior position to the supplicant who is reduced to taking the offerings from the employer. Unlike workers, employers are not expected to be grateful to their workers for their efforts.

This inequality between job givers and job takers presumably explains why society is expected to shower the generous job givers with so many benefits, such as subsidies and tax write offs. In contrast, social programs, directed at the people who actually do the work, seem to be nothing more than impositions by ungrateful wretches, who are trying to extort excessive benefits from the already overburdened taxpayer—a code word for the wealthy, who, following in the footsteps of Samuel Read, see themselves as the real creators of value.

The focus of this book has been the destructive nature of the relationship between capital and labor. The ingrained Procrustean perspective is doubly destructive in this respect. First, business fails to take advantage of, and even stifles, the potential of the working class. Second, the Procrustean ideology blinds much of society, including a good part of the working class, to the possibility of a different system, one that could allow for a more productive economy—and more important—a more fulfilling life.

Self-Imprisonment

Many working-class people have unconsciously accepted the Procrustean perspective that they should find their fulfillment as consumers, while putting up with their jobs as the necessary precondition of consumption. For workers, left without appropriate outlets for self-expression and drained by stressful work, consumptionism becomes a major vehicle of self-definition.

Consumption generally fails to provide lasting satisfaction. Instead, the initial pleasure is often fleeting, especially after the consumer sees advertisements for new-and-improved products or, worse, a neighbor with a better version. Satisfaction rapidly turns into dissatisfaction, creating an emotional emptiness. This emptiness feeds on itself, creating a craving for additional consumption.

Harriet Lerner, a noted psychologist, once observed, "Our society doesn't promote self-acceptance and it never will. First of all, self-acceptance doesn't sell products. Capitalism would fall if we liked ourselves the way we are now."[3] This negativity becomes contagious. Lerner said that "people who feel shamed and inadequate themselves tend to pass it on. I'm sure you've noticed that many individuals and groups try to enhance their self-esteem by diminishing others, "This behavior often takes the form of outdoing others in consumption."[4] People's attempt to self-medicate with consumptionism may improve the immediate performance of the economy by creating more demand for commodities, but at a cost of diminishing its long-term potential.

Continually chasing a better lifestyle puts many consumers in a precarious financial state that makes the hold of Procrusteanism even tighter. Any interruption in income—or just a slowdown in the rate of growth of income—can spell economic disaster. Such continual economic insecurity makes workers fearful. In this sense, consumptionism increases the vulnerability of workers to traumatization.

Even more corrosively, fear sometimes makes people more likely to crave authority. Whether or not this craving is operational, people come to feel unworthy and doubt their own capacities. Though they might be disgruntled about their personal condition, on a deeper level people seem to accept the status quo as inevitable, if not just, in effect, internalizing the Procrustean ethic by donning the invisible handcuffs.

Politically, people in such a state become vulnerable to the deadening mantra of "jobs, jobs, jobs." The idea of change, even when it might be in their self-interest, cannot overcome the underlying state of fearfulness. Besides, too many promises have already been broken. Better the devil you know than the one you don't.

In contrast, those born in more favorable conditions come to see themselves as entitled to the privileges they enjoy. They rarely recognize how they have profited from the network of friends and family that have opened the corridors of power to them. Such people often learn to carry themselves in a way that effectively signals their status to the rest of the world. The confidence that they exude often intimidates some of the less fortunate.

This discouraging mindset induces many people to become disengaged, or worse, to collaborate in their own oppression. In some cases, people succumb to patterns of behavior that prevent them from enjoying even a working-class standard of living. For the most part, however, fearing the consequences of destitution, the great mass of the population continues to perform the work necessary to fuel the same Procrustean economy that imprisons them.

Politically, the great challenge is to win the support of the majority of the population—those people who would stand to benefit the most from a progressive reorganization of society, but who still unquestioningly submit to Procrusteanism.

A Meritocracy of Fools

Unlike a crude caste system, the current social organization is partially permeable. A few exceptional people from the bottom manage to claw their way up to a relatively high position. These infrequent successes of a few token people of merit reinforce the existing class system by giving an appearance of fairness. The lesson for the less fortunate is that challenges to the system are unjustified: they too could stand among the victors, if only they had made the right decisions in their lives.

More often than not, modern institutions identify merit by looking for characteristics associated with upper-class life. Once people become conditioned to accept this pecking order, the system takes on the appearance of a meritocracy. In effect, appealing to merit as a guiding principle can be a pretense for keeping existing class structures in place.

In fact, the word *meritocracy* is of relatively recent vintage. In 1958, Michael Young, a British sociologist, coined the term in a satiric novel, *The Rise of the Meritocracy*, set in 2033. Looking back, Young reported that he was "sadly disappointed" that the term has now taken on favorable connotations. Young admits:

> It is good sense to appoint individual people to jobs on their merit. It is the opposite when those who are judged to have merit of a particular kind harden into a new social class without room in it for others. . . . The new class has the means at hand, and largely under its control, by which it reproduces itself.[5]

Young's worst fears seem to have been realized. Those on the top appear to naturally inhabit their elevated perches; those further down also appear to belong just where they are. Given this mindset, polite society naturally dismisses questions about outsized incomes enjoyed by the privileged class as impertinent. Such rewards seem suitable for those who have risen to the pinnacle of an aristocracy of talent.

Nobody dares to expect the same harsh Procrustean demands of the corporate elite that this privileged group would routinely impose on everybody else. The public may delight in seeing celebrities experience embarrassment or upon rare occasions fall into hard times, but corporate leaders rarely fall under the harsh scrutiny of the public, possibly because most are too boring to interest many people.

This permissive attitude toward corporate leaders might make some sense in those cases when a chief executive officer successfully leads a corporation to greater profits without harming too many people, but as we have seen, CEOs still profit handsomely even when getting fired for poor performance or worse.

Every few decades, after a major economic downturn reveals waves of grotesque corporate behavior, few executives are brought to account. After the crisis subsides, once again the executives can do what they want as long as the financial markets are satisfied.

Merit or Class?

Virtually everybody accepts that some form of real meritocracy is desirable; however, nobody has ever succeeded in explaining just how a meritocracy should function. People have an easier time declaring that success (in the absence of government interference) ultimately depends upon merit.

Just what constitutes merit? Are those in a position of power qualified to determine how merit should be determined? How can society ensure that everybody has the same opportunity to develop their merit, say, through good education? In fact, society today has an almost hereditary system in which children of the affluent have easy access to the elite universities, which then presumably certify merit.[6]

For the most part, talent and a strong work ethic alone are rarely enough to ensure success. Successful people almost invariably have received a crucial boost from some preexisting connections. The importance of such connections becomes obvious when well-connected people, no matter how undeserving, enjoy meteoric success.

The fate of these people brings to mind the biblical injunction (Deuteronomy 8:17):

> When you have eaten your fill and have built fine houses and live in them, and when your herds and flocks have multiplied, and your silver and gold is multiplied, and all that you have is multiplied, Do not say to yourself, "My power and the might of my own hand have gotten me this wealth."

Despite the admonition of the Bible, the illusory merit of such people becomes self-confirming; at that same time it sends a signal of futility to others. The result is that many exceptionally talented people fall between the cracks. Poverty and other social pressures discourage many talented people from even trying to develop their abilities. Some of those left at the bottom of the scale internalize the perverted values of the system, becoming convinced that their fate in life is inevitable, or even well deserved.

Of course, many cases do exist in which very bright, hardworking people are able to leverage their talents and opportunities into positions of authority. These exceptions serve to make the existing social pyramid less vulnerable to questions about fairness.

Even if society could somehow reach a unanimous agreement about how to measure merit, it would still face another serious question: How should the rewards associated with various degrees of merit be distributed? For example, everybody could earn the same income, though positions associated with greater merit might offer more prestige. Alternatively, one could argue that great differences in income are necessary to induce people to prepare themselves to function effectively in positions of high responsibility. These differentials could range from modest amounts to the spectacular gaps between salary levels found in contemporary society.

In the United States today, rewards are certainly not commensurate with contributions to society. How could anyone rationally explain why schoolteachers or nurses earn less than advertising executives or stockbrokers?

In short, on closer inspection, many of those people who rise to the top of their professions frequently do not seem to be any more distinguished than their peers. A cynic might even label our present world a *kakistocracy*, a Greek term that means government by the least qualified or most unprincipled citizens. Although that verdict might be too extreme, the absurd distortions that Procrusteanism imposes on society should be beyond dispute.

Obviously, leaders of society would be unlikely to appreciate being compared with Procrustes. Many would protest that they generously donate time and money to charitable causes. Unfortunately, some of these causes, but certainly not all, are devoted to nothing more than instilling Procrustean values in the less fortunate. What is more, the wealth that the successful people donate—more often than not with fanfare—owes a great deal to the sweat of others, just as the hard work of others makes possible the free time our affluent philanthropists devote to their charities.

Such displays of conscience may help some people view themselves as philanthropists, a word that implies "lovers of people." But the love that these people shower on others seems less admirable when put in a larger context. Donating substantial amounts of money on Sunday may be eye-catching, but with few exceptions such donations typically constitute a relatively small share of the wealth that was accumulated from the work of others during the rest of the week.

Any connection between their own privileges and the undesirable conditions of the less fortunate is lost on the successful. But, as Adam Smith's friend Lord Kames once observed, "If there were no luxury, there would be no poor."[7] Not only do the masses perform the work that makes the affluence of the rich possible, but their low incomes leave more of the economic pie for the elites.

Powerful politicians and business leaders often brag about their rise from poverty, real or imagined. They almost invariably attribute their success to their own hard work and determination, qualities they find lacking among the poor. They avoid seeing themselves as part of a larger process in which the fortunes of a few depend upon the misfortunes of the many.

Of course, extraordinarily hard work was essential for many people who rose from unfavorable circumstances, although their good fortune almost invariably owed much to a strong dose of luck and/or a helping hand from the higher ranks. These exceptions hardly prove the nonexistence of the harsh forces that consign many people to a particular class. Nonetheless, many people use such cases to hammer home a strong ideological lesson: those who stay mired in the lower reaches of society owe their fate to their own personal deficiencies. Given that the majority supposedly lacks the qualities to ascend beyond their proletarian existence, how could such people ever function effectively in an environment that offered them more freedom?

Crooked Timber

Isaiah Berlin, a widely respected scholar, attempted to give a philosophical luster to Procrusteanism by insisting that people are too imperfect to flourish without the imposition of discipline. Berlin repeatedly cited Immanuel Kant, the great German philosopher, who used a metaphor from forestry:

> It is just as with the trees in the forest, which need each other, for in seeking to take in the air and sunlight from each other, each obtains a beautiful, straight shape, while those that grow in freedom and separate from one another branch out randomly, and are stunted, bent, and twisted.[8]

Kant concluded: "Out of the crooked timber of humanity no straight thing was ever made." Indeed, Berlin even titled a 1991 collection of his essays *The Crooked Timber of Humanity*.

Perry Anderson took Berlin to task for his appropriation of Kant's metaphor:

> By dint of repetition—it is cited once in *Russian Thinkers*, twice in *Against the Current*, three times in *Four Essays on Liberty*, and twice more in *The Crooked Timber* itself—Berlin has virtually made of this a saw. Here, we are given to understand, is a signal expression of that rejection of all perfectionist utopias which defines a humane pluralism. But what was the actual force of the text from which the sentence is taken? *The Idea for a Universal History in a Cosmopolitan Perspective* is a terse, incandescent manifesto for a world order still to be constructed, and a world history yet to be written.[9]

Russell Jacoby went further, noting that Kant's meaning was the inverse of Berlin's. Kant was writing at a time when the Germans were pioneering what purported to be scientific forestry. The state saw the forests "through its fiscal lens into a single number" representing potential revenue from timber and firewood:

> Missing, of course, were all those trees, bushes, and plants holding little or no potential for state revenue. Missing as well were all those parts of trees, even revenue-bearing trees, which might have been useful to the population but whose value could not be converted into fiscal receipts. Here I have in mind foliage and its uses as fodder and thatch; fruits, as food for people and domestic animals; twigs and branches, as bedding, fencing, hop poles, and kindling; bark and roots, for making medicines and for tanning; sap, for making resins; and so forth. Each species of tree—indeed, each part or growth stage of each species—had its unique properties and uses.[10]

The fiscal foresters adopted an almost economistic perspective, ignoring the larger environment. They grew straight but unhealthy trees. This effort to control the forests proved counterproductive:

A new term, Waldsterben (forest death), entered the German vocabulary to describe the worst cases. An exceptionally complex process involving soil building, nutrient uptake, and symbiotic relations among fungi, insects, mammals, and flora—which were, and still are, not entirely understood—was apparently disrupted, with serious consequences. Most of these consequences can be traced to the radical simplicity of the scientific forest.[11]

For example, Rosa Luxemburg, an important revolutionary leader, wrote to her friend Sophie Liebknecht about the destructive nature of scientific forestry:

> Yesterday I was reading about the reasons for the disappearance of song birds in Germany. The spread of scientific forestry, horticulture, and agriculture, have cut them off from their nesting places and their food supply. More and more, with modern methods, we are doing away with hollow trees, waste lands, brushwood, fallen leaves. I felt sore at heart. I was not thinking so much about the loss of pleasure for human beings, but I was so much distressed at the idea of the stealthy and inexorable destruction of these defenceless little creatures, that the tears came into my eyes.[12]

Similarly, the Procrusteans may be able to enforce discipline, but only at the cost of strangling more productive capacities that could make life better. John Maynard Keynes was one of the few economists who occasionally grasped the unhealthy nature of the Procrustean system, although not from the perspective of this book.

A Non-Procrustean World for Our Grandchildren

In the midst of the Great Depression, John Maynard Keynes published an engaging essay titled "Economic Possibilities for Our Grandchildren."[13] Keynes was not just some woolly-minded intellectual, isolated in an ivory tower. He was the editor of possibly the most important professional economics journal in the world. People in the highest levels of government and business also regularly turned to him. During the Second World War, Keynes was the most important representative of his government in coordinating British and American economic policy.

In a sense, this essay prefigured Keynes's later work, where he explained how depressions occurred because market forces were unable to produce enough jobs. This article, however, went much further, striking at the very heart of economic theory, which purports to be an analysis of how to deal with scarcity.

Although Keynes was relatively conservative, he adopted a revolutionary position for an economist, launching a powerful attack on Procrusteanism. He suggested that the overriding problem that the world faced was not scarcity, but abundance. Keynes realized that, at least in the developed world, society would soon possess more than enough means to produce a good standard of living for everybody with a minimum effort.

Almost two decades before, just after resigning from the British delegation for the international negotiations following the devastation of the First World War, Keynes had already speculated about his hope for the post-Procrustean future:

> Perhaps a day might come when there would at last be enough to go round, and when posterity could enter into the enjoyment of our labours. In that day overwork, overcrowding, and underfeeding would come to an end, and men, secure of the comforts and necessities of the body, could proceed to the nobler exercises of their faculties.[14]

In effect, Keynes was speculating on the possibility of going beyond Adam Smith's vision of four stages, moving into a fifth and higher stage of human development in which traditional methods of control have no justification. With the commencement of this new stage, modern technology could provide a good standard of living with a minimum of effort.

At the same time, Keynes seemed to accept that, for the time being, the inelegant and inefficient Procrustean basis of economic growth would have to remain in place. A decade and a half after the publication of "Economic Possibilities" Keynes stepped down from his long-standing position as the editor of the Royal Economic Society's *Economic Journal*, Britain's premier economics journal. On the occasion of his retirement in 1945, the society gave a dinner in his honor. Keynes gave a speech apparently calling upon economists to make sure that people continue to keep their noses against the grindstone, ending with a toast: "To economists, who are the trustees, not of civilisation, but of the possibility of civilisation."[15] Unfortunately, this trusteeship has fallen short of its obligation. At least Keynes, while he was congratulating his fellow economists for having played such a key role in promoting economic progress, had the good sense to realize that this current progress was something different from what he considered to be civilization. Unfortunately, his idea of civilization, like his rejection of Procrusteanism, was largely cultural.

Even earlier than Keynes, his teacher Alfred Marshall, who set the tone for much of the narrow, formalized, early twentieth-century economics, wrote in a similar vein:

> Now at last we are setting ourselves seriously to inquire whether there need to be large numbers of people doomed from their birth to hard work in order to provide for others the requisites for a refined and cultured life; while they themselves are prevented by their poverty and toil from having any share or part in that life. [16]

Keynes and Marshall both anticipated that this new stage of development would permit all people to enjoy the opportunity to develop their human capacities. Although they looked forward to the disappearance of crude Procrusteanism in the future, neither gave any hint that society was ready to ease the discipline at the time they were writing.

In the case of Keynes, this narrow vision is understandable. Besides being a great economist, he was an upper-class snob. In his essay, as well as in most of his work, Keynes never really seemed to be thinking about the actual lives of working people or their preferences. Although Keynes was formally somewhat solicitous of the material welfare of the working class, he certainly held himself aloof from workers, whom he contemptuously regarded as "boorish."[17] He wrote to a friend, "I have been having tea with working men; I suppose that they're virtuous enough fellows, not as ugly as they might be, and that it amuses them to come to Cambridge and be entertained for a fortnight—but I don't know what good it does."[18] Except for such brief moments spent with workers on farms that his college owned, Keynes seems to have had almost no later personal association with those who were obliged to work for wages.[19]

Instead of a positive vision of multifaceted human flourishing, Keynes's vision reflected an aesthetic revulsion toward unattractive elements of his world. As a close colleague noted, "He hated unemployment because it was stupid and poverty because it was ugly."[20] The hard business values of untrammeled capitalism also repulsed Keynes. In the concluding remarks to *The General Theory*, Keynes justified private business only on the tenuous grounds that it allowed otherwise "dangerous human proclivities" to be "canalised into comparatively harmless channels . . . It is better that a man should tyrannize over his bank balance than over his fellow-citizens."[21] In the same spirit, he belittled "the management of stock exchange investments of any kind as a low pursuit having little social value and partaking (at best) of the nature of a game of skill."[22] Despite his contempt for what he presumed to be the present personalities both of the working class and the capitalists, Keynes, like Marshall, believed that a better society could produce better sorts of people—at least the sort of people with whom Keynes enjoyed associating.

Keynes gave no hint that he was sensitive to the main point of this book—that the economic policies intended to spur economic development may actually impair the rate of economic growth by failing to take advantage of the potential of those the Procrustean economy typically leaves behind. Although Keynes looked forward to a time when people could flourish, his vision of flourishing almost seemed to be limited to those already living in a more refined manner.

In the end, despite their limited concern with the broader possibilities of human flourishing, over and beyond cultural niceties, neither

Keynes nor Marshall ever did much to challenge the Procrustean thinking. Instead, they only dreamed about a time when humanity could move on to the next stage.

Keynes even indicated that for the time being the Procrustean path was humanity's only choice and that path would be a long one:

> For at least a hundred years we must pretend to ourselves and to everyone that fair is foul and foul is fair; for foul is useful and fair is not. Avarice and usury and precaution must be our gods for a little longer still. For only they can lead us out of the tunnel of economic necessity into daylight.[23]

This reluctance to challenge the existing system is not surprising. People like Keynes or Marshall were hardly revolutionaries. They were not about to make common cause with the unwashed working class. Nor were they likely to risk ostracism by the comfortable elites, who were unlikely to welcome the new stage of society that Keynes and Marshall imagined.

The Recalcitrance of the Elites

Keynes was realistic enough to recognize that the transition to the post-Procrustean stage of development would be met with stiff resistance. In particular, the most desirable aspects of the transition for the majority would threaten the position of the powerful minority—whom Keynes strangely enough calls "ordinary men." Here Keynes's words are worth citing at length:

> I think with dread of the readjustment of the habits and instincts of the ordinary man, bred into him for countless generations, which he may be asked to discard in a few decades. . . . For the first time since his creation man will be faced with his real, his permanent problem—how to use his freedom from pressing economic cares, how to occupy his leisure, which science and compound interest will have won for him, to live wisely and agreeably and well.

> Yet there is no country and no people, I think, who can look forward
> to the age of leisure and of abundance without a dread. [24]

Surely Keynes would have known that the elites would resist losing something far dearer to them than their work habits—the prestige and authority they held over others. The elites would not welcome an egalitarian society that would whittle away at their status. Why should anybody else have the same opportunity that the elites now enjoy? What gives common people the right to participate in activities that are now the exclusive domain of the better sort of people? How could such people expect equal access to the elevated positions in society? Here again, Keynes's concern was largely cultural, with little thought to the potential contributions of the "boorish" masses.

Even more seriously, the erosion of the work habits of the masses would be a matter of great concern for the elites. To imagine that their authority to order other people around would no longer exist would be a bitter pill for the elites to swallow.

Although Keynes was not explicit about the class-based nature of the resistance he expected, his description of the dread of the new stage of development does not ring true for poor working-class people. We could reasonably expect that most of the less fortunate people would not put up much resistance to the opportunities Keynes described—more leisure and a higher standard of living for everybody, including the working class. Even so, Keynes's negative assessment of the cultural dimension of Procrusteanism actually went much further than Sen:

> When the accumulation of wealth is no longer of high social importance, there will be great changes in the code of morals. We shall be able to rid ourselves of many of the pseudo-moral principles which have hag-ridden us for two hundred years, by which we have exalted some of the most distasteful of human qualities into the position of the highest virtues. We shall be able to afford to dare to assess the money-motive at its true value. The love of money as a possession—as distinguished from the love of money as a means to the enjoyments and realities of life—will be recog-

nised for what it is, a somewhat disgusting morbidity, one of those semi-criminal, semi-pathological propensities which one hands over with a shudder to the specialists in mental disease. [25]

Keynes's description of "the pseudo-moral principles which have hag-ridden us for two hundred years, by which we have exalted some of the most distasteful of human qualities into the position of the highest virtues" is one of the most accurate depictions of the cultural basis of Procrusteanism that I have seen.

Based on Keynes's perspective, the prospects of a future that would satisfy him would make good Procrusteans shudder, especially because Keynes believed that working hours could dramatically shrink:

> Three-hour shifts or a fifteen-hour week may put off the problem for a great while. For three hours a day is quite enough to satisfy the old Adam in most of us![26]

Keynes's hundred-year estimate for the duration of the existing state proved overly optimistic. Unfortunately, in the more than three-quarters of a century that has passed since Keynes wrote, society seems to keep drifting further and further from the future he sketched.

Working hours keep increasing, and virtually everyone but the wealthy has an increasingly hard time making ends meet. In addition, global economic forces are making more and more people within the advanced market economies redundant, replacing them with much cheaper labor from the poorer regions of the world. Even people with professional skills are coming under intense pressure.

Reason should dictate that the people who are falling under the wheels of this juggernaut would question the prevailing Procrusteanism, but for the most part they have not yet succeeded in identifying their underlying problem. Alas, despite the fact that the existing economic system is not working for the benefit of the majority, Procrusteanism now has a tighter hold on society than Keynes could ever imagine.

The underlying force preventing the transition Keynes envisioned is not, as he thought, one of economic necessity, but rather a system of power and class, which consigns the majority of people to constrained lives that block the mobilization of their potential, whether to create a better way of life or to meet the growing challenges that endanger humanity.

Unless the people in power are willing to abandon the present system of class and control that hobbles society, ultimately even those whom the present system seems to benefit may well suffer the same fate as the admiral on the ill-fated ship who failed to heed a call from an ordinary member of the crew. Will the powers-that-be hang those future unauthorized navigators who report that the ship is off course?

What is needed to navigate the difficult waters that lie ahead is something entirely new—an equal opportunity social order that allows all people to develop their talents—a society that breaks down the mind-numbing confines of class. But what are the alternatives?

A Musical Interlude

A system as complex as a modern economy requires some system of coordination, but economics teaches that markets, without any external form of coordination, are the most efficient way of organizing an economy. In contrast, economics seems virtually unanimous that, within the economy as a whole, complex production units require top-down managerial controls. This book takes the position that neither markets nor managerial controls are particularly efficient and that cooperation offers a better alternative.

Calls for a cooperative organization of production will sound hopelessly utopian to some ears. The production of symphonic music, where a conductor prevents the musicians from creating a cacophony of sounds, is a common metaphor for the need for authority. Rarely have people raised the question of whether all that power and control is required. Even Karl Marx suggested the necessity of a conductor:

In all labour where many individuals cooperate, the interconnection and unity of the process is necessarily represented in a governing will, and in functions that concern not the detailed work but rather the workplace and its activity as a whole, as with the conductor of an orchestra.[27]

Certainly, the conductor presents an imposing figure:

There is no more obvious expression of power than the performance of a conductor. Every detail of his public behavior throws light on the nature of power. Someone who knew nothing about power could discover all its attributes, one after another, by careful observation of a conductor. The reason why this has never been done is obvious: the music that a conductor evokes is thought to be the only thing that counts; people take it for granted that they go to concerts to hear symphonies and no-one is more convinced of this than the conductor himself. He believes that his business is to serve music and to interpret it faithfully.[28]

Surprisingly, conductors were a fairly new innovation at the time Marx was writing. Only a few decades before, conductors wielding a baton did not lead the orchestra. Instead, musicians themselves, usually the first violinist, took on that responsibility while they were performing. Bach, Mozart, and Beethoven all conducted their own works—often from the keyboard.

According to Urs Frauchiger, previously director of Bern's music conservatory, the composer Carl Maria von Weber was the first to serve as a conductor standing in front of the musicians in a performance at Dresden in 1817. Later, Ludwig Spohr conducted a performance. Felix Mendelssohn soon followed.

The creation of the dictatorship of the conductor did not occur without resistance. The famous composer Robert Schumann protested that the conductor's baton contradicted republican principles.[29] Within a short time, republican principles were soon forgotten and the conductor became accepted as a central figure in symphonic productions.

One factor that promoted the role of the conductor was the development of Romanticism in the late nineteenth century. This genre often involved more complexity, which reinforced the perceived need for a conductor. As Igor Stravinsky asserted:

> It was Romantic music that unduly inflated the personality of the KAPELLMEISTER, even to the point of conferring upon him—along with the prestige that he today enjoys on his podium, which in itself concentrates attention upon him—-the discretionary power that he exerts over the music committed to his care. Perched on his sibylline tripod, he imposes his own movements, his own particular shadings upon the compositions he conducts, and he even reaches the point of talking with a naive impudence of his specialties, of HIS fifth, of HIS seventh, the way a chef boasts of a dish of his own concoction. Hearing him speak, one thinks of the billboards that recommend eating places to automobilists: "At so-and-so's restaurant, his wines, his special dishes."
>
> There was never anything like it in the past, in times that nevertheless already knew as well as our time go-getting and tyrannical virtuosos, whether instrumentalists or prima donnas. But those times did not suffer yet from the competition and plethora of conductors, who almost to a man aspire to set up a dictatorship over music.[30]

Conducting Against Democracy

Something less romantic than Romanticism was also at work. In the United States during and after the Civil War, as larger-scale methods of production displaced the traditional craft and agrarian economies in the United States, the elites were accumulating enormous fortunes, often with questionable ethics.

They acquired a certain degree of respectability through philanthropy. Some chose to become patrons of the arts to advertise their culture as well as their wealth. These wealthy "philanthropists" provided the capital to erect symphony halls as new temples of culture, which stood as a boundary marking off the distance between the masters of Procrusteanism and ordinary people.

In Europe, the symphony orchestra had been a poor stepchild compared to the opera, which had a popular following.[31] Unlike today, the wealthy regarded opera as an excessively democratic art form. Ordinary people, without sufficient funds to purchase expensive instruments, could and often did sing the arias themselves.

In the United States, only a few decades earlier in 1842, symphonic music also had a democratic aura. The Philharmonic Society of New York was initially founded as a cooperative enterprise. The musicians elected the conductor, chose the repertory, and shared the receipts.[32] The funders of this new symphonic music regarded such democratic rule as inappropriate.

In contrast, the patrons of U.S. symphonies wanted to promote "high culture," which had the added attraction that it seemed to require the imposition of a strict hierarchy. They built "new temples exclusively for this orchestral music . . . a higher form of art, which (supposedly) reflected the moral character of the city."[33]

Romantic music was ideal for the patrons of this "high culture." The spirit of Romanticism elevated the undemocratic idea of the heroic creator who rose above the crowd. In a sense, this image of the composer parallels the later vision of the influential economist Joseph Schumpeter, who popularized the image of the heroic entrepreneur as a central figure in economic progress. These entrepreneurs create enormous value by developing new products or great efficiencies.[34] Schumpeter's idea became popular in the business press toward the end of the twentieth century, during the height of the dot-com boom.

In the United States, the expense of this capital-intensive system of production elevated the wealthy philanthropist as a heroic figure. As a symbol of this new musical mode of production, the conductor attained a position of great importance.

For example, when in 1906, Wilhelm Gericke resigned as music director of the Boston Symphony Orchestra, a Cleveland reporter commented on the enormity of the event: "In Boston the leader of the orchestra is a good deal bigger than the mayor." Two years later, romantic composer Gustav Mahler advised Willem Mengelberg to accept the same job: "The Boston position is the finest imaginable for a musician. An orchestra of the first rank. Unlimited sovereign power. A social standing such as the musician cannot obtain in Europe."[35] In effect, the nameless musicians were to go about their work under the close supervision of the conductor, culturally instructing the public about the correctness of this new phase of the capitalist mode of production.

In this new environment, "sacralization increased the distance between amateur and professional." The popular "traditional practice of mixing musical genres and presenting audiences with an eclectic feast" became obsolete.[36] After all, the symphonies could enjoy the support of wealthy patrons who often contributed their names as well as their money to the grand culture temples. Symphonies had no need to appeal to popular tastes. Besides, this kind of performance would be too expensive for popular audiences to support.

Even Marx thought that the role of the conductor revealed that the capitalist was an unnecessary figure in production of music:

> Capitalist production has itself brought it about that the work of supervision is readily available, quite independent of the ownership of capital. It has therefore become superfluous for this work of supervision to be performed by the capitalist. A musical conductor need in no way be the owner of the instruments in his orchestra, nor does it form part of his function as a conductor that he should have any part in paying the "wages" of the other musicians.[37]

Some musical leaders are coming to question the dictatorship of the conductor. Leon Fleisher, a renowned pianist and conductor himself, now advocates a return to the earlier tradition. *The Economist* reported on Fliesher's experience during a rehearsal of Beethoven's "Emperor" Concerto, while working with the Orpheus Chamber Orchestra, which functions without a conductor. Fleisher exclaimed, "This part is always screwed up with a conductor, but we've played it perfectly twice. This is proof that conductors should just sit down."

The article cites Eric Bartlett, a cellist with both Orpheus and the New York Philharmonic Orchestra, who described the lower level of individual intensity in the latter organization: "If even a great conductor is empowered to make all the important decisions musicians start to play in a more passive way. Orpheus has removed a barrier between the audience and the music, the conductor himself." The article concludes: "So why aren't there more conductor-less orchestras? Star conductors sell more tickets than co-operatives."[38]

Stravinsky observed how such commercial considerations reinforce this artistic dictatorship:

> A quip that was passed on to me years ago clearly shows the importance which the conductor has come to take on in the preoccupations of the musical world. One day a person who presides over the fortunes of a big concert agency was being told about the success obtained in Soviet Russia by that famous conductorless orchestra of which we have already spoken: "That doesn't make much sense," declared the person in question, "and it doesn't interest me. What I'd really be interested in is not an orchestra without a conductor, but a conductor without an orchestra."[39]

As Stravinsky suggested, the prestige of the conductor is, at least in part, another case of markets triumphing over art, hardly an unknown outcome.

Summing up, the power of the conductor, which seemed almost natural even to as critical a thinker as Marx, seems to be integrally connected with the whole system of Procrusteanism. Romanticism, reflecting the unleashing of bourgeois individualism, played a role.

In contrast, Fleisher's experience with the Orpheus Orchestra suggests that forms of organization ordinarily taken for granted may not be the best way of organizing society. Just as centuries ago capitalism set free bourgeois energies that had been repressed under feudalism, a new form could be equally liberating for the masses of people presently trapped in their Procrustean beds.

A Window to the Future

Just as musical Procrusteanism cut into the creative powers of musicians, class lines restricted participation in the creativity of symphonic music. An experiment in Venezuela suggests the degree to which breaking down such barriers can contribute to the pool of creativity.

In 1975, when Venezuela had only two symphony orchestras, José Antonio Abreu founded the Youth Orchestra of Venezuela to give poor, disadvantaged youth an opportunity to become acquainted with symphonic music—the same genre that such people were supposed to be incapable of appreciating. By the time that one of these children, Gustavo Dudamel, became twenty-six, the *New York Times* described him as the most-talked-about young musician in the world. Sir Simon Rattle, the principal conductor of the Berlin Philharmonic, has called him "the most astonishingly gifted conductor I have ever come across." At a time when recording companies are cutting back on orchestral releases, Dudamel has received a coveted contract with Deutsche Grammophon and has released two CDs of Beethoven and Mahler symphonies. Already a frequent presence in European halls, he began his most extended appearance in the United States in 2010, performing in Los Angeles, San Francisco, Boston—and, for the first time, in New York, with the New York Philharmonic and, at Carnegie Hall, with his own Simón Bolívar Youth Orchestra of Venezuela.

Dudamel is still a conductor, but a different kind of conductor. Igor Lanz, the executive director of the private foundation that administers the now government-financed program, explained, "They learn that the most important thing is to work together in one common aim." This ethic seems to come across to Dudamel's colleagues. One of his fellow musicians explained how he breaks with the traditional mold of the Procrustean conductor:

> "We used to believe that a conductor is an old, introverted guy," says Rafael Payares, who plays French horn in the orchestra and is one of Dudamel's closest friends. "But this is the same Gustavo you used to see playing the violin or throwing parties. He's still the same—crazy."[40]

Dudamel made his reputation outside of Venezuela at the first Gustav Mahler International Conducting Competition in 2004. Ironically, Mahler's symphonies were at the forefront of the Romantic movement that produced complex symphonies that seemed to demand a domineering conductor.

Dudamel's achievements raise a question central to this book: how many poor children languishing in slums around the world might be potential symphony conductors, scientists, doctors, or inventors? The Venezuelan experiment suggests that people should begin to consider the answer to that question.

Freedom in a Procrustean State

If the only alternatives are a Procrustean state or a willy-nilly world of everybody "doing their own thing," then Isaiah Berlin and the more extreme Procrusteans may have a legitimate point. If, however, people have the potential to cooperate without harsh authority, then Berlin's work is misleading.

For example, many communities have symphony orchestras made up of volunteers. Their music would not be very enjoyable if all the musicians were free to play whatever they wanted regardless of anyone else. Not only do such musicians agree to play the same score, but they also generally work under the direction of a conductor—often a volunteer, who helps to coordinate their performances. As in the case of Venezuela, the conductor often also serves as a teacher, since many of the performers are still learning their craft.

Everybody in the orchestra shares the same goal of creating an enjoyable musical experience for both the audience and the musicians. When the orchestra musicians become sufficiently skilled, they might even do without the conductor. Procrustes certainly has no place at such an event.

Similarly, some communities have volunteer fire departments, which protect the straitened timbers of buildings. These volunteers do quite well, even though the logic of the market would lead "rational" people to conclude that they have no incentive to participate— better to wait for others to take their place.

Some hard-minded Procrusteans might admit that such activities might be possible under exceptional circumstances. After all, the core of Procrustean philosophy is the belief that selfishness and egotism are hard-wired into human brains and that without strong discipline the law of the jungle will prevail. Of course, proof or disproof of opinions about human nature is impossible.

The Procrusteans go further by imagining a fantasy world in which everybody prospers by following the law of the market. Even ignoring the damage done to workers, the evidence that the market operates efficiently is questionable. Most of these inefficiencies pass unnoticed until a large number of them come together in the form of a strong recession or even depression. Franklin Roosevelt illustrated this delayed recognition of the defects of the market in his Second Inaugural Address, when he said, "We have always known that heedless self-interest was bad morals; we know now that it is bad economics."[41] I explored the questionable efficiency of markets elsewhere, especially in *The Natural Instability of Markets* (1999).

Regardless of whether markets work well or not, contemporary market society has gone well beyond the ideas of Adam Smith, whose *Theory of Moral Sentiments* emphasized that market society would only function well if people exercised a degree of moral restraint. Smith proposed that people would behave that way in order to protect their reputation.

A person's reputation may be important in a small community, where people have to repeatedly interact with one another. In contrast, in a global economy where people are mobile, the concept of community means less. Failed CEOs can earn multimillion-dollar bonuses. Less "successful" people can repeatedly reinvent themselves, leaving their previous reputations behind. Disgraced corporations can adopt a new name, with the expectation that the public will soon forget their past misdeeds. As a result, protecting one's good name means far less than Smith once imagined.

Here we come to the central irony of the "Crooked Timber" perspective. When the Procrusteans worry about the need for discipline, their concerns are not consistent across class lines. Yes, ordinary people must be held in check, but the rich and powerful must be free to do what they please. Burdensome regulation will imperil the economy.

When financial scandals occur, we hear that only a few bad apples were involved. Why in the world should anybody believe that only a few bad apples exist within the upper reaches of society, while the rest of the population, which did not cause the problem, requires strict discipline?

Under the bright glare of the scandals, superficial regulations will be put in place, but only for a short period. A barrage of propaganda will eventually assure the public that such regulation is counterproductive. The war cry of "jobs, jobs, jobs" will come into play—unless the regulations are loosened, jobs are certain to be lost.

In his presidential address to the American Economic Association, recent Nobel Prize–winner Daniel McFadden warned against this perverted market fundamentalism: "Romantics of the economic right would carry the concepts of self-interested consumers and free markets even further, embracing a withering of authority and a nirvana of . . . self-reliance."[42] Of course, the authority that would wither away is the authority of the state to interfere with business. The Procrustean state would remain intact to protect the authority of those with capital.

Just What Is Work?

To understand the potential for transforming the economy, consider a simple example that does not require much of a stretch of the imagination. Just think of the enormous contrast between farm work for wages and gardening as a hobby. Farm work is considered to be so abhorrent in the United States that we regularly hear that only foreign-born workers are willing to perform it. Supposedly, upstanding citizens of the United States would never subject themselves to the life of a farm worker for poverty wages.

While farm labor may be among the hardest, most dangerous work in our society, many people regard gardening as a pleasant diversion.

While the United Farm Workers Union represents mostly downtrodden workers, a good number of wealthy people are proud affiliates of their blue-blood garden clubs. Over and above the time they spend in their gardens, many gardeners enthusiastically devote considerable leisure time to conversing or reading in order to become better gardeners. In addition, many gardeners also willingly spend substantial sums for equipment and supplies to use in their gardens.

What, then, is the underlying difference between farm work and gardening? Farm work typically entails hard physical labor, but many gardeners also exert themselves in their gardens. The difference lies in the context of gardening. Gardeners, unlike farm workers, freely choose to be gardeners. During the time they work in their gardens, they want to be gardening. Nobody tells them what to do. Gardeners are producing for themselves rather than for someone else who will benefit from their work.

As the psychologist John Neulinger says: "Everyone knows the difference between doing something because one has to and doing something because one wants to."[43] We should also keep in mind that society respects gardeners. Our newspapers regularly print features of interest to gardeners. Some even have special sections to appeal to their affluent gardening readers. All the while, the lives of farm workers pass virtually unnoticed. In our society, farm work is never "respectable" work; well-to-do families would not approve of their children becoming farm workers.

Of course, gardeners are not entirely free to follow their whims. The rhythms of the seasons and the sudden shifts in the weather dictate some of what the gardeners do, but gardeners generally accept these demands beforehand.

The pleasures of gardening are not some recent discovery. For example, Adam Smith attempted to justify the low earning of farm workers. According to Smith, farm work is so enjoyable that too many people rush to take up such work, pushing wages down. He wrote:

> Hunting and fishing, the most important employments of mankind in the
> rude state of society, become in its advanced state their most agreeable

amusements, and they pursue for pleasure what they once followed from necessity. In the advanced state of society, therefore, they are all very poor people who follow as a trade, what other people pursue as a pastime.[44]

Gardening is not the only manual work that can be appealing. Some wealthy executives restore old cars, run vineyards, or make fine furniture. Recently, the *Wall Street Journal* published a story about executives who "find inner peace in carpentry." One of these people declared that there's nothing like the deep rumble of a $2,700 Powermatic table saw.[45]

If we paid farm workers as well as those who labor on Wall Street and accorded them the sort of dignity that college professors enjoy, parents might still try to steer their children away from farm work because of the frequent exposure to potentially lethal toxins. But then, if society esteemed farm workers, their employers would not and could not spray them with impunity.

One cannot turn farm workers into gardeners or CEOs into carpenters overnight. Some work is inherently unpleasant. The method of creating a decent society will not be found in a book.

The importance of this discussion is to illustrate the destructive influence of social hierarchies, whether or not they are the formal product of a capitalist system of production. The process of organizing a good society will require much struggle, even after the creation of a socialist republic.

Madmen in Authority

As suggested earlier, the key to the Procrustean trap is not the threat of physical force but rather the inability to imagine anything outside of the constrained present circumstances. The willingness to take seriously Margaret Thatcher's preposterous claim—"There is no alternative"—perfectly sums up this state of mind.

A writer for Bloomberg.com reminisced about Thatcher's Procrustean destructive success:

Of course, it's possible to change a society and to drag it into the global economic monoculture. Mrs. Thatcher showed how: Break up collectives and make people feel a little bit more alone in the world. Cut a few holes in the social safety net. Raise the status of money-making, and lower the status of every other activity. Stop giving knighthoods to artists and start giving them to department-store moguls. Stop listening to intellectuals and start listening to entrepreneurs and financiers.

Stick to the plan long enough and the people who are good at making money acquire huge sums and, along with them, power. In time, they become the culture's dominant voice. And they love you for it.[46]

Thatcher's scheme actually worked. Her acolytes were so convinced that the mere utterance of Thatcher's acronym TINA seemed sufficient to cut off any debate with skeptics. In the process, the long-term prospects of the British economy suffered, while great wealth flowed to a minority. I am reminded of the comment of an early British leader about the victories of the invading Roman army: "They create a desolation, they call it peace."[47]

Thatcher was an exceptional Procrustean in one respect. Her certainty consciously fed off economic theory. More often, people absorb their economic thinking unconsciously. As John Maynard Keynes wrote in one of his more famous passages:

Practical men, who believe themselves to be quite exempt from any intellectual influences, are usually the slaves of some defunct economist. Madmen in authority, who hear voices in the air, are distilling their frenzy from some academic scribbler of a few years back. I am sure that the power of vested interests is vastly exaggerated compared with the gradual encroachment of ideas. Not, indeed, immediately, but after a certain interval.[48]

However, even those who happily echo economists' ideas rarely pay any attention to the unrealistic assumptions on which these theories stand.

Keynes, if anything, was too conservative in one respect about the influence of economics. Even many of the most skilled practitioners working inside sophisticated financial markets can fall under the spell of economic theory. For example, the sociologist Donald MacKenzie published an in-depth study of the co-evolution of modern financial markets and the academic work leading up to the highly mathematical Black-Scholes-Merton option-pricing model, which analyzed how speculators would behave in an abstract world subject to a number of assumptions.

Relatively quickly, speculators took the emerging theoretical model to be a formula for success. They began to develop investment strategies based on the principles of the model, in effect transforming financial markets to conform to the model. Alas, because the model was not an entirely accurate representation of the real world, it misled the speculators, eventually helping to set off a massive stock market crash in 1987.[49]

Not only speculators, but economists themselves fall victim to their own theories. In this vein, modern economists have the tendency to classify everything productive as capital. The concept of human capital is a case in point.

The Dead End of Human Capital

Some early economists understood the importance of workers' productive capacities. Adam Smith, in listing the kinds of fixed capital stock of the country, included machines, buildings used for commercial reasons, improvements of the land, and finally:

> the acquired and useful abilities of all the inhabitants or members of the society. The acquisition of such talents, by the maintenance of the acquirer during his education, study, or apprenticeship, always costs a real expense, which is a capital fixed and realized, as it were, in his person. Those talents, as they make a part of his fortune, so do they likewise of that of the society to which he belongs. The improved dexterity of a workman may be considered in the same light as a machine or instrument of trade which facilitates and abridges labour, and which, though it costs a certain expense, repays that expense with a profit.[50]

Elsewhere, Smith defined the worker as a "living instrument" and compared educated workers with "expensive machines," as might be expected from someone who conflated workers and laboring cattle.[51] These observations were made in passing and had little effect on the core of Smith's theory, except to reinforce the idea that appropriate individual behavior would open up the road to success.

For more than a century, those economists who tried to look at workers' productive capacity followed Smith's lead in not going beyond vague speculations about how the qualities of the workforce increased a nation's capacity to produce. Often economists would frame such discussions in terms of crude speculations about the racial and ethnic heritage of the workforce.

Within this aggregated mass, considerations of the potential capabilities of individual workers are nowhere to be found. By the 1960s, statistical models that were explaining the growth of the GDP by increases in capital and labor needed some sort of adjustment. Economists began using measures of education as a reflection of human capital.

In what was called "the most comprehensive effort to develop an estimate of the value of human capital in the United States,"[52] economists Dale Jorgensen and Barbara Fraumeni calculated that human capital constituted over 70 percent of the U.S. capital stock.[53]

But what is this human capital—a term that seems to merge human existence and inanimate objects? Economists tell us that "human capital refers to the productive capacities of income producing agents in the economy."[54]

Human capital, of course, is unmeasurable. A similar difficulty of measurement is part of the reason that economists avoid the subjects of work, workers, and working conditions. Economists found a way around the measurement problem by assuming that people accumulated their human capital in schools.

Years of schooling, although a crude and often misleading measure of workers' capabilities, offer a convenient quantitative measure. This method of calculating human capital emphasizes what has happened—almost passively—to the worker prior to entering the workplace. People may have accumulated more human capital—for example, by following an educational program—but at the precise moment when the economist looks at the economy an individual's human capital is fixed.

Consider the fate of a person without education condemned to a career of drudgery. The lack of human capital seems to confirm the appropriateness of the position that person holds, even though education is largely rationed by race, class, and (until fairly recently) gender rather than merit.

This approach to measuring human capital also reinforces the practice of ignoring work, workers, and working conditions, since learning on the job never enters into the picture. The concept of human capital, in effect, dehumanizes the human and collapses everything else into something akin to the sort of inert capital goods that might be found on the factory floor. To the extent that people exist solely as human capital, they should merely adapt themselves to the demands of their work.

Emphasizing the human rather than the capital in human capital would recognize that workers are not merely passive instruments. To do so would mean understanding workers as human beings with hopes and desires who have capacities that go far beyond simply taking orders. That realization would undermine centuries of economic theory, which has studiously avoided looking at work, workers, or the labor process.

The individualistic perspective of human capital makes this concept still more flawed. To begin with, young people who enter the schoolroom are not passive vessels. They are part of a larger community that includes other students, family, friends, and the world at large. These relationships go a long way to conditioning the education that a person receives. In addition, insofar as an individualistic perspective conditions the way education is offered, it becomes less relevant as a measure of productive potential because work is generally a collective activity.

Fleas, Rabbits, and Elephants

Surprisingly, Robert Lucas, mentioned earlier in terms of his very conservative analysis, wrote perceptively about the social nature of human capital formation: "A general fact that I will emphasize again and again: that human capital accumulation is a social activity, involving groups of people in a way that has no counterpart in the accumulation of physical capital."[55] Unfortunately, Lucas was not intending to make a crucial point about "human capital" but merely to justify an abstract model in which each generation could benefit by the human capital accumulated by an earlier generation.

Had Lucas realized the importance of what his words might have meant, he would have understood how workplaces, free of Procrusteanism, might be a valuable source of human development, which, among other benefits, would make the economy more productive. Instead, the concept of human capital reduces humans to just another form of capital.

Besides human capital, economists and some other social scientists drain the meaning of many other parts of life by reducing them to a form of capital. One article even complained of "a plethora of capitals."[56] Another study found sixteen different capitals, including, besides the familiar economic terms—financial, real, public, venture, human, social capital—"religious, intellectual, natural, digital, psychological, linguistic, emotional, symbolic, cultural, moral, political, endogenous, network, family, knowledge, and organizational capital."[57] Gary Becker and George Stigler, two conservative Nobel Prize–winning economists, have actually used consumption capital to indicate consumers' capacity to engage in more productive forms of consumption.[58] Nor should we forget self-command capital.

One should not be surprised that a capitalist society should adopt the investment idiom (as) a dominant way of understanding the individual's place in society. Personality and talent become "human capital"; homes, families, and communities become "social capital."[59] No wonder that Virginia Woolf, the British novelist, confessed to her diary after a dinner party at Keynes's home that she did not know how to invest her "emotional capital."[60]

This tendency to try to reduce all dimensions of human existence into capitals helps to reinforce Thatcher's TINA. Nothing has meaning except as it fits into the logic of the market.

For example, Bill Watson's coworkers, described in chapter 2, counted for little human capital—at least in the way economists conceptualize it. They probably lacked a dozen of the other aforementioned capitals as well. Yet they knew more about the products being produced than the management, which was running the automobile industry into the ground. Unfortunately, management denied them a modicum of dignity and denied the firm the benefit of their potential contributions.

In return, the workers subjected management to their pranks. Although such behavior probably appeared to be nothing more than immaturity to their employers, it was more likely a statement of their humanity. By expressing their creativity in this way, they were stating emphatically that they were much more than human capital.

Just as Watson's employers shut down the line rather than respect their employees' humanity, economists, since the time of the rebuke of Jevons, have shut down research regarding the inner workings of the labor process, including workers' subjective concerns.

Although shutting down an assembly line the way that Watson and his cohorts did might appall good Procrusteans, capitalism itself depends upon far more extensive forms of shutdowns. What is the prevention of sharing music but a shutdown? Musicians deserve to enjoy the fruits of their labors, but is it a law of nature that such rewards come in the form of the commodification of art?

The Federal Reserve practices a more destructive form of shutdown, by manufacturing unemployment, with disastrous human consequences. This kind of shutdown makes Watson's pranks shrink into insignificance.

Tragically, the Procrustean system shuts down enormous amounts of human potential. Economist Jaroslav Vanek once compared the losses due to interference with the market system with the losses due to unemployment and the even greater losses due to the prevention of a system of cooperative production to fleas, rabbits, and elephants.[61] In effect, Vanek was saying that Procrusteanism puts the world to work producing fleas in a way that slaughters the rabbits and elephants.

Dignity as a Factor of Production

Following the economic practice of considering everything productive as capital, this book is a tongue-in-cheek call to acknowledge "dignity capital," or dignity as a major factor of production—to adopt the stilted economic jargon for reducing everything to a form of capital.

In contrast to economists' traditional factors of production—land, labor, and capital—dignity emphasizes the value of individual people as part of society rather than treating them as nothing more than abstract agents engaged in market activities. Certainly, dignity implies breaking out of the narrow confines of a Procrustean economy.

Of course, dignity is not really capital. Indeed, dignity may be the opposite of capital—a form of anti-capital. Unlike dignity, capital is naturally scarce. If you burn a ton of coal, that coal is no longer available. In contrast, dignity, like respect, can be contagious. If I have a sense of dignity, I have no need to demean you; instead, I can treat you with dignity. In addition, a sense of dignity can empower people to resist the entreaties of the market.

Dignity does have something in common with capital in the sense that acknowledging people's dignity would probably go a great way toward increasing the productive potential of society. Watson's employers should have learnt as much.

The concept of dignity is not exactly new to economics. Adam Smith credited the displacement of the feudal economy by the market with increasing dignity, although he did not use that term. Certainly, Smith rankled against the remnants of the caste-like hierarchy of the feudal economy he saw around him. He celebrated markets' potential to rupture the stifling constraints on less fortunate, but deserving people. Surely he hoped that less deserving people, such as those in the urban mobs that disturbed him so much, would eventually embrace and be embraced by the market system. If so, Smith's hopes were never completely fulfilled.

Just as Smith's market did succeed in rupturing feudal society, the time has come for a new rupture—one that would break down the new restraints on human existence created by the corporate market economy. Economists tell the story that the rupture of feudalism elevated the productive activities of mankind from pervasive drudgery to hard work. The next stage in human development will go as far as possible in elevating work to pleasure—the kind of pleasure that scientists enjoy when making a discovery or the thrill that athletes or artists feel after a great success.

More than a century ago, the British novelist H. G. Wells, while capturing the technical shortcomings of Procrusteanism, certainly exaggerated, when he suggested:

> Were our political and social and moral devices only as well contrived to their ends as the linotype machine, an antiseptic operating plant, or an electric streetcar, there need now be no appreciable toil in the world and only the smallest fraction of the pain, the fear, and the anxiety that now makes human life so doubtful in value.[62]

Wells seems to imagine that the problem is technical—something that could be taught in a business class on human relations. Life will always contain a certain amount of hard work, and even drudgery, but modern technology is rapidly diminishing the necessary amounts of both. This decline would be far greater in a more rational society without the unnecessary trappings of Procrusteanism.

Going beyond Procrusteanism, a more sophisticated society would make work conform more to the needs of the workers rather than the reverse, which is the norm today. The resulting freedom and creativity could unleash a burst of productivity, that could actually diminish the need for drudgery.

No Fairy-Tale Ending

Mythological metaphors, such as the story of Procrustes, may be particularly appropriate for getting a handle on a society with a less-than-firm grasp of reality. This book has argued that the fate of working people is Procrustean: they are expected to sacrifice themselves to work in order that the market can provide them with things. The market is supposed to care for their needs in this way, but in reality, working people merely function as a means to an end (human capital), rather than as an end in themselves.

The Procrustean analogy does fall short in one sense. The current economy certainly stretches the poor to conform to the iron bed; at the same time, the rich can recline on a comfortable bed that is decidedly not Procrustean. Rather than cutting down the rich to fit them into a restrictive iron bed, the economy showers them with even more rewards, according to the earlier-discussed Matthew Effect.

The saving grace of the Procrustean economy is supposedly its capacity to mobilize labor and resources efficiently. Instead, the case is made in this book that the Procrustean economy fails miserably in that respect, especially in its ability to take advantage of the full capacities of the people who do the work.

A post-Procrustean economy would value possessions only if they elevate the quality of life. Anyone who suffers under the illusion that markets adequately supply the means to improve the quality of life needs only turn on a television set. Here is a technology with the capacity to uplift and enlighten people. Instead, it becomes nothing more than a means to promote consumption, while distracting and misinforming us.

How do we go about creating a non-Procrustean economy that could actually accommodate people? In such an economy, new technology would not threaten people with unemployment or reduced wages but instead would offer them an opportunity for more leisure or at least better working conditions. On a more profound level, a non-Procrustean economy would be arranged so that people would have an opportunity to find fulfillment on the job—not just satisfying themselves with monetary rewards for following the commands of their superiors, but also providing a chance to act creatively in a way that actually provides enjoyment and a sense of accomplishment.

Just as Procrustes turned the countryside into a wasteland, the modern Procrusteans are doing enormous damage to the economy, which, ironically, is their pride and joy. So while the Procrusteans can bask amid the luxury that the economy provides them, they do nothing to maintain the real foundation of the economy that ultimately sustains them—the people who do the work and the environment in which they live. As a result, a creeping depression has been engulfing an increasing share of the population in the United States for almost four decades.

In contrast to the shock of the Great Depression, a slow decline can cause acquiescence, like the proverbial frog that fails to react when the temperature of water gently rises to the boiling point. In any case, under no circumstance will the story end like the Procrustes myth. No heroic young king will bring retribution. Only with hard work, courage, and imagination will people be able to slay the monster and begin to create a wholesome way of life.

Any efforts to create a better way of life will meet considerable resistance from people who presently enjoy a disproportionate share of wealth and privilege. Support for Procrustean ethic will not come just from the rich and powerful. Many of the less fortunate, who will benefit the most from a new system, will also remain unconvinced of any benefits, or even fearful of change.

However, with enough patience and dedication, change is possible. We will begin to see that a more equitable society actually improves our physical and mental health, even for those of us who would otherwise sit near the peak of the social pyramid. In fact, in a post-Procrustean economy, the class lines, which economics has worked so hard to mantain, would finally disappear.

Conclusion

This book offers a dual critique of both economics and market relations. Its message is that because of the exclusion of the issues of work, workers, and working conditions, both economics and market relations impede the development of the human, as well as the productive, potential of society.

Economists generally accept Lionel Robbins's definition of their discipline as "the science which studies human behaviour as a relationship between ends and scarce means that have alternative uses."[63] Economists find confirmation in this approach in their experiments with rats, but neither their studies of humans or rats offer much insight into human behavior. Instead, most economists fail to understand the pitfalls of their restrictive vision.[64]

Rather than studying human life, economists have created a fictional concept of the *homo economicus*, in which commercial activity exists separate from the rest of life. Fictions are often necessary abstractions to help people get a grasp on a complex subject, but simplifications should not come at the expense of excluding essential aspects. This book concentrated on only one: the absence of work, workers, and working conditions.

The concept of an economy is another example of a simplification that obscures reality. I can do no better than cite the words of the French historian Fernand Braudel:

> The worst error of all is to suppose that capitalism is simply "an economic system," whereas in fact it lives off the social order, standing almost on a footing with the state, whether as adversary or accomplice; it is and always has been a massive force, filling the horizon. Capitalism also benefits from all the supports that culture provides for the solidity of the social edifice.[65]

A person who cooks a meal at home for a worker contributes to productive activity just as certainly as the worker in the factory. A parent who nurtures a child is making an investment in future production, as much as an executive who decides to invest in a new piece of equipment. Leisure-time experiences that make workers fuller people are also productive.

Of course, non-commercial activities, such as food preparation or the nurturing of children, are more than acts of economic production, but the exclusion of their contribution contaminates much economic analysis.

Yet economists often become indignant when people question their approach, in effect treating skeptics as either fools or enemies of science. This stance reminds me of the Hindu fable about a group of blind men feeling different parts of an elephant, each convinced that the animal is something altogether different—a snake, a rope, a tree. Although they "feel" part of the elephant, they stand convinced that they alone understand the elephant. Unlike the blind men, who must have been aware of their physical limitations, economists put themselves forward as objective scientists, who see no need to engage those who fail to appreciate their rigor—which sometimes resembles rigor mortis.

The blindness of economics is self-inflicted. Many economists are absolutely brilliant. As people, many economists are also warm, generous, and socially conscious. Yet the discipline maims itself by imposing a restrictive frame of analysis that narrowly defines its boundaries.

The blindness of business is somewhat different. The human relations perspective described in the previous chapter is correct. Business often leaves money on the table because of its short-sighted practices. But I argue that the problem goes deeper—that markets have something tyrannical embedded into their DNA.

The blindness of market society is even more troubling. The modern world faces urgent global challenges, such as global warming. Finding solutions will require a better system of social organization than relying on individualistic, profit-maximizing behavior.

Environmentalists have long recoiled at the way economists have downplayed negative environmental consequences as externalities because they are non-priced. Feminists have resented the absence of women's (and men's) non-commercial activities from economic analysis. In the same spirit, this book has criticized the intentional exclusion of work, workers, and working conditions, reminding us, as Marx recognized, that "the secret of bourgeois production [is] that it is dominated by exchange-value."[66] Solutions depend on the creation of a cooperative system that can take a long-term perspective, nurturing both people and the environment. At this moment, I think back to Michelangelo's *Bearded Slave*, hoping that this book has contributed to the realization that Procrusteanism is a dangerous barrier to progress in meeting the pressing problems that face the world today. I can only hope that the message of this book might contribute to a rethinking of economics, releasing it from its stolid ideological confines.

Notes

INTRODUCTION: SETTING THE STAGE

1. Jacob August Riis, *The Making of an American* (New York: Macmillan, 1922), 253.

2. Paul Krugman and Robin Wells, *Macroeconomics*, 2nd ed. (New York: Macmillan, 2009), 488.

ONE: THE ANTI-WORKER THEOLOGY OF MARKETS

1. Robert Harris, "How Kinnock Could Ruin the Lady's Waltz, Labour's Challenge," *The Times* (London), May 7, 1989.

2. Charles Darwin, *The Descent of Man and Selection in Relation to Sex* (1871; Princeton: Princeton University Press, 1981), 3.

3. Edmund Burke, *Thoughts and Details on Scarcity*, in *The Writings and Speeches of Edmund Burke, The Revolutionary War, 1794–1797, and Ireland*, Vol. 9, ed. R. B. McDowell and Paul Langford (1795; Oxford: Oxford University Press, 1992), 137.

4. Howard E. Fischer, *Arizona Star*, December 8, 1999, quoted in John E. Schwarz, *Freedom Reclaimed: Rediscovering the American Vision* (Baltimore: Johns Hopkins University Press, 2005), 6.

5. Frederick Winslow Taylor, *The Principles of Scientific Management* (1911; New York: W. W. Norton, 1967), 7.

6. Max Weber, *Economy and Society: An Outline of Interpretive Sociology*, 3 vols., eds. Guenther Roth and Claus Wittich (1921; New York: Bedminster Press, 1968), 636–37.

7. Max Weber, *The Protestant Ethic and the Spirit of Capitalism and Other Writings* (1904–5; New York: Penguin Classics, 2002), 121, 13.

8.   Albert O. Hirschman, *The Passions and the Interests: Political Arguments for Capitalism Before Its Triumph* (Princeton: Princeton University Press, 1977).

9.   Adam Smith, *An Inquiry into the Nature and Causes of the Wealth of Nations*, 2 vols., eds. R. H. Campbell and A. S. Skinner (1789; New York: Oxford University Press, 1976), I.ii.2, 26–27 [Note that the *Wealth of Nations* references are to book, section, and paragraph].

10.   John Maynard Keynes, *The General Theory of Employment, Interest and Money* (London: Macmillan, 1936), 374.

11.   F. Y. Edgeworth, *Mathematical Psychics: An Essay on the Application of Mathematics to the Moral Sciences* (London: Kegan Paul, 1881), 16–17.

12.   See Michael Perelman, *The Invention of Capitalism: The Secret History of Primitive Accumulation* (Durham, N.C.: Duke University Press, 2000).

13.   Thomas Robert Malthus, *An Essay on the Principle of Population: Text, Sources and Background, Criticism*, ed. Philip Appleman (1798; New York: Norton, 1967), 100.

14.   Lawrence A. Weschler, *A Miracle, A Universe: Settling Accounts with Torturers* (New York: Pantheon Books, 1990), 147; also cited in Naomi Klein, *The Shock Doctrine: The Rise of Disaster Capitalism* (New York: Henry Holt, 2007), 116.

TWO: DISCIPLINING WORKERS IN THE PROCRUSTEAN BED

1.   Greg LeRoy, *The Great American Jobs Scam: Corporate Tax Dodging and the Myth of Job Creation* (San Francisco: Berrett-Koehler, 2005).

2.   Sarah Anderson and John Cavanagh, *The Top 200: The Rise of Global Corporate Power* (Washington, D.C.: Institute for Policy Studies, 2000).

3.   LeRoy, *The Great American Jobs Scam.*

4.   Greg LeRoy, *No More Candy Store: States and Cities Making Job Subsidies Accountable* (Chicago and Washington D.C.: Federation for Industrial Retention and Renewal, 1994); Robert Guskind, "Dead before Arrival," *National Journal*, Vol. 25, No. 20 (May 15, 1993): 1171–75.

5.   "Northwest Advised Workers to See Treasure in Trash," *Reuters*, August 15, 2006.

6.   Abigail Goldman and Nancy Cleeland, "The Wal-Mart Effect" (first of three-part series), *Los Angeles Times*, November 23, 2003; cited in Holly Sklar and Paul Sherry, *A Just Minimum Wage: Good for Workers, Business and Our Future* (American Friends Service Committee/National Council of Churches, 2005).

7.   George Miller, "Everyday Low Wages: The Hidden Price We All Pay for Wal-Mart's Labor Record," Committee on Education and the Workforce, U.S. House of Representatives, February 16, 2004.

8.   President of the United States, *Economic Report of the President* (Washington, D.C.: U.S. Government Printing Office, 2008), Table B-47, 282.

9.   G. Pascal Zachary, "Study Predicts Rising Global Joblessness," *Wall Street Journal,* February 22, 1995, A 2; see also William Bridges, *Job Shift: How to Prosper in a Workplace without Jobs* (New York: Addison-Wesley, 1994); and "The End of the Job," *Fortune,* September 19, 1994.

10.   Edmund L. Andrews, "Don't Go Away Mad, Just Go Away; Can AT&T Be the Nice Guy as It Cuts 40,000 Jobs?," *New York Times,* February 13, 1996, D 1.

11.   Cited in Keith Thomas, "Work and Leisure," *Past and Present,* No. 29 (December 1964): 63; see also H. Wilensky, "The Uneven Distribution of Leisure: The Impact of Economic Growth on 'Free Time'," *Social Problems,* Vol. 9 (1961): 35-56.

12.   Karl Kautsky, *The Agrarian Question,* tr. Pete Burgess (1899; London: Zwan, 1988), 107.

13.   Bill Watson, "Counter-Planning on the Shop Floor," *Radical America,* Vol. 5, No. 3 (May-June 1971): 76-77, http://www.zabalaza.net/pdfs/varpams/counterplanningontheshopfloor.pdf.

14.   Ibid., 80.

15.   Ibid., 80-81.

16.   James P. Womack, Daniel T. Jones, and Daniel Roos, *The Machine that Changed the World: The Story of Lean Production* (New York: Harper Perennial, 1990), 57.

17.   Niccolo Machiavelli, *The Prince,* ed. Peter Bondanella (New York: Oxford University Press, 1984), 59.

18.   Martin Mayer, *The Bankers* (New York: Ballantine, 1976), 410-11.

19.   See Joseph Stiglitz, *The Roaring Nineties: A New History of the World's Most Prosperous Decade* (New York: W. W. Norton, 2004), 81.

20.   Bob Woodward, *Maestro: Greenspan's Fed and the American Boom* (New York: Simon & Schuster, 2000).

21.   Paul Volcker, Chairman of the Board of Governors of the Federal Reserve System, "Testimony before the Committee on Banking, Finance and Urban Affairs of the U.S. House of Representatives, 21 July 1981," *Federal Reserve Bulletin,* Vol. 67, No. 8 (August 1981): 614; and "Testimony before the Joint Economic Committee, 26 January 1982," *Federal Reserve Bulletin,* Vol. 68, No. 2 (February 1982): 89.

22.   Herbert Stein, *Presidential Economics: The Making of Economic Policy from Roosevelt to Reagan and Beyond* (New York: Simon and Schuster, 1984), 149; also cited in Ann May and Randy Grant, "Class Conflict, Corporate Power, and Macroeconomic Policy: The Impact of Inflation in the Postwar Period," *Journal of Economic Issues,* Vol. 25, No. 2 (June 1991): 373.

23.   David Ricardo, "Letter to the Editor," *Morning Chronicle,* September 6, 1810; reprinted in ed. Piero Sraffa, *The Works and Correspondence of David Ricardo,* Vol. 3, *Pamphlets and Papers, 1809-1811* (Cambridge: Cambridge University Press, 1951), 136.

24. George Akerlof, William Dickens, and George Perry, "The Macroeconomics of Low Inflation," *Brookings Papers on Economic Activity*, No. 1 (1996): 1–60.

25. See May and Grant, "Class Conflict, Corporate Power, and Macroeconomic Policy."

26. Edwin Dickens, "The Great Inflation and U.S. Monetary Policy in the Late 1960s: A Political Economy Approach," *Social Concept*, Vol. 9, No. 1 (July 1995): 49–82; and "The Federal Reserve's Tight Monetary Policy During the 1973–75 Recession: A Survey of Possible Interpretations," *The Review of Radical Political Economics*, Vol. 29, No. 3 (Summer 1997): 79–91.

27. James K. Galbraith, Olivier Giovannoni, and Ann J. Russo, "The Fed's Real Reaction Function: Monetary Policy, Inflation, Unemployment, Inequality, and Presidential Politics," Levy Economics Institute Working Paper, No. 511 (August 2007), http://www.levy.org/pubs/wp_511.pdf.

28. Valerie Cerra and Sweta Chaman Saxena, "Growth Dynamics: The Myth of Economic Recovery," *American Economic Review*, Vol. 98, No. 1 (March 2008): 439–57.

29. John Maynard Keynes, "The Economic Consequences of Mr. Churchill," in *The Collected Works of John Maynard Keynes*, Vol. 9, *Essays in Persuasion*, ed. Donald Moggridge (London: Macmillan, 1972), 218.

30. Ibid., 211.

31. Ibid., 218.

32. *Wall Street Journal*, October 9, 1979.

33. George Melloan, "Some Reflections on My 32 Years with Bartley," *Wall Street Journal*, December 16, 2003.

34. William Greider, *Secrets of the Temple* (New York: Simon and Schuster, 1987), 429.

35. Michael Mussa, "U.S. Monetary Policy in the 1980s" in ed. Martin Feldstein, *American Economic Policy in the 1980s* (Chicago: University of Chicago Press, 1994), 81, 112.

36. Louis Uchitelle, "Advocate of Paying Chiefs Well Revises Thinking," *New York Times*, September 28, 2007.

37. Warren Buffett, "Annual Letter to the Shareholders of Berkshire Hathaway Inc." (2005), http://www.berkshirehathaway.com/letters/2005ltr.pdf.

38. Walter Hamilton and Kathy M. Kristof, "Merrill Lynch Chief Resigns," *Los Angeles Times*, October 31, 2007.

39. Harry G. Johnson, "Problems of Efficiency in Monetary Management," *Journal of Political Economy*, Vol. 76, No. 5 (September 1968): 986.

40. Andrew Clark and James Oswald, "Unhappiness and Unemployment," *The Economic Journal*, Vol. 104, No. 424 (May 1994): 658.

41. Richard Layard, *Lessons from a New Science* (New York: Penguin Press 2005), 67.

42. George Orwell, "Looking Back on the Spanish War," in *The Collected*

Essays, Journalism and Letters, Vol. 2, *My Country Right or Left,* *1940–1943* (New York: Harcourt Brace and World, 1968), 265.

43. Woodward, *Maestro,* 163.

44. Alan Greenspan, "Testimony Before the Subcommittee on Domestic and International Monetary Policy of the Committee on Banking and Financial Services House of Representatives," March 5, 1997, http://commdocs. house.gov/committees/bank/hba38677.000/hba38677_0f.htm.

45. Ibid., 254.

46. Greenspan, "The Interaction of Education and Economic Change: Address to the 81st Annual Meeting of the American Council on Education," Washington, D.C., February 16, 1999.

47. Governor Edward W. Kelley, Jr., "Federal Open Market Committee Meeting Transcripts," August 22, 1995, http://www.federalreserve.gov/ FOMC/transcripts/1995/950822Meeting.pdf.

48. Paul Samuelson and William D. Nordhaus, *Macroeconomics,* 16th ed. (New York: McGraw Hill, 1998), 36.

49. United States Department of Labor, Bureau of Labor Statistics, *Major Work Stoppages in 2007,* http://www.bls.gov/news.release/pdf/wkstp.pdf.

50. Derek Rucker and Adam Galinsky, "Desire to Acquire: Powerlessness and Compensatory Consumption," *Journal of Consumer Research,* Vol. 35, No. 2 (August 2008): 257.

51. Jared Bernstein, *All Together Now: Common Sense for a Fair Economy* (San Francisco, CA: Berrett-Koehler, 2006).

52. Audrey Laporte, "Do Economic Cycles Have a Permanent Effect on Population Health? Revisiting the Brenner Hypothesis," *Health Economics,* Vol. 13 (August 2004): 767–79.

53. Daniel Sullivan and von Wachter, "Mortality, Mass-Layoffs, and Career Outcomes: An Analysis Using Administrative Data," National Bureau of Economic Research, Working Paper No. 13626, 2007.

54. Richard G. Wilkinson, *Unhealthy Societies: The Afflictions of Inequality* (London: Routledge, 1997).

55. Robert Sanders, "EEGs Show Brain Differences Between Poor and Rich Kids," December 2008, http://www.berkeley.edu/news/media/releases/ 2008/12/02_cortex.shtml; Mark M. Kishiyama et al., "Socioeconomic Disparities Affect Prefrontal Function in Children," *Journal of Cognitive Neuroscience,* Vol. 21, No. 6 (June 2009): 1106–1115.

56. Greg Ip, "His Legacy Tarnished, Greenspan Goes on Defensive," *Wall Street Journal,* April 8, 2008.

57. Karl Marx, *Capital,* Vol. 1 (New York: Vintage, 1977), 896ff.

THREE: HOW ECONOMICS MARGINALIZED WORKERS

1. Lionel Charles Robbins, *An Essay on the Nature and Significance of Economic Science,* 2nd ed. (London, Macmillan, 1969), 1, 65.

2. Frank Knight, "Cost of Production and Price Over Long and Short Periods," *Journal of Political Economy*, Vol. 29, No. 4 (April 1921): 73.

3. Marc Linder, *Labor Statistics and Class Struggle* (New York: International Publishers 1994), 57; citing United States House of Representatives, *Occupational Safety and Health Act of 1969: Hearings before the Select Subcommittee on Labor of the House Committee on Education and Labor*, 91st Congress, 1st Session, 1969, 112.

4. Centers for Disease Control, "Nonfatal Occupational Injuries and Illnesses among Workers Treated in Hospital Emergency Departments–United States, 2003," April 28, 2006, http://www.cdc.gov/mmwr/preview/mmwrhtml/mm5516a2.htm; "Workers' Memorial Day," April 28, 2008, http://www.cdc.gov/Features/WorkersMemorialDay.

5. Centers for Disease Control, "Workers' Memorial Day"; J Paul Leigh et al., "Occupational Injury and Illness in the United States: Estimates of Costs, Morbidity and Mortality," *Archives of Internal Medicine*, Vol. 167 (July 1997): 1557–68.

6. Kris Maher, "Black Lung on Rise in Mines, Reversing Trend," *Wall Street Journal*, December 15, 2009, A 5.

7. Philip J. Landrigan, "Commentary: Environmental Disease—A Preventable Epidemic," *American Journal of Public Health*, Vol. 82, No. 7 (July 1992): 941–43.

8. Centers for Occupational and Environmental Health, *Green Chemistry: Cornerstone to a Sustainable California*, University of California, 2008, http://coeh.berkeley.edu/docs/news/green_chem_brief.pdf.

9. David Barstow, "U.S. Rarely Seeks Charges for Deaths in Workplace," *New York Times*, December 22, 2003.

10. David Uhlmann, "The Working Wounded," *New York Times*, May 27, 2008.

11. David Barstow and Lowell Bergman, "At a Texas Foundry, an Indifference to Life," *New York Times*, January 8, 2003.

12. Kenneth D. Rosenman et al., "How Much Work-Related Injury and Illness Is Missed by the Current National Surveillance System?," *Journal of Occupational and Environmental Medicine*. Vol. 48, No. 4 (April 2006): 357–65.

13. Christopher J. Ruhm, "Are Recessions Good for Your Health?," *Quarterly Journal of Economics*, Vol. 115, No. 2 (May 2000): 617–650.

14. Ken Ward, Jr., "Congressional Report: Bayer Blast 'Could Have Eclipsed' Bhopal," *The Charleston Gazette*, April 21, 2009.

15. Chesley B. Sullenberger, "Statement before the Subcommittee on Aviation Committee on Transportation and Infrastructure," United States House of Representatives, February 24, 2009, http://transportation.house.gov/Media/file/Aviation/20090224/Sullenberger.pdf.

16. Andy Pasztor, "Crash Probe Examines Pilot Fatigue," *Wall Street Journal*, May 14, 2009, A 1.

17. Andy Pasztor, "Captain's Training Faulted in Air Crash that Killed 50," *Wall Street Journal,* May 11, 2009, A 1.

18. Sholnn Freeman, "Colgan Air Pilots Faced Long Commutes, Low Pay, Second Jobs," *Washington Post,* May 13, 2009.

19. Adam Smith, *An Inquiry into the Nature and Causes of the Wealth of Nations,* 2 vols., eds. R. H. Campbell and A. S. Skinner (1789; New York: Oxford University Press, 1976), II.ii.7, 287, II.v. 12, 363.

20. Sir William Petty, *Treatise of Taxes and Contributions* (1662) in *The Writings of Sir William Petty,* Vol. 1, ed. C. H. Hull (Cambridge: Cambridge University Press, 1899; New York: Augustus M. Kelley, 1963), 44–45.

21. Smith, *An Inquiry into the Nature and Causes of the Wealth of Nations,* I.v.2, 47.

22. Ibid., I.viii.44, 99.

23. Robert H. Wiebe, *The Search for Order, 1877–1920* (New York: Hill and Wang, 1967), xiii.

24. Arthur Twining Hadley, *Railroad Transportation: Its History and Its Laws,* 10th ed. (New York: G. P. Putnam's and Sons, 1903), 65.

25. Stanley Lebergott, *The Americans: An Economic Record* (New York: Norton, 1984), 131.

26. David Nasaw, *Andrew Carnegie* (New York: Penguin, 2006), 99.

27. Henry Adams, *The Education of Henry Adams* (1918; Boston: Houghton Mifflin, 1961), 249–50.

28. Anthony Patrick O'Brien, "Factory Size, Economies of Scale, and the Great Merger Wave of 1898–1902," *Journal of Economic History,* Vol. 48, No. 3 (September 1988): 639–49.

29. Francis Wheen, *Karl Marx: A Life* (New York: Norton 2000), 330–35.

30. John Rae, "The Socialism of Karl Marx and the Young Hegelians," *Contemporary Review,* Vol. 40 (October 1881): 585.

31. Alfred Marshall, "Letter to Herbert Somerton Foxwell" (October 6, 1903), in ed. John K. Whitaker, *The Correspondence of Alfred Marshall,* Vol. 3, *Towards the Close, 1903–1924* (Cambridge: Cambridge University Press, 1996), 61–63.

32. Senator George Hoar, "Speech on Wages and Hours of Labor: United States Congress," *The Congressional Globe,* December 13, 1879, Vol. 27, Part 2, 102.

33. Arthur Twining Hadley, "Letter to E. D. Worcester" (July 29, 1879); cited in Hadley, Morris, *Arthur Twining Hadley* (New Haven: Yale University Press, 1948), 32.

34. See Michael Perelman, *Railroading Economics: The Creation of the Free Market Mythology* (New York: Monthly Review Press, 2006), 98–99.

35. Ronald L. Meek, "Marginalism and Marxism," *History of Political Economy,* Vol. 4 (1972): 499–511; reprinted in Ronald Meek, *Smith,*

Marx, and After: Ten Essays in the Development of Economic Thought (New York: Wiley, 1977): 165–75.

36. William Stanley Jevons, *The Theory of Political Economy* (1871; Baltimore: Penguin, 1970), 86.

37. William Stanley Jevons, "The Mathematical Theory of Political Economy," *Journal of the Statistical Society of London*, Vol. 37, No. 4 (December 1874): 485.

38. William Stanley Jevons, *The State in Relation to Labour* (New York: A. M. Kelley, 1968), 100–101.

39. Armen A. Alchian and Harold Demsetz, "Production, Information Costs, and Economic Organization," *American Economic Review*, Vol. 62, No. 5 (December 1972): 777.

40. Gregory Clark, "Factory Discipline," *Journal of Economic History*, Vol. 54, No. 1 (March 1994): 128.

41. Clark Nardinelli, "Corporal Punishment and Children's Wages in 19th Century Britain," *Explorations in Economic History*, Vol. 19, No. 3 (July 1982): 289.

42. Steven Cheung, "The Contractual Nature of the Firm," *Journal of Law and Economics*, Vol. 26, No. 1 (April 1983): 5.

43. Abba Lerner, "The Economics of Politics and Consumer Sovereignty," *American Economic Review*, Vol. 62, No. 2 (May 1972): 259.

44. William Stanley Jevons, "Opening Address as President of Section F (Economic Science and Statistics) of the British Association for the Advancement of Science," *Methods of Social Reform and Other Papers* (London: Macmillan and Co., 1883), 195.

45. Walter Bagehot, *The Postulates of English Political Economy* (New York and London: G. P. Putnam, 1885), 4.

46. Henry Varnum Poor, *Money and Its Laws, Embracing a History of Monetary Theories and a History of the Currencies of the United States* (London: C. Kegan Paul and Co., 1877), 392.

47. Robert Solow, "What Do We Know that Amasa Walker Didn't?" *History of Political Economy*, vol. 19, No. 2 (Summer 1987); 183–89.

48. Francis Amasa Walker, "The Present Standing of Political Economy," *Sunday Afternoon* (May): 432–41.

49. John Maloney, *Marshall, Orthodoxy and the Professionalisation of Economics* (Cambridge: Cambridge University Press, 1985), 9; citing Leslie Stephen, *The Life of Henry Fawcett* (London: Smith, Elder & Co., 1885), 123.

50. Peter D. Groenewegen, *A Soaring Eagle: Alfred Marshall, 1842–1924* (Brookfield, VT: Edgar Elgar, 1995), 532–34.

51. Ibid., 129.

52. H. S. Foxwell, "The Economic Movement in England," *Quarterly Journal of Economics*, Vol. 2, No. 1 (October 1887): 92.

53. Alfred Marshall and Mary Paley Marshall, *The Economics of Industry* (London: Macmillan 1879), 2.

54. See Maloney, *Marshall, Orthodoxy and the Professionalisation of Economics,* 130–33.

55. Joseph A. Schumpeter, *History of Economic Analysis* (New York: Oxford University Press, 1954), 1115.

56. Henry Dunning Macleod, *On the Modern Science of Economics* (London: John Heywood, 1887), 111.

57. Henry Dunning Macleod, *An Address to the Board of Electors to the Professorship of Political Economy in the University of Cambridge* (London, 1884), 12; cited in Timothy Alborn, "Review of Philip Mirowski's *More Heat than Light: Economics as Social Physics, Physics as Nature's Economics,*" *Isis*, Vol. 82, No. 2 (June 1991): 354.

58. Philip Mirowski, *More Heat than Light: Economics as Social Physics, Physics as Nature's Economics* (Cambridge: Cambridge University Press, 1989), 217.

59. Ibid., 31.

60. Ibid., 241–49.

61. Alfred Marshall, *Principles of Economics: An Introductory Volume,* 8th ed. (London: Macmillan & Co., 1920), 1.

62. Groenewegen, *A Soaring Eagle,* 323 and ch. 15.

63. Maloney, *Marshall, Orthodoxy and the Professionalisation of Economics,* 24.

64. Joan Robinson, *Economic Philosophy* (Chicago: Aldine, 1962), 74.

65. Mirowski, *More Heat than Light,* 264.

66. Alfred Marshall, "Fragment," reprinted in Alfred C. Pigou, ed., *Memorials of Alfred Marshall* (New York: Kelley and Millman, 1956; 1st ed., 1925), 366–67.

67. Groenewegen, *A Soaring Eagle,* 729.

68. Martin S. Feldstein, "Reducing Poverty Not Inequality," *Public Interest* (Fall 1999): 34.

69. Richard A. Lester, "Notes of Wages and Labor Costs," *Southern Economic Journal*, Vol. 10, No. 3 (January 1944): 235–38.

70. Thomas Sowell, "A Student's Eye View of George Stigler," *Journal of Political Economy*, Vol. 101, No. 5 (October 1993): 787.

71. Craig Freedman, "The Economist as Mythmaker—Stigler's Kinky Transformation," *The Journal of Economic Issues*, Vol. 29, No. 1 (1995): 194.

72. George J. Stigler, *The Theory of Price,* 4th ed. (New York: Macmillan, 1987), 99.

73. George J. Stigler, *The Citizen and the State: Essays on Regulation* (Chicago: University of Chicago Press, 1975), x.

74. George J. Stigler, "Do Economists Matter?," *Southern Economic Journal*, Vol. 42, No. 3, (1976): 347–54; reprinted in *The Economist as Preacher* (Oxford: Basil Blackwell, 1982): 54–67.

75. David Card and Alan B. Krueger, "Minimum Wages and Employment: A Case Study of the Fast-Food Industry in New Jersey and Pennsylvania," *American Economic Review*, Vol. 84, No. 4 (September 1994): 772-93.

76. Douglas Clement, "Interview with David Card," *The Region* (a publication of the Federal Reserve Bank of Minneapolis): December 2006.

77. Merton Miller, "Commentary on the Minimum Wage," *Wall Street Journal*, April 25, 1996, A 20.

78. James M. Buchanan, "Commentary on the Minimum Wage," *Wall Street Journal*, April 25, 1996, A 20.

79. Clement, "Interview with David Card."

80. Cited in Paul Diesing, "Hypothesis Testing and Data Interpretation: The Case of Milton Friedman," *Research in the History of Economic Thought and Methodology*, Vol. 3 (Greenwich, CT: JAI Press, 1985), 61.

81. Craig Freedman, personal communication, August 18, 2008.

82. Donald N. McCloskey, *The Rhetoric of Economics* (Madison: The University of Wisconsin Press, 1985), 140.

83. Melvin W. Reder, "Chicago Economics: Permanence and Change," *Journal of Economic Literature*, Vol. 20, No. 1 (March 1982): 13, 18, 19.

84. Charles Kindleberger, *Manias, Panics, and Crashes* (New York: Basic Books, 2000), 235.

85. George J. Stigler, "Charles Babbage (1791 + 200 = 1991)," *Journal of Economic Literature*, Vol. 29, No. 3 (September 1991): 1149.

86. Charles Babbage, *On the Economy of Machinery and Manufactures* (1835; New York: Augustus M. Kelley, 1971), 156; cited in Stigler, "Charles Babbage (1791 + 200 = 1991)," 1150.

87. Research Center for Behavioral Economics and Decision-Making, Federal Reserve Bank of Boston, "Implications of Behavioral Economics for Economic Policy," Conference, September 27-28, 2007, http://www.bos.frb.org/economic/conf/BehavioralPolicy2007/index.htm.

88. "The Perils of Prosperity: Can You Be Too Rich?," *The Economist*, April 27, 2006.

89. Martin S. Feldstein, "Structural Reform of Social Security," *The Journal of Economic Perspectives*, Vol. 19, No. 2 (Spring 2005): 36.

90. Frank H. Knight, "Ethics and Economic Reform," *Economica*, Vol. 6, No. 21 (February 1939): 21.

91. Norman Joseph Ware, *The Industrial Worker, 1840-1860* (Boston: Houghton-Mifflin, 1924), 76-77.

92. Kenneth Warren, *Industrial Genius: The Working Life of Charles Michael Schwab* (Pittsburgh: University of Pittsburgh Press, 2007), 77.

93. Michael J. Piore, "The Impact of the Labor Market upon the Design and Selection of Productive Techniques within the Manufacturing Plant," *Quarterly Journal of Economics*, Vol. 82, No. 4 (November 1968): 610.

94. J. Cox, "The Evolution of Tomato Canning Machinery"; quoted in Peter

Phillips and Martin Brown, "The Historical Origin of Job Ladders on the U.S. Canning Industry and Their Effects on the Gender Division of Labour," *Cambridge Journal of Economics*, Vol. 10, No. 2 (June 1986): 134.

95. Frederick Winslow Taylor, *The Principles of Scientific Management* (1911; New York: W. W. Norton & Co., 1967), 7, 65–67.

96. Robert Kanigel, *The One Best Way: Frederick Winslow Taylor and the Enigma of Efficiency* (New York: Viking, 1997).

97. William Stanley Jevons, "On the Natural Laws of Muscular Exertion," *Nature*, Vol. 2 (June 30, 1870): 158–60; see also Harro Maas, *William Stanley Jevons and the Making of Modern Economics* (Cambridge: Cambridge University Press, 2005), 200.

98. Jevons, *The Theory of Political Economy*, 189.

99. See Michael V. White, "In the Lobby of the Energy Hotel: Jevons's Formulation of the Postclassical 'Economic Problem'," *History of Political Economy*, Vol. 36, No. 2 (Summer 2004): 227–71.

100. Anson Rabinbach, *The Human Motor: Energy, Fatigue, and the Origins of Modernity* (New York: Basic Books, 1990), 46.

101. Alfred Marshall, "Letter to Francis Ysidro Edgeworth" (August 28, 1892), in ed. John K. Whitaker, *The Correspondence of Alfred Marshall*, Vol. 2, *At the Summit, 1891–1902* (Cambridge: Cambridge University Press, 1996): 71–72.

102. David Spencer, *The Political Economy of Work* (London: Routledge, 2009), ch. 5.

103. Karl Marx, *Capital*, Vol. 1 (New York: Vintage, 1977), 279.

104. Arnold C. Harberger, "Monopoly and Resource Allocation," *American Economic Review*, Vol. 44, No. 2 (May 1954): 77.

105. Arnold C. Harberger, "Using the Resources at Hand More Effectively," *American Economic Review*, Vol. 49, No. 2 (May 1959): 134–46.

106. Harberger, "Monopoly and Resource Allocation," 87.

107. Robert Mundell, "Book Review: L. H. Janssen, "Free Trade, Protection and Customs Union," *American Economic Review,* Vol. 52, No. 3 (June 1962): 622.

108. Harvey Leibenstein, "Allocative Efficiency vs. 'X-Efficiency'," *American Economic Review*, Vol. 56, No. 3 (June 1966): 392–415.

109. Leo Tolstoy, *War and Peace* (New York: Modern Library, 2004), Part XIV, II.

110. John R. Hicks, "Annual Survey of Economic Theory: The Theory of Monopoly," *Econometrica*, Vol. 3, No. 1 (January 1935): 8; and *Value and Capital* (Oxford: Clarendon Press, 1935), 265.

111. Mark Perlman and J. W. Dean, "Harvey Leibenstein as a Pioneer of Our Time," *The Economic Journal*, Vol. 108, No. 446 (January 1998): 141.

112. George J. Stigler, "The Xistence of X-Efficiency," *American Economic Review*, Vol. 66, No. 1 (1976): 213.

113. Michael Perelman, *The Confiscation of American Prosperity: From*

Right-Wing Extremism and Economic Ideology to the Next Great Depression (New York: Palgrave, 2007), 9.

114. George J. Stigler, "The Xistence of X-Efficiency," 216.

115. Arnold C. Harberger, "A Vision of the Growth Process," *American Economic Review*, Vol. 88, No. 1 (March 1998): 1.

116. Ibid., 3.

117. Ibid., 4.

118. Leo Ernest Durocher, *Nice Guys Finish Last* (New York: Simon & Schuster, 1975), 13.

119. Richard Thaler, "Mortgages Made Simpler," *New York Times*, July 5, 2009.

120. See Richard Thaler and Sherwin Rosen, "The Value of Saving a Life: Evidence from the Labor Market," in ed. N. Terleckyj, *Household Production and Consumption* (New York: Columbia University Press, 1976), 265–98.

121. Centers for Disease Control and Prevention, *Morbidity and Mortality Weekly Report,* June 6, 2008, "Work-Related Injury Deaths among Hispanics–United States, 1992–2006," http://www.cdc.gov/mmwr/preview/mmwrhtml/mm5722a1.htm.

122. Roger Lowenstein, "Exuberance Is Rational or at Least Human," *New York Times Magazine*, February 11, 2001.

123. See Michael Perelman, *Manufacturing Discontent: The Trap of Individualism in a Corporate Society* (London: Pluto, 2005), 123–29, 163–67.

124. See Seth Borenstein, "How to Value Life? EPA Devalues Its Estimate," *Sacramento Bee,* July 13, 2008, D 1.

125. John D. Graham, *Comparing Opportunities to Reduce Health Risks: Toxin Control, Medicine and Injury Prevention* (Dallas: National Center For Policy Analysis, 1995).

126. Richard Thaler and Cass R. Sunstein, *Nudge: Improving Decisions about Health, Wealth, and Happiness* (New Haven, CT: Yale University Press, 2008).

127. Upton Sinclair, *American Outpost: A Book of Reminiscences* (1932; Port Washington, New York: Kennikat Press, 1969), 175.

128. Eric Schlosser, *Fast Food Nation: The Dark Side of the All-American Meal* (Boston: Houghton Mifflin, 2001), 172.

129. Conference Board, "U.S Job Satisfaction Declines, the Conference Board Reports," February 23, 2007.

130. Burt Helm, "It's Not A McJob, It's A McCalling," *Business Week*, June 4, 2007, 13.

131. Conference Board, "U.S Job Satisfaction Declines, the Conference Board Reports."

132. Roddy Boyd, "N.Y. Exec Knew of Problems: Ex-Honcho," *New York Post*, January 5, 2006.

133. Charles Babbage, *On the Economy of Machinery and Manufactures* (1835; New York: Augustus M. Kelley, 1971), 54.

134. Amanda Schaffer, "Fighting Bedsores with a Team Approach," *New York Times,* February 19, 2008.

FOUR: EVERYDAY LIFE IN A PROCRUSTEAN WORLD

1. Frank H. Knight, "Cost of Production and Price over Long and Short Periods," *Journal of Political Economy,* Vol. 29, No. 4 (April 1921): 313.
2. See Robert E. Lucas, Jr., *Models of Business Cycles. The Yjiro Jannson Lectures* (Oxford: Basil Blackwell, 1987), 54.
3. Simon Nelson Patten, *The New Basis of Civilization* (Cambridge, MA: Belknap Press, 1968), 141 and 137.
4. United States Census Bureau, *Statistical Abstract of the United States, 2007* (Washington, D.C.: United States Census Bureau, 2007), Table 587.
5. Lawrence Mishel, Jared Bernstein, and Sylvia Allegretto, *The State of Working America, 2006/2007* (Ithaca, New York: Cornell University Press, 2007), 38.
6. Edward C. Prescott, "Why Do Americans Work So Much More than Europeans?," *Federal Reserve Bank of Minneapolis Quarterly Review,* Vol. 28, No. 1 (July 2004): 2–13.
7. Adam Smith, *Early Draft of The Wealth of Nations* in *Lectures on Jurisprudence,* eds. R. L. Meek, D. D. Raphael, and P. G. Stein (1758; Oxford: Clarendon Press, 1978), IV.i.9, 183.
8. Ibid., IV.i.6, 180.
9. Ibid., IV.i.8, 181.
10. Ibid.
11. Ibid., 182.
12. Adam Smith, *An Inquiry into the Nature and Causes of the Wealth of Nations,* 2 vols., eds. R. H. Campbell and A. S. Skinner (1789; New York: Oxford University Press, 1976), I.x.b.26, 124.
13. Mark Twain, *The Autobiography of Mark Twain* (New York: Harper Perennial Modern Classics, 2000), 32.
14. Robert Whaples, "Winning the Eight-Hour Day, 1909–1919," *Journal of Economic History,* Vol. 50, No. 2 (June 1990): 393; see also Daniel T. Rogers, *The Work Ethic in Industrial America, 1850–1920* (Chicago: University of Chicago Press, 1978), 157 ff.
15. John Kenneth Galbraith, The *New Industrial State* (1967; Princeton, New Jersey: Princeton, 2007), 334.
16. Daniel T. Rogers, *The Work Ethic in Industrial America, 1850–1920* (Chicago: University of Chicago Press, 1978), 156; citing the Ohio Bureau of Labor Statistics, *Second Annual Report* (Columbus, 1879), 281.
17. David Montgomery, *Beyond Equality* (New York: Knopf, 1967), 236; citing the Massachusetts Bureau of Statistics of Labor, *Annual Report* (Boston, 1870), 221.

18. James Warren Prothro, *The Dollar Decade: Business Ideas in the 1920's* (Baton Rouge: Louisiana State University Press, 1954), 6–7.

19. Janny Scott, "Cities Shed Middle Class, and Are Richer and Poorer for It," *New York Times*, July 23, 2006.

20. William Temple, *Essay on Trade and Commerce* (London, 1770), 266; see also Edgar Furniss, *The Position of the Laborer in a System of Nationalism* (New York: Augustus M. Kelley, 1965), 14–15.

21. Maurice Cranston, *John Locke: A Biography* (New York: Macmillan, 1957), 425.

22. See John Brown, *A Memoir of Robert Blincoe, An Orphan Boy, Sent from the Workhouse at St. Pancras, London at Seven Years of Age to Endure the Horrors of a Cotton Mill* (Manchester: J. Doherty, 1832).

23. See Michael Perelman, *The Invention of Capitalism: The Secret History of Primitive Accumulation* (Durham: Duke University Press, 2000), 64.

24. Gary M. Anderson and Robert D. Tollison, "Ideology, Interest Groups, and the Repeal of the Corn Laws," *Zeitschrift für die gesamte Staatswissenschaft*, Vol. 141, No. 2 (June 1985): 197–212; Friederich Engels, "The English Ten Hours' Bill," *Neue Rheinische Zeitung Politisch-ökonomische Revue,* No. 4, March 1850 in Karl Marx and Friederich Engels, *Collected Works*, Vol. 10, September 1849–June 1851 (New York: International Publishers, 1978), 288–300.

25. Paul Glader, "At 78, Bonnie Rooks Likes a 'Dirty Old Job' in an Ohio Steel Mill: Great-Grandmother Enjoys a Paycheck, Younger Pals; Paying a Child's Mortgage," *Wall Street Journal,* August 10, 2005, A 1.

26. Mitra Toossie, "Labor Force Projections to 2016: More Workers in Their Golden Years," *Monthly Labor Review*, Vol. 130, No. 11 (November 2007): 33–52.

27. Quoted in Susan George and Fabrizio Sabelli, *Faith and Credit: The World Bank's Secular Empire* (Boulder, CO: Westview Press, 1994), 106.

28. Nassau Senior, "Letter to Charles Poulett Thompson" (March 28, 1837), in *Letters on the Factory Act, As it Affects the Cotton Manufactures*; reprinted in Nassau Senior, *Selected Writings on Economics, a Volume of Pamphlets, 1827–1852* (New York: Augustus M. Kelley, 1966), 12.

29. Karl Marx, *Capital*. Vol. 1 (New York: Vintage, 1977), ch. 9.

30. Hans Staehle, "Technology, Utilization and Production," *Bulletin de l'Institut Internationale de Statistique*, Vol. 34, Part 4 (1955): 127, 133.

31. Michael Perelman, *The Pathology of the U.S. Economy Revisited: The Intractable Contradictions of Economic Policy* (New York: Palgrave, 2001), 117–19.

32. Joseph A. Schumpeter, *Business Cycles: A Theoretical, Historical, and Statistical Analysis of the Capitalist System*, 2 vols. (New York: McGraw Hill, 1939), v.

33. "The Treaty of Detroit," *Fortune*, Vol. 62, No. 1, July 1950; see also William Serrin, *The Company and the Union* (New York: Vintage, 1974), 170.

34. George Fitzhugh, *Cannibals All! Or, Slaves Without Masters*, ed. C. Vann Woodward (1857; Cambridge, MA: Belknap Press, 1980).

35. Robert K. Merton, "The Matthew Effect in Science," *Science*, Vol. 159, No. 3810 (January 5, 1968): 58; quoting Matthew 25:29.

36. Milton Friedman, "Introduction," in Frederick A. Hayek, *The Road to Serfdom*, 50th anniversary edition (Chicago, IL: University of Chicago Press, 1994); reprinted in *The Road to Serfdom: Text and Documents—The Definitive Edition*, ed. Bruce Caldwell (Chicago, IL: University of Chicago Press, 2007).

37. Quoted in Randall Parker, *The Economics of the Great Depression: A Twenty-first Century Look Back at the Economics of the Interwar Era* (Cheltenham: Edward Elgar, 2007), 10.

38. Quoted in Eric Foner, *Free Soil, Free Labor, Free Men: The Ideology of the Republican Party before the Civil War* (New York: Oxford University Press, 1970), 25.

39. Anatole France, *The Red Lily*, tr. Winifred Stephens (1894; New York: Dodd, Mead and Co., 1925), 91.

FIVE: INTERNATIONAL PROCRUSTEANISM

1. "Venezuela: The Busy Bs," *Time*, September 21, 1953.

2. Adam Smith, *An Inquiry into the Nature and Causes of the Wealth of Nations*, 2 vols., eds. R. H. Campbell and A. S. Skinner (1789; New York: Oxford University Press, 1976), III.iv.17, 422.

3. Sol Tax, *Penny Capitalism: A Guatemalan Indian Economy* (Smithsonian Institution Institute of Social Anthropology, Publication No. 16, Washington, D.C.: U.S. Government Printing Office; reprinted New York: Octagon Books, 1972).

4. Thomas Friedman, *The Lexus and the Olive Tree* (New York: Farrar Straus & Giroux, 1999), 86–87.

5. Ibid., 90–91, 115.

6. Walter B. Wriston, *The Twilight of Sovereignty: How the Information Revolution Is Transforming Our World* (New York: Scribner, 1992), 8–9, 61–62.

7. See William Darity, Jr., and Bobbie L. Horn, *The Loan Pushers: The Role of Commercial Banks in the International Debt Crisis* (Cambridge, MA: Ballinger, 1988).

8. Phillip L. Zweig, *Wriston: Walter Wriston, Citibank, and the Rise and Fall of American Financial Supremacy* (New York: Crown Publishers, 1995), 867, 872.

9. Bob Woodward, *Maestro: Greenspan's Fed and the American Boom* (New York: Simon & Schuster, 2000), 73.

10. Thomas Friedman, "A Race to the Top," *New York Times*, June 3, 2005.

SIX: ADAM SMITH'S HISTORICAL VISION

1. Jacob Viner, "Adam Smith and Laissez Faire," *Journal of Political Economy*, Vol. 35, No. 2 (April 1927): 189–232; reprinted in *The Long View and the Short* (Glencoe, IL: The Free Press, 1958).

2. Adam Smith, *An Inquiry into the Nature and Causes of the Wealth of Nations*, 2 vols., eds. R. H. Campbell and A. S. Skinner (1789; New York: Oxford University Press, 1976), I.viii.13, 84.

3. Ibid., IV.i.32, 448.

4. Anthony Waterman, personal communication, 1998.

5. Salim Rashid, "Charles James Fox and *The Wealth of Nations*," *History of Political Economy*, Vol. 24, No. 2 (Summer 1992): 493.

6. John Rae, *The Life of Adam Smith* (1895; New York: Augustus M. Kelley, 1965), 291.

7. Anthony Waterman, "Reappraisal of 'Malthus the Economist,' 1933-1997," *History of Political Economy*, Vol. 30, No. 2 (Summer 1998): 295.

8. Emma Rothschild, "Adam Smith and Conservative Economics," *Economic History Review*, Vol. 45, No. 1 (February 1992): 74.

9. Quoted in Francis Horner, *Memoirs and Correspondence of Francis Horner, M.P.*, 2 vols., ed. Leonard Horner (London: John Murray, 1843), 1: 229.

10. Jeffrey Young, "Accounting for Adam Smith," Summer Institute for the Preservation of the Study of the History of Economics, George Mason University, June 4, 2007.

11. Adam Smith, *The Theory of Moral Sentiments* (1759), V.I.25, http://www.econlib.org/library/Smith/smMS5.html.

12. George J. Stigler, *Five Lectures on Economic Problems* (London: Longmans, Green and Co., 1949), 4.

13. From a lost manuscript of 1749, quoted in Dugald Stewart, "Account of the Life and Writings of Adam Smith, L.L.D," in *The Works of Dugald Stewart*, Vol. 5 (London: T. Caddell and W. Davies, 1811), 400–552; reprinted in *Adam Smith, Essays on Philosophical Subjects*, ed. W. P. D. Wightman and J. C. Bryce (Oxford: Clarendon Press, 1980), 269–352.

14. Arnold Toynbee, *Lectures on the Industrial Revolution of the Eighteenth Century in England: Popular Addresses, Notes, and Other Fragments* (London: Rivingtons, 1884), 8.

15. John Ramsay McCulloch, *Treatise on the Rate of Wages and the Condition of the Labouring Classes* (1826; New York: Kelley, 1967), 16–17.

16. See Michael Perelman, *Transcending the Economy: On the Potential of Passionate Labor and the Wastes of the Market* (New York: St. Martin's Press, 2000), 201; Adam Smith, *Lectures on Jurisprudence*, eds. R. L. Meek, D. D. Raphael, and P. G. Stein (1762-1766; Oxford: Clarendon Press, 1978), 563.

17. Frederick Law Olmsted, *A Journey in the Seaboard Slave States in the Years 1853–1854* (New York: Dix and Edwards, 1856), 46–47.

18. Rae, *The Life of Adam Smith*, 8.

19. T. S. Ashton, *The Industrial Revolution, 1760–1830* (London: Oxford University Press, 1948), 47.

20. Ibid., 15.

21. Roy Hutcheson Campbell, *Carron Company* (Edinburgh: Oliver and Boyd, 1961), 18.

22. John Roebuck, "Letter to Adam Smith" (November 1, 1775), in *The Correspondence of Adam Smith*, eds. Ernest Campbell Mossner and Ian Simpson Ross (Oxford: Clarendon Press, 1977), 182–84.

23. Richard L. Hills, *Power from Steam: A History of the Stationary Steam Engine* (Cambridge: Cambridge University Press, 1989), 55.

24. David Hume, "Letter to Adam Smith" (June 27, 1772), in *The Correspondence of Adam Smith*, eds. Mossner and Ross, 161–63.

25. Adam Smith, *An Inquiry into the Nature and Causes of the Wealth of Nations*, 2 vols., eds. R. H. Campbell and A. S. Skinner (1789; New York: Oxford University Press, 1976), I.viii, 94.

26. John H. Clapham, "Review of Werner Sombart. *Luxus und Capitalismus. Krieg und Capitalismus,*" *The Economic Journal*, Vol. 23, No. 91 (September 1913): 401.

27. James Boswell, *Boswell's Life of Johnson*, Vol. 5, *The Life, 1780–1784* (Oxford: Oxford University Press, 1934–64), 188.

28. Jonathan Williams, Jr., *Journal of Jonathan Williams, Jr., of His Tour with Franklin and Others through Northern England, May 28, 1771*, in Benjamin Franklin, *The Papers of Benjamin Franklin*, Vol. 18, eds. Leonard W. Larabee and William B. Wilcox (New Haven: Yale University Press, 1959), 114–16.

29. Adam Smith, *An Inquiry into the Nature and Causes of the Wealth of Nations*, I.i.5, 17.

30. A. W. Coats, "Adam Smith: The Modern Appraisal," *Renaissance and Modern Studies*, Vol. 6 (1962): 47; see also E. R. A. Seligman, "Introduction" in Adam Smith, *An Inquiry into the Nature and Causes of the Wealth of Nations* (London: Everyman's Edition, 1910), xi.

31. Richard Koebner, "Adam Smith and the Industrial Revolution," *Economic History Review*, 2nd series, Vol. 11, No. 3 (1959): 381–91.

32. Charles Kindleberger, "The Historical Background: Adam Smith and the Industrial Revolution" in *The Market and the State: Essays in Honour of Adam Smith*, eds. Thomas Wilson and Andrew S. Skinner (Oxford: Clarendon Press, 1976), 1–25.

33. Smith, *Lectures on Jurisprudence*, 338.

34. Ibid., 339.

35. Ibid., 340–41.

36. Ibid., 341.

37. Ibid., 351.

38. Smith, *An Inquiry into the Nature and Causes of the Wealth of Nations*, I.i.3, 14–15.

39. Smith, *Lectures on Jurisprudence*, vi.34, 343; and *An Inquiry into the Nature and Causes of the Wealth of Nations*, I.i.3, 14–15.

40. Jean-Louis Peaucelle, "Adam Smith's Use of Multiple References for His Pin Making Example," *European Journal of the History of Economic Thought*, Vol. 13, No. 4 (December 2006): 494; Smith, *An Inquiry into the Nature and Causes of the Wealth of Nations*, I.i.3, z. 14–15.

41. Adam Smith, *Early Draft of The Wealth of Nations* in *Lectures on Jurisprudence*, eds. R. L. Meek, D. D. Raphael, and P. G. Stein (Oxford: Clarendon Press, 1978), 564.

42. Adam Ferguson, *An Essay on the History of Civil Society*, ed. Duncan Forbes (1793; Edinburgh: Edinburgh University Press, 1966).

43. Alexander Carlyle, *Autobiography of the Rev. Dr. Alexander Carlyle* (Boston: Ticknor and Fields, 1861), 231.

44. Rae, *The Life of Adam Smith*, 264.

45. Ferguson, *An Essay on the History of Civil Society*, 181.

46. Ibid., 186.

47. Ibid., 218.

48. Ibid., 230.

49. Campbell, *Carron Company*, 79.

50. Ibid., 80–81.

51. Henri-Louis Duhamel du Monceau, *Art de l'e'pinglier* (Paris: Saillant et Noyon, 1761); tr. in Peaucelle 2006, "Adam Smith's Use of Multiple References for His Pin Making Example," 502.

52. Henry Hamilton, *English Brass and Copper Industries to 1880* (New York: Augustus M. Kelley, 1967), 103.

53. Kirk Willis, "The Role in Parliament of the Economic Ideas of Adam Smith, 1776–1800," *History of Political Economy*, Vol. 11, No. 4 (Summer 1979): 505–44.

54. Arthur Young, *A Six Months Tour through the Southern Counties of England and Wales*, 3rd ed. (London: W. Straham, 1772), 170–74.

55. Robert C. Allen, *The British Industrial Revolution in Global Perspective* (Cambridge: Cambridge University Press, 2009), 147.

56. Smith, *An Inquiry into the Nature and Causes of the Wealth of Nations* (Oxford University Press, 1976), IV.viii.42, 658.

57. Ibid., I.i.9, 20–21.

58. Smith, *An Inquiry into the Nature and Causes of the Wealth of Nations* (Modern Library, 1937), n. 10.

59. Smith, *Lectures on Jurisprudence*, 1762–1766, 343–47.

60. Smith, *Early Draft of The Wealth of Nations* in *Lectures on Jurisprudence*, 567–9.

61. Smith, "Letter to Lord Carlisle" (November 8, 1779) in *The Correspondence of Adam Smith*, eds. Ernest Campbell Mossner and Ian Simpson Ross (Oxford: Clarendon Press, 1977), 242–43.

62. Ibid., 240–42,

63. See Jacob Viner, *The Role of Providence in the Social Order: An Essay in Intellectual History* (Philadelphia: American Philosophical Library, 1972), 80.

64. Smith, *The Theory of Moral Sentiments*, eds. D. D. Raphael and A. L. Macfie (Oxford: Clarendon Press, 1976), ii, II, 3, 2, 86; see also Smith, *Lectures on Jurisprudence*, 539.

65. Smith, *An Inquiry into the Nature and Causes of the Wealth of Nations* (Oxford University Press, 1976), I.iii.1, 31.

66. Ibid., I.iv.1, 37.

67. Sarah Jordon, *The Anxieties of Idleness: Idleness in Eighteenth-Century British Literature and Culture* (Lewisburg, PA: Bucknell University Press, 2003), 55.

68. Smith, *An Inquiry into the Nature and Causes of the Wealth of Nations* (Oxford University Press, 1976), I.x.c.27, 145.

69. Freeman Dyson, *Disturbing the Universe* (New York: Harper Colophon, 1979), 51.

SEVEN: THE DARK SIDE OF ADAM SMITH

1. Adam Smith, *Lectures on Jurisprudence*, eds. R. L. Meek, D. D. Raphael, and P. G. Stein (1762–1766; Oxford: Clarendon Press, 1978), 205 and 487.

2. Edward Thompson, "The Moral Economy of the English Crowd in the Eighteenth Century," *Past and Present*, Vol. 50 (February 1971): 76–136.

3. Smith, *Lectures on Jurisprudence*, iii, 143, 197; and Smith, *An Inquiry into the Nature and Causes of the Wealth of Nations*, 2 vols., eds. R. H. Campbell and A. S. Skinner (1789; New York: Oxford University Press, 1976), IV.v.b.8, 527. See also David Hume, "An Inquiry Concerning the Principles of Morals" in *The Philosophical Works of David Hume*, Vol. 4, eds. T. H. Green and T. H. Gross (New York: Scientia Verlag, 1964), book 3, para. 147.

4. Martin J. Sklar, *The Corporate Reconstruction of American Capitalism: 1890–1916* (Cambridge: Cambridge University Press, 1988), 103.

5. Smith, *An Inquiry into the Nature and Causes of the Wealth of Nations*, IV.v.b.26, 534.

6. Ibid., IV.v.a.3, 524.

7. Ibid, I.x.c.24, 144.

8. Smith, *Lectures on Jurisprudence*, 539.

9. Smith, *An Inquiry into the Nature and Causes of the Wealth of Nations*, V.i.f.51, 783; almost repeated verbatim at V.i.f.61, 788.

10. Smith, *Lectures on Jurisprudence,* V.i.f.61, 788.

11. Ibid., V.i.g.12, 795.

12. Smith, *An Inquiry into the Nature and Causes of the Wealth of Nations,* V.i.b.2, 709-10.

13. Ibid., I.vii.27, 78-79.

14. Ibid., I.viii.44, 99.

15. Ibid., IV.ii.30: 464-65.

16. Smith, *Lectures on Jurisprudence,* 189, 202.

17. Smith, *An Inquiry into the Nature and Causes of the Wealth of Nations,* V.i.f.49, 781.

18. Ibid., V.i.f.50, 781-82.

19. Ibid., V.i.a.21, 699.

20. Ibid., V.i.a.14, 697.

21. Ibid., V.i.f.53, 784-85; V.i.a.15, 697.

22. Ibid., V.i.f.57, 786.

23. Ibid., V.i.f.58, 786.

24. Leonidas Montes, "Adam Smith and the Militia Debate in Context," History of Economics Society Annual Meeting, June 29, 2008; see also R. B. Sher, "Adam Ferguson, Adam Smith, and the Problem of National Defense," *The Journal of Modern History*, vol. 61, No. 1 (June 1989): 240-68.

25. Adam Smith, *The Correspondence of Adam Smith*, eds. Ernest Campbell Mossner and Ian Simpson Ross (Oxford: Clarendon Press, 1977), n. 22.

26. Ibid., 21-22.

27. Smith, *An Inquiry into the Nature and Causes of the Wealth of Nations,* V.i.g.14, 796.

28. See Gary M. Anderson, "Mr. Smith and the Preachers: The Economics of Religion in the *Wealth of Nations*," *Journal of Political Economy*, Vol. 96, No. 5 (October 1988): 1066-88. See also Charles and Patrick Raines, "Adam Smith on Competitive Religious Markets," *History of Political Economy*, Vol. 24, No. 2 (Summer 1992): 499-513; and "The 'Protective State' Approach to the 'Productive State' in *The Wealth of Nations*: The Odd Case of Lay Patronage," *Journal of the History of Economic Thought*, Vol. 24, No. 4 (December 2002): 427-41.

29. Smith, 1759, 3.5.8, 166.

30. Jacob Viner, "Adam Smith and Laissez Faire," *Journal of Political Economy*, Vol. 35, No. 2 (April 1927): 189-232; reprinted in *The Long View and the Short* (Glencoe, IL: The Free Press, 1958).

31. Smith, *An Inquiry into the Nature and Causes of the Wealth of Nations,* III.iv.10, 419.

32. Ibid., V.i.f-g.61, 788.

33. Adam Ferguson, *An Essay on the History of Civil Society,* ed. Duncan Forbes (1793; Edinburgh: Edinburgh University Press, 1966), 182-83.

34. Smith, *An Inquiry into the Nature and Causes of the Wealth of Nations,*
     I.5.2, 47.

35. Ibid., I.v.7, 50.

36. Ibid., V.i.f.7, 760.

37. Ibid., Book 1, Chapter 10, Part 2.

38. Samuel Read, *The Political Economy* (Edinburgh: Oliver & Boyd, 1829),
     xxix–xxxiv.

39. David Ricardo, *On Protection to Agriculture* in eds. Piero Sraffa and
     Maurice Dobb, *Pamphlets and Papers, The Works and Correspondence of
     David Ricardo,* Vol. 4 (Cambridge: Cambridge University Press), 235, 237.

40. Smith, *An Inquiry into the Nature and Causes of the Wealth of Nations,*
     I.viii.36, 96.

41. Smith, "The Principles which Lead and Direct Philosophical Enquiries;
     Illustrated by the History of Astronomy," in *Essays on Philosophical
     Subjects,* eds. W. P. D. Wightman and J. C. Bryce (New York: Clarendon
     Press, 1980), 105.

42. Margaret C. Jacob and Larry Stewart, *Practical Matter: Newton's Science in
     the Service of Industry and Empire, 1687–1851* (Cambridge: Harvard
     University Press, 2004).

43. Elie Halévy, *The Growth of Philosophical Radicalism,* tr. Mary Morris
     (London: Faber and Faber, 1928), 3.

44. Stephen Edelston Toulmin, *Return to Reason* (Cambridge, MA: Harvard
     University Press, 2001).

45. Alberto Alesina and George-Marios Angeletos, "Fairness and
     Redistribution," *American Economic Review,* Vol. 95, No. 4 (September
     2005): 960–80.

46. Smith, *An Inquiry into the Nature and Causes of the Wealth of Nations,*
     II.iii.2, 331.

EIGHT: KEEPING SCORE

1.   Guy Routh, *The Origin of Economic Ideas* (New York: Vintage, 1977), 45.

2.   Carol S. Carson, "The History of the United States National Income and
     Product Accounts: The Development of an Analytical Tool," *The Review
     of Income and Wealth* (June 1975): 153–81.

3.   See Clifford Cobb, Ted Halstead, and Jonathan Rowe, "If the GDP Is Up,
     Why Is America Down?," *Atlantic Monthly,* October 1995; and Jonathan
     Rowe, "Rethinking the Gross Domestic Product as a Measurement of
     National Strength," Testimony before the United States Senate Committee
     on Commerce, Science and Transportation, Subcommittee on Interstate
     Commerce, March 12, 2008.

4.   United States Department of Commerce, *National Income: 1929–32,*

Senate Doc. 124, 73rd Congress, 2nd Session, 1934, 5–6.

5.   Ibid., 6–7.

6.   Mark Perelman, "Political Purpose and the National Accounts" in eds. William Alonso and Paul Starr, *The Politics of Numbers* (New York: Russell Sage Foundation, 1987), 144.

7.   Robert W. Fogel, "Academic Economics and the Triumph of the Welfare State," Association of American Universities Centennial Meeting, April 17, 2000.

8.   Simon Kuznets, *National Income and Its Composition, 1919–1935*, 2 vols. (New York: National Bureau of Economic Research, 1941), 10.

9.   Simon Kuznets, *National Product in Wartime* (New York: National Bureau of Economic Research, 1945), 26.

10. Paul A. Samuelson and William D. Nordhaus, *Macroeconomics*, 16th ed. (New York: McGraw Hill, 1998), 390.

11. Stanley Lebergott, *Manpower in Economic Growth: The American Record since 1800* (New York: McGraw-Hill, 1964), 31.

12. Arthur Cecil Pigou, *Economics of Welfare* (London: Macmillan, 1920), 32.

13. See Scott Burns, *Household, Inc.* (New York: Doubleday, 1976), 22; Tibor Scitovsky, *The Joyless Economy: An Inquiry into Human Satisfaction* (New York: Oxford University Press, 1976), 86–89; and Robert Eisner, "Total Income, Total Investment and Growth," paper presented at the annual meetings of American Economic Association, December 29, 1979.

14. Robert Eisner, "Extended Accounts for National Income and Product," *Journal of Economic Literature*, Vol. 26, No. 4 (December 1988): 1161–84.

15. Lena Graber and John Miller, "Wages for Housework: The Movement and the Numbers," *Dollars and Sense* (September/October 2002): 45–46.

16. United States Department of Labor, Bureau of Labor Statistics, *Occupational Outlook Handbook*, 2009, http://www.bls.gov/oco/.

17. See Barbara R. Bergman, *The Economic Emergence of Women* (New York: Palgrave Macmillan, 2005), ch. 9.

18. William Nordhaus and James Tobin, "Is Growth Obsolete?" in *The Measurement of Economic and Social Performance*, National Bureau of Economic Research, *Studies in Income and Wealth*, No. 38, ed. Milton Moss (New York: Columbia University Press, 1972), 518.

19. Katheryn E. Walker and Margaret E. Woods, *Time Use: A Measure of Household Production of Family Goods and Services* (Washington, D.C.: Center for the Family of the American Home Economics Association, 1976).

20. Michael Aglietta, *A Theory of Capitalist Exploitation: The U.S. Experience*, tr. David Fernbach (London: New Left Books, 1979), 158; Andre Gorz, *Strategy for Labor* (Boston: Beacon Press, 1968), 88 ff.

21. Eisner, "Extended Accounts for National Income and Product."

22. See the introduction in Anwar Shaikh and Ertugrul Ahmet Tonak, *Measuring the Wealth of Nations: The Political Economy of National Accounts* (Cambridge: Cambridge University Press, 1994).

23. On the "Genuine Progress Indicator" see http://www.rprogress.org/sustainability_indicators/genuine_progress_indicator.htm.

24. Jane Spencer, "Why Beijing Is Trying to Tally the Hidden Costs of Pollution as China's Economy Booms," *Wall Street Journal*, October 2, 2006, A 2.

25. Luigino Bruni, "The 'Technology of Happiness' and the Tradition of Economic Science," *Journal of the History of Economic Thought*, 26: 1 (March, 2004): 19–44.

26. Earlene Craver, "Patronage and the Direction of Research in Economics," *Minerva*, Vol. 24, No. 2-3 (Summer-Autumn 1986): 214.

27. Anon., *The Character and Qualifications of an Honest Loyal Merchant* (London: Robert Roberts, 1686), 11.

28. Bruni, "The 'Technology of Happiness' and the Tradition of Economic Science," 25.

29. Anson Rabinbach, *The Human Motor: Energy, Fatigue, and the Origins of Modernity* (New York: Basic Books, 1990), 203.

30. Marc Linder and Ingrid Nygaard, *Void Where Prohibited: Rest Breaks and the Right to Urinate on Company Time* (Ithaca, New York: ILR Press, 1998), 21.

31. Charles Barzillai Spahr, *America's Working People* (London: Longmans and Green, 1900), 177.

32. Amartya K. Sen, "Mortality as an Indicator of Economic Success and Failure," *The Economic Journal*, Vol. 108, No. 446 (January 1998): 9.

33. Amartya K. Sen, *Development as Freedom* (New York: Knopf, 1999), 75.

34. David P. Levine and S. Abu Turab Rizvi, *Poverty, Work and Freedom: Political Economy and the Moral Order* (Cambridge: Cambridge University Press, 2005), 47.

35. See http://www.bhutanstudies.org.bt/publications/gnh/gnh.htm.

36. Cathy Scott-Clark and Adrian Levy, "Fast Forward into Trouble," *Guardian*, June 14, 2003, http://www.guardian.co.uk/weekend/story/0,3605,975769,00.html; Ross McDonald, "Television, Materialism and Culture: An Exploration of Imported Media and its Implications for GNH," *Journal of Bhutan Studies*, Vol. 11, No. 4 (Winter 2004): 68–88.

37. United Nations Development Programme, *United Nations Human Development Report, 2004: Cultural Liberty in Today's Diverse World* (New York: Oxford University Press, 2004), 139.

38. World Bank, Development Committee Press Conference, April 30, 2001, http://web.worldbank.org/WBSITE/EXTERNAL/NEWS/0,,contentMDK:20025769~pagePK:64257043~piPK:437376~theSitePK:4607,00.html.

39. Richard Layard, *Happiness: Has Social Science a Clue?*, Lionel Robbins

Memorial Lectures 2002/3, Lecture 1: "What Is happiness? Are We Getting Happier?," http://www.stoa.org.uk/topics/happiness/Happiness%20-%20Has%20Social%20Science%20A%20Clue.pdf. See also Bruno S. Frey and Alois Stutzer, *Happiness and Economics: How the Economy and Institutions Affect Well-Being* (Princeton: Princeton University Press, 2002), 8; and Richard A. Easterlin, "Will Raising the Incomes of All Increase the Happiness of All?," *Journal of Economic Behavior and Organization*, Vol. 27, No. 1 (June 1995): 1–34.

40.   Robert H. Frank, *Choosing the Right Pond: Human Behavior and the Quest for Status* (New York: Oxford University Press, 1985), 31.

41.   Henry Louis Mencken, *A Mencken Chrestomathy* (1949; New York: A. A. Knopf, 1956).

42.   Juliet Schor, *The Overspent American: Upscaling, Downshifting, and the New Consumer* (New York: Basic Books, 1998), 14; Alois Stutzer, "The Role of Income Aspirations in Individual Happiness," *Journal of Economic Behavior and Organization*, Vol. 54, No. 1 (May 2004): 89–109.

43.   Daniel Defoe, *Robinson Crusoe: An Authoritative Text, Contexts, Criticism*, ed. Michael Shinagel (1719; New York: Norton, 1994), 121.

44.   Daniel Kahneman and Alan B. Krueger, "Developments in the Measurement of Subjective Well-Being," *The Journal of Economic Perspectives*, Vol. 20, No. 1 (Winter 2006): 3.

45.   Daniel Kahneman, Alan B. Krueger et al., "Toward National Well-Being Accounts," *American Economic Review*, 94: 2 (May 2004): 429–34.

46.   Ibid., 432.

NINE: THE DESTRUCTIVE NATURE OF PROCRUSTEANISM

1.   David Noble, *Forces of Production: A Social History of Industrial Automation* (New York: Oxford University Press, 1984).

2.   Andrew Pickering, *The Mangle of Practice* (Chicago: University of Chicago Press, 1995), 160.

3.   Babbage, *On the Economy of Machinery and Manufactures* (1835; New York: Augustus M. Kelley, 1971), 250.

4.   Alfred Marshall, *Principles of Economics: An Introductory Volume* (London: Macmillan & Co., 1920), 284.

5.   Stephen Hymer, "The Multinational Corporation and the Law of Uneven Development," in Jagdish Bhagwati, *Economics and the World Order* (New York: Macmillan), 122, 124.

6.   Patrick Wright, *On a Clear Day You Can See General Motors: John Z. DeLorean's Look Inside the Automotive Giant* (New York: Avon, 1979), 137.

7.   Ibid., 7.

8.   David Kiley, "The New Heat on Ford," *Business Week*, June 4, 2007, 33–38.

9.   Steven Rattner, "The Auto Bailout: How We Did It," *Fortune*, Vol. 160, No. 9, November 9, 2009.

10.   Peter Huber, "The Unbundling of America," *Forbes*, April 13, 1992, 118.

11.   Lawrence H. Summers and Victoria P. Summers, "When Financial Markets Work too Well: A Cautious Case for a Securities Transactions Tax," *Journal of Financial Services Research*, Vol. 3, Nos. 2 and 3 (December 1989): 271.

12.   Steven Mufson, "Breaking Own Record, Exxon Sets Highest U.S. Profit Ever; Second-Quarter Earnings Total $11.68 Billion," *Washington Post*, August 1, 2008, D 1.

13.   Leonhardt, "3,400 Layoffs Send a Message to Millions," *New York Times*, April 4, 2007, C 1.

14.   Darius Mehri, *Notes From Toyota-Land: An American Engineer in Japan* (Ithaca: Cornell University/ILR Press, 2005).

15.   James Surowiecki, "The Open Secret of Success: Toyota Turns the Concept of Innovation on Its Head, Shares It and Still Wins," *The New Yorker*, May 12, 2008.

16.   Teri Evans, "Entrepreneurs Seek to Elicit Workers' Ideas," *Wall Street Journal*, December 22, 2009, B 8.

17.   Jim B. Bushnell and Catherine D. Wolfram, "The Guy at the Controls: Labor Quality and Power Plant Efficiency," University of California Energy Institute, Center for the Study of Energy Markets, Paper CSEMWP-168, 2007, http://repositories.cdlib.org/cgi/viewcontent.cgi?article=1071& context=ucei/csem.

18.   Michael L., Dertouzos et al., *Made in America: Regaining the Productive Edge* (Cambridge, MA: The MIT Press, 1989), 82.

19.   Shoshana Zuboff, *In the Age of the Smart Machines: The Future of Work and Power* (New York: Basic Books, 1988), 255–67.

20.   Jeffrey Pfeffer, "Human Resources from an Organizational Behavior Perspective: Some Paradoxes Explained," *Journal of Economic Perspectives*, Vol. 21, No. 4 (Fall 2007): 123.

21.   Richard Sennett, *The Culture of the New Capitalism* (New Haven: Yale University Press, 2005), 67.

22.   Todd Bishop, "Microsoft Adds a Record 11,200 Employees," *Seattle Post Intelligencer*, June 20, 2008, http://seattlepi.nwsource.com/business/367743_msftemploy20.html.

23.   Stephen H. Wildstrom, "Firefox Keeps Nipping at Microsoft," *Business Week*, June 23, 2008, 78; "Mozilla Message Card," Mozilla Foundation, 2009, http://www.spreadfirefox.com/node/238.

24.   Pfeffer, "Human Resources from an Organizational Behavior Perspective: Some Paradoxes Explained," 115.

25.   Pfeffer, *Competitive Advantage through People: Unleashing the Power of the Work Force* (Boston: Harvard Business School Press, 1994), 110.

26. Ibid.,111.

27. Tore Ellingsen and Magnus Johannesson, "Paying Respect," *Journal of Economic Perspectives*, Vol. 21, No. 4 (Fall 2007): 144.

28. Edward P. Lazear and Kathryn L. Shaw, "Personnel Economics: The Economist's View of Human Resources," *Journal of Economic Perspectives*, Vol. 21, No. 4 (Fall 2007): 110.

29. Ibid.

30. Lazear, "The Future of Personnel Economics," *Economic Journal*, Vol. 110 (2000): 611.

31. Leo Panitch, "Ralph Miliband: Socialist Intellectual, 1924–1994" in *Socialist Register 1995: Why Not Capitalism?* (New York: Monthly Review Press, 1995), 4.

32. David Packard, *The HP Way* (New York: HarperCollins, 1995), 135.

33. Stanley Mathewson, *Restriction of Output among Unorganized Workers* (1939; Carbondale: Southern Illinois University Press, 1969), 125.

34. Harrison Emerson, *The Twelve Principles of Scientific Management* (New York: Engineering Company, 1912), 67; cited in Bryan Palmer, "Class, Conception and Conflict: The Thrust for Efficiency, Managerial Views of Labor and the Working Class Rebellion, 1903–22," *Review of Radical Political Economy*, Vol. 7, No. 2 (Summer 1975): 37.

35. Seymour Hersh, "The Next Act," *The New Yorker*, November 27, 2006.

36. Pam Galpern, "Working to Rule Builds Pressure from Within," *Labor Notes,* December 2005.

37. Ibid.

38. Harley Shaiken, *Work Transformed: Automation and Labor in the Computer Age* (New York: Holt, Rinehart & Winston, 1985), 19–20.

39. Joan Greenbaum, *Windows on the Workplace: Computers, Jobs, and the Organization of Office Work in the Late Twentieth Century* (New York: Monthly Review Press, 1995), 4; citing, Juliet Webster, *Office Automation: The Labour Process and Women's Work in Britain* (London: Harvester Wheatsheaf, 1990), 118.

40. Sennett, *The Culture of the New Capitalism*, 34.

41. Frank Bruni, "Bush Promotes Education, and in a Calculated Forum," *New York Times*, August 2, 2001, A 14.

42. U.S. Department of Labor, Bureau of Labor Statistics, Current Population Survey, 2009, Table 2: "Families by presence and relationship of employed members and family type, 2005–06 annual averages," http://www.bls.gov/news.release/famee.t02.htm.

43. Harold Hotelling, "Stability in Competition," *Economic Journal*, Vol. 39, No. 153 (March 1929): 41–57.

44. U.S. Department of Labor, Bureau of Labor Statistics, Current Population Survey, 2009.

45. James O'Connor, "Productive and Unproductive Labor," *Politics and Society*, Vol. 5, No. 3 (1975): 303.

46. Samuel Bowles and Arjun Jayadev, "Garrison America," *The Economists'
     Voice*, Vol. 4, Issue 2, Article 3 (2007): 1.

47. Wolfgang Saxon, "John S. Morrison, Scholar, 87, Rebuilt a Lost Greek
     Warship," *New York Times*, November 12, 2000.

48. Samuel Bowles and Arjun Jayadev, "Guard Labor," *Journal of
     Development Economics*, Vol. 79, No. 2 (April 2006): 337, Table 1.

49. Ibid., 338, Table 2.

50. Ibid., 341, Figure 1.

51. Frederic Natusch Maude, *War and the World's Life* (London: Smith, Elder,
     and Co., 1907), 13, 92.

52. Mehri, *Notes From Toyota-Land*, 31–32.

53. Samuel Gompers, *Seventy Years of Life and Labour: An Autobiography*, 2
     vols. (1925; New York: Kelley, 1967), 45.

54. Samuel Gompers, "Testimony" (1883) in ed. John A. Garraty, *Labor and
     Capital in the Gilded Age: Testimony Taken by the Senate Committee upon
     the Relations between Labor and Capital* (Boston: Little, Brown, 1968), 16.

55. Lynn Bauer and Steven Owens, *Justice Expenditure and Employment
     Statistics* (Washington, D.C.: U.S. Department of Justice, Bureau of Justice
     Statistics, 2006), 1.

56. U.S. Department of Justice, Office of Justice Programs, Bureau of Justice
     Statistics, 2006, http://www.ojp.usdoj.gov/bjs.

57. Marc Mauer, *Comparative International Rates of Incarceration: An
     Examination of Causes and Trends Presented to the U.S. Commission on
     Civil Rights* (Washington, D.C.: The Sentencing Project, 2003).

58. Peter Pae, "Aerospace Legend Looks Back at the Time He Wasted—in
     Meetings," *Los Angeles Times*, November 6, 2005.

59. Alexandra Luong and Steven G. Rogelberg, "Meetings and More
     Meetings: The Relationship between Meeting Load and the Daily
     Well-Being of Employees," *Group Dynamics: Theory, Research, and
     Practice*, Vol. 9, No. 1 (2005): 58.

60. Ibid.

61. Charles T. Munger, "Academic Economics: Strengths and Faults After
     Considering Interdisciplinary Needs," Herb Kay Undergraduate Lecture,
     University of California, Santa Barbara Economics Department, October
     3, 2003, http://www.tilsonfunds.com/MungerUCSBspeech.pdf.

62. John Huston and Nipoli Kamdar, "$9.99: Can 'Just-Below' Pricing Be
     Reconciled with Rationality?," *Eastern Economic Journal*, Vol. 22, No. 2
     (Spring 1996): 137–38.

63. Robert H. Frank, *The Economic Naturalist: In Search of Explanations for
     Everyday Enigmas* (New York: Basic Books, 2007), 61.

64. Raymond E. Lombra, "Eliminating the Penny from the U.S. Coinage
     System: An Economic Analysis," *Eastern Economic Journal*, 2001, Vol.
     27, Issue 4 (Fall 2001): 433–42.

65. Milton Friedman and Anna Jacobson Schwartz, *A Monetary History of the United States, 1867–1960* (1963; Princeton: Princeton University Press, 1971), 240.

66. Milton Friedman, "The Fed Has No Clothes," *Wall Street Journal*, April 15, 1988, 15.

67. Milton Friedman, "The Fed's Thermostat," *Wall Street Journal*, August, 19, 2003.

68. John Maynard Keynes, *The General Theory of Employment, Interest and Money* (London: Macmillan, 1936).

69. Robert E. Lucas, Jr., "The Death of Keynesian Economics," *Issues and Ideas* (Winter 1980).

70. Justin Fox, "The Comeback of Keynes," *Time*, October 23, 2008, http://www.time.com/time/printout/0,8816,1853302,00.html.

71. Lawrence H. White, "The Federal Reserve System's Influence on Research in Monetary Economics," *Econ Journal Watch*, Vol. 2, No. 2 (August 2005): 325–54, http://www.econjournalwatch.org/pdf/WhiteInvestigating August2005.pdf; Robert D. Auerbach, *Deception and Abuse at the Fed: Henry B. Gonzalez Battles Alan Greenspan's Bank* (Austin, TX: University of Texas Press, 2008), 141.

72. Alan Greenspan, "Opening Remarks," *Rethinking Stabilization Policy: A Symposium Sponsored by the Federal Reserve Bank of Kansas City, Jackson Hole, Wyoming* (Kansas City, MO: Federal Reserve Bank of Kansas City, 2002), 4–5, http://www.kansascityfed.org/publicat/Sympos/2002/sym02prg.htm.

73. Alan Greenspan, *The Age of Turbulence: Adventures in a New World* (New York: Penguin Press, 2007), 202.

74. Kevin P. Phillips, *Wealth and Democracy: A Political History of the American Rich* (New York: Broadway Books, 2002), 236.

75. Adam Smith, *An Inquiry into the Nature and Causes of the Wealth of Nations*, 2 vols., eds. R. H. Campbell and A. S. Skinner (1789; New York: Oxford University Press, 1976), I.xi,10, 267.

76. Ibid., V.i.e.18, 741.

77. See John M. Barry, *The Great Influenza: The Epic Story of the Deadliest Plague in History* (New York: Viking, 2004).

TEN: WHERE DO WE GO FROM HERE?

1. Fredric Jameson, "Future City," *New Left Review*, Vol. 21 (May–June 2003), http://www.newleftreview.org/?view=2449.

2. John Adams, "Letter to Thomas Jefferson" (February 2, 1816) in *The Writings of Thomas Jefferson* (Washington, D.C., Thomas Jefferson Memorial Association of the United States, 1907), 426–67.

3. Harriet Lerner, *Fear and Other Uninvited Guests* (New York: HarperCollins Publishers, 2004), 161.

4. Ibid.

5. Michael Dunlop Young, "Down with Meritocracy," *The Guardian*, June 29, 2001.

6. Jerome Karabel, *The Chosen: The Hidden History of Admission and Exclusion at Harvard, Yale, and Princeton* (Boston: Houghton Mifflin, 2005).

7. Henry Home Kames, *Introduction to the Art of Thinking* (Edinburgh: W. Creech and T. Caddell, 1789), 57.

8. Russell Jacoby, *Picture Imperfect: Utopian Thought for an Anti-Utopian Age* (New York: Columbia University Press, 2005), 65.

9. Perry Anderson, *Zone of Engagement* (London: Verso, 2002), 232.

10. James C. Scott, *Seeing like a State: How Certain Schemes to Improve the Human Condition Have Failed* (New Haven: Yale University Press, 1998), 12.

11. Ibid., 20.

12. Rosa Luxemburg, "Letter to Sophie Liebknecht" (May 2, 1917), http://www.marxists.org/archive/luxemburg/1917/05/02.htm.

13. John Maynard Keynes, "Economic Possibilities for Our Grandchildren," *Nation and Athenaeum*, October 11 & 18, 1930; reprinted in Keynes, *Essays in Persuasion* (New York: W. W. Norton, 1963), 358–73.

14. Keynes, *The Economic Consequences of the Peace* (1919) in *The Collected Works of John Maynard Keynes*, Vol. 2, ed. Donald Moggridge (London: Macmillan, 1971), 12.

15. Roy F. Harrod, *The Life of John Maynard Keynes* (New York: Harcourt, Brace & Co., 1951), 194.

16. Alfred Marshall, *Principles of Economics* (London: Macmillan, 1890), 3.

17. Keynes, "A Short View of Russia," *Nation and Athenaeum*, October 10, 17 and 25, in *Essays in Persuasion* (1931); republished as *The Collected Works of John Maynard Keynes*, Vol. 9, ed. Donald Moggridge (London: Macmillan, 1972), 297–311.

18. Keynes to Duncan Grant, July 31, 1908; quoted in Robert Skidelsky, *John Maynard Keynes: Hopes Betrayed* (New York: Viking, 1986), 195.

19. George Rylands, "The Kingsman" in ed. Milo Keynes, *Essays on John Maynard Keynes* (Cambridge: Cambridge University Press, 1975), 47.

20. Joan Robinson, "What Has Become of the Keynesian Revolution?" in Milo Keynes, *Essays on John Maynard Keynes*, 128.

21. John Maynard Keynes, *The General Theory of Employment, Interest and Money* (London: Macmillan, 1936), 374.

22. Keynes, "Memorandum for the Estates Committee, King's College, Cambridge, May 8, 1938," *Collected Writings*, Vol. 12 (London: Macmillan), 109.

23. Keynes, "Economic Possibilities for Our Grandchildren" in *Essays In Persuasion*, 372.

24. Ibid., 366.

25. Ibid., 369.

26. Ibid.

27. Karl Marx, *Capital*, Vol. 3 (New York: Vintage, 1981), 507.

28. Elias Canetti, *Crowds and Power*, tr. Carol Stewart (New York: The Viking Press, 1962), 395.

29. Urs Frauchiger, *Was zum Teufel ist mit der Musik los* (Bern: Zyglogge, 1982), 69.

30. Igor Stravinsky, *Poetics of Music in the Form of Six Lessons*, tr. Arthur Knodel and Ingolf Dahl (Cambridge: Harvard University Press, 1947), 167–69.

31. José Antonio Bowen and David Mermelstein, "The American Tradition" in *The Cambridge Companion to Conducting*, ed. José Antonio Bowen (Cambridge: Cambridge University Press, 2003), 164.

32. Lawrence W. Levine, *Highbrow/Lowbrow: The Emergence of Cultural Hierarchy in America* (Cambridge, MA: Harvard University Press, 1988), 129.

33. Bowen and Mermelstein, *The Cambridge Companion to Conducting*, 164.

34. Joseph Schumpeter, *Capitalism, Socialism and Democracy* (New York: Harper & Row, 1950).

35. H. Earle Johnson, *Symphony Hall, Boston* (Boston: Little, Brown, 1950), 52, 47.

36. Levine, *Highbrow/Lowbrow*, 134, 139.

37. Marx, *Capital*, Vol. 3, 511.

38. "Headless," *The Economist*, August 3.

39. Stravinsky, *Poetics of Music in the Form of Six Lessons*, 169.

40. Arthur Lubow, "Conductor of the People," *New York Times*, October 28, 2007.

41. Franklin D. Roosevelt, *Second Inaugural Address*, 1937, http://avalon. law.yale.edu/20th_century/froos2.asp.

42. Daniel McFadden, "Free Markets and Fettered Consumers," *American Economic Review*, Vol. 96, No. 1 (March 2006): 6.

43. John Neulinger, *The Psychology of Leisure*, 2nd ed. (Springfield, IL: Charles C. Thomas, 1981), 15.

44. Adam Smith, *An Inquiry into the Nature and Causes of the Wealth of Nations*, 2 vols., eds. R. H. Campbell and A. S. Skinner (1789; New York: Oxford University Press, 1976), I.x.b.3., 117–8.

45. George Anders, "Cutting-Edge Executives: Top Managers Find Inner Peace in Carpentry; A $700 Sander that Eats Its Own Dust," *Wall Street Journal*, August 10, 2007.

46. Michael Lewis, "Sarkozy Forces the French to Join the 1980s," *Bloomberg*, August 6, 2008, http://www.bloomberg.com/apps/news?pid=20601039& refer=columnist_lewis&sid=azEdlWcgsj5M.

47. Cornelius Tacitus, *The Agricola and The Germania*, tr. H. Mattingly (New York: Penguin Books, 1970), ch. 30, 81.

48. Keynes, *The General Theory of Employment, Interest and Money*, 383.

49. Donald A. MacKenzie, *An Engine, Not a Camera* (Cambridge: MIT Press, 2006).

50. Smith, *An Inquiry into the Nature and Causes of the Wealth of Nations*, II.i.17, 282.

51. Ibid., IV.viii. 44, 659, and I.x.b.6, z 118.

52. Robert H. Haveman, Andrew Bershadker, and Jonathan A. Schwabish, *Human Capital in the United States from 1975 to 2000: Patterns of Growth and Utilization* (Kalamazoo, MI: W.E. Upjohn Institute for Employment Research, 2003), 68.

53. Dale Jorgenson and Barbara Fraumeni, *The Accumulation of Human and Non-Human Capital, 1948–84* (Cambridge: Harvard University Press, 1987).

54. Sherwin Rosen, "Human Capital," *The New Palgrave: A Dictionary of Economics*, vol. 2 (New York: Palgrave Macmillan, 1987), 681–90.

55. Robert E. Lucas, Jr., "On the Mechanics of Economic Development," *Journal of Monetary Economics*, Vol. 22, No. 1 (July 1988): 19.

56. James N. Baron and Michael T. Hannan, "The Impact of Economics on Contemporary Sociology," *Journal of Economic Literature*, Vol. 32, No. 3 (September 1994): 112.

57. Gunnar Lind Haase Svendsen and Gert Tinggaard Svendsen, "On the Wealth of Nations: Bourdieuconomics and Social Capital," *Theory and Society*, Vol. 32, No. 5/6 (December 2003): 627.

58. Gary Becker and George J. Stigler, "De Gustibus Non Est Disputandum," *American Economic Review*, Vol. 67, No. 2 (March 1977): 78.

59. Gerald Fredrick Davis, *Managed by the Markets: How Finance Reshaped America* (Oxford: Oxford University Press, 2009), 6.

60. Virginia Woolf, *The Diary of Virginia Woolf*, Vol. 2, 1920–1924, eds. Anne Olivier Bell and Andrew McNeillie (New York: Harcourt Brace Jovanovich, 1978), 231.

61. Jaroslav Vanek, *Crisis and Reform: East and West* (Ithaca, New York: Cornell University Press, 1989), 93.

62. H. G. Wells, *A Modern Utopia* (New York: Charles Scribner's Sons, 1905), 102.

63. Lionel Charles Robbins, *An Essay on the Nature and Significance of Economic Science*, 2nd ed. (London: Macmillan, 1969), 16.

64. See J. Kagel, "Economics According to the Rats (and Pigeons Too): What Have We Learned and What Can We Hope to Learn?" in ed. A. Roth, *Laboratory Experimentation in Economics: Six Points of View* (Cambridge: Cambridge University Press, 1987), 99–130.

65. Fernand Braudel, *The Perspective of the World*, Vol. 3, *Civilization and Capitalism: 15th–18th Century* (New York: Harper and Row, 1982).

66. Karl Marx, *Contribution to the Critique of Political Economy* (New York: International Publishers, 1970), 158.

Index